THE COMPLETE
IDIOT'S
GUIDE® TO

Psychic Intuition

Third Edition

by Lynn A. Robinson, M.Ed., and LaVonne Carlson-Finnerty
Revised with Katherine A. Gleason

ALPHA

A member of Penguin Group (USA) Inc.

For Shiri Hughes, my dear friend and mentor. I know you're up in heaven and surely giving the angels their instructions!

ALPHA BOOKS

Published by Penguin Group (USA) Inc.

Penguin Group (USA) Inc., 375 Hudson Street, New York, New York 10014, USA • Penguin Group (Canada), 90 Eglinton Avenue East, Suite 700, Toronto, Ontario M4P 2Y3, Canada (a division of Pearson Penguin Canada Inc.) • Penguin Books Ltd., 80 Strand, London WC2R 0RL, England • Penguin Ireland, 25 St. Stephen's Green, Dublin 2, Ireland (a division of Penguin Books Ltd.) • Penguin Group (Australia), 250 Camberwell Road, Camberwell, Victoria 3124, Australia (a division of Pearson Australia Group Pty. Ltd.) • Penguin Books India Pvt. Ltd., 11 Community Centre, Panchsheel Park, New Delhi—110 017, India • Penguin Group (NZ), 67 Apollo Drive, Rosedale, North Shore, Auckland 1311, New Zealand (a division of Pearson New Zealand Ltd.) • Penguin Books (South Africa) (Pty.) Ltd., 24 Sturdee Avenue, Rosebank, Johannesburg 2196, South Africa • Penguin Books Ltd., Registered Offices: 80 Strand, London WC2R 0RL, England

Previous edition originally published as *The Complete Idiot's Guide to Psychic Awareness*.

Copyright © 2012 by Amaranth

International Standard Book Number: 978-1-61564-195-6

Library of Congress Catalog Card Number: 2011945186

19 18 17   9 8 7

Interpretation of the printing code: The rightmost number of the first series of numbers is the year of the book's printing; the rightmost number of the second series of numbers is the number of the book's printing. For example, a printing code of 12-1 shows that the first printing occurred in 2012.

Printed in the United States of America

Note: This publication contains the opinions and ideas of its authors. It is intended to provide helpful and informative material on the subject matter covered. It is sold with the understanding that the authors, publisher, and book producer are not engaged in rendering professional services in the book. If the reader requires personal assistance or advice, a competent professional should be consulted.

The authors, publisher, and book producer specifically disclaim any responsibility for any liability, loss, or risk, personal or otherwise, which is incurred as a consequence, directly or indirectly, of the use and application of any of the contents of this book.

Most Alpha books are available at special quantity discounts for bulk purchases for sales promotions, premiums, fund-raising, or educational use. Special books, or book excerpts, can also be created to fit specific needs.

For details, write: Special Markets, Alpha Books, 375 Hudson Street, New York, NY 10014.

Publisher: *Marie Butler-Knight*

Associate Publisher: *Mike Sanders*

Executive Managing Editor: *Billy Fields*

Executive Acquisitions Editor: *Lori Cates Hand*

Book Producer: *Lee Ann Chearneyi/ Amaranth@LuminAreStudio*

Development Editor: *Megan Douglass*

Senior Production Editor: *Janette Lynn*

Copy Editor: *Lisanne V. Jensen*

Cover Designer: *Kurt Owens*

Book Designers: *William Thomas, Rebecca Batchelor*

Indexer: *Julie Bess*

Layout: *Brian Massey*

Senior Proofreader: *Laura Caddell*

Contents

Appendixes

Introduction

It's easy to imagine why you picked up this book. After all, who hasn't heard of, or doesn't actually know, someone who has had a psychic (or what we prefer to call intuitive) experience? In all likelihood, you yourself have had such an experience. Who isn't familiar with the feeling that they've sensed something unusual—something beyond the reach of their ordinary senses, and yet just as real?

Attitudes have changed a lot since we wrote the first edition of this book back in 1999. Many more people have opened their minds and understand the value that their wise inner guidance can bring to their lives. We've changed our book as well. First, we changed the title from *The Complete Idiot's Guide to Being Psychic* to *The Complete Idiot's Guide to Psychic Awareness* for the second edition, and now *The Complete Idiot's Guide to Psychic Intuition* for this third edition. For each edition, the new title more accurately reflects our intention to help you become aware of the many ways to use your psychic intuitive skills. To that end, we've given you more fabulous exercises that you can do by yourself or with friends. We've also updated the material with new psychic resources and a host of online links for further study. We predict you'll enjoy the results!

Whether using your intuition is familiar to you or you just want to check out what you've heard from others, you're probably still wondering whether your experience was "real." Maybe your intuitive experience was just a hyperactive imagination or a hypersensitive mind at work?

Trust your intuition on that one. It *was* real. And after you've read through this book, you'll have a much better sense of what to call these experiences and a greater understanding of why they occur. We're here to offer insight into the various types of psychic abilities and how to put them to use in your own life.

First, let us explain who we are. Lynn is one of the nation's leading experts on intuition. She's a best-selling author of six books, including *Listen: Trusting Your Inner Voice in Times of Crisis*, *Trust Your Gut: How the Power of Intuition Can Grow Your Business*, and *Divine Intuition: Your Guide to Creating a Life You Love*. She has been an intuitive consultant for more than 25 years, working as an advisor to both businesses and individuals. LaVonne is an editorial consultant and writer who has a strong religious upbringing that she often resists in favor of her rational side. Through the experience of working on the first edition of this book, she has learned much about intuition and has no doubt about its awesome power. Katherine, who has written numerous titles on her own and with co-authors, including the best-selling

The Complete Idiot's Guide to Wicca and Witchcraft, Third Edition (with Denise Zimmermann) and *The Complete Idiot's Guide Numerology Workbook* (with Patricia Kirkman), had a great time working with Lynn on the revised and updated text for the third edition of this book. We worked together, culling the best from our different backgrounds, to show you how easy it can be to tap into your intuition.

When Lynn was a young girl, she was just as curious as you are now—but books like this one weren't as readily available. Lynn haunted libraries (so to speak) and started reading the few materials she could find. The more she discovered about the psychic world, the more she wanted to know. Lynn developed and practiced her own methods for strengthening psychic intuition. Eventually, of course, Lynn wanted to try doing readings herself.

Readings seemed to come naturally: Lynn didn't have to work too hard to receive information. Friends who agreed to be subjects for her early experiments at giving psychic intuitive readings were often shocked by what Lynn seemed to know about their private lives. And Lynn's sure that a few of her friendships cooled because certain friends became convinced she could read their minds.

Well, it wasn't so then, and it isn't so now (although you'd have a hard time convincing her husband of that). Lynn can't read your mind, but she can tell you a lot about what's going on in your world, what could occur in your future, and how you can shape your life into something much closer to what you'd like it to be.

Not long into her journey as a psychic intuitive, Lynn made a startling discovery. She learned that her maternal grandfather—a family member her English-born mother rarely spoke of—had been a practicing psychic. That suddenly seemed to explain Lynn's early and abiding interest in psychic phenomena. But she had decided that although she might have a genetic, intuitive advantage, Lynn's not all that different from anyone else who works at being good at what they love.

Make no mistake, Lynn did work at developing and fine-tuning her psychic skills to become highly intuitive. And because she did, she can help guide you there easily and quickly. Lynn knows the shortcuts. All it takes from you is the same curiosity Lynn had as a child (and that you had when you were a child). It also benefits from an openness to the possibility of creating a better life through developing your own "sixth" sense.

Has Lynn been able to "see into a person's life"? Yes. Has Lynn amused, amazed, and astounded some of her clients? Definitely. Has she won the lottery? Well, yes—and no. What Lynn has done most consistently is help people learn some important things about themselves and their current situations and then suggest ways to improve their lives. When her clients listen with open minds and hearts, they almost always learn something of value to them personally. That's what Lynn wishes for you as you read *The Complete Idiot's Guide to Psychic Intuition, Third Edition.*

William James, a famous American psychologist, said, "The greatest discovery of my generation is that human beings, by changing the inner attitudes of their minds, can change the outer aspects of their lives."

Developing your psychic abilities can definitely help you change your attitudes—and your life. Lynn can personally vouch for that. And if you read this guide and apply what you learn, you, too, will find your life changing for the better. You might even help other people to change theirs.

So now, open your mind—and your heart—and let's begin.

How This Book Is Organized

Before you jump right in, we'd like to offer some basic information to get you started. Here's how the book is organized:

Part 1, What Does It Mean to Have Psychic Intuition?, presents an overview of all things psychic, including how science sees psychic ability and a focus on how you access your own psychic intuition. We want to get you grounded in the basic facts about intuitive ability, including ways to recognize your own.

Part 2, Building Your Psychic Intuition, focuses on developing your psychic senses. Once you become aware of being surrounded—and infused—with natural intuitive ability, you'll find yourself opening up to entirely new levels of experience.

Part 3, Intuitive Intelligence, offers more advanced steps toward involving your mind in the process of psychic development. Here's where we get into the fascinating facts about altered states of consciousness, visions, dreams, and communication between minds.

Part 4, Leaping the Barriers of Space and Time, gets a pretty spiritual vibration going. We talk about accessing information from far away and long ago, channeling messages from spirits, and out-of-body experiences. It's absolutely fascinating—and something you can learn to do yourself!

Part 5, Listening to Your Intuition, includes what probably matters most to you: a chapter on conducting your own psychic consulting sessions. So what are you waiting for? It's time to get started! You'll also find lots of exercises that you can use to hone your intuitive abilities, enhance your spirituality, and improve your life.

Extras

Throughout this book, you'll find boxes that explain unfamiliar terms, give you helpful tips, point out warnings or pitfalls, or give you further information. Here's what to look for:

DEFINITION

These sidebars help you talk the talk. They'll bring you up to speed on technical terms we use in the text by giving you simple, straightforward definitions.

GUIDED INTUITION

These sidebars make simple suggestions for using intuition in your own life.

MIXED MESSAGES

It's often wise to see two sides of a situation. Some material that may sound pretty simple at first should be taken with a little caution. These sidebars offer an extra warning.

ARE YOU AWARE?

These sidebars present tidbits and trivia about the history and/or study of psychic phenomena.

Acknowledgments

Last but certainly not least, we want to thank many tremendous people who have helped create or inspire this book. As we say later in the book, everyone and everything is connected: the hearts, minds, and spirits of all those who have come together to create this book are proof of that. May the light of the universe bless you all.

Lynn: I would like to thank my husband, Gary, for all his support. I appreciate all the proofreading and late-night discussions.

Thank you also to Shiri Hughes. You helped me proofread the first two editions. I felt your spirit whispering corrections on this third edition!

Thanks also to Katherine A. Gleason for her fabulous writing and quick wit. You've been a joy to work with!

LaVonne would like to thank the following people for their contributions to the book: Lee Walker for his expertise as a physicist and dreamer; Ruth Seeliger for sharing "the way;" K. Lavonne for her courage and encouragement; and Joanne Go for her inspiration and support. Big hugs go to Brian, Elizabeth, and Patrick for their patience, faith, and love (and sharing computer time!). A huge thank you goes to Lynn Robinson, who always anticipated just what was needed next, whether it was extra information or enthusiastic support.

At Alpha Books, publisher Marie Butler-Knight and Executive Acquisitions Editor Lori Cates Hand offered ongoing and invaluable support. We both would like to acknowledge Lee Ann Chearneyi of Amaranth@LuminAreStudio for providing the vision for this book and for keeping us on track throughout and Katherine A. Gleason for her terrific work on the third edition.

Special Thanks to the Technical Reviewer

The Complete Idiot's Guide to Psychic Intuition, Third Edition, was reviewed in its first edition by two experts who double-checked the accuracy of what you'll learn here to help us ensure that this book gives you everything you need to know about using your psychic talents. Special thanks are extended to Shiri Hughes and Belleruth Naparstek.

Shiri Hughes had been a practicing psychic and medium for more than 30 years. Living well into a graceful old age, she was grateful that her intuitive ability saved her life at least three times during World War II. Shiri studied astrology and metaphysics with the famous astrologer Isabel Hickey, then studied mediumship with the brilliant medium Sophie Busch. In 1970, the Spiritualist Church ordained Shiri as a minister. Shiri passed away in 2011. However, we know she's continuing her teaching and counseling work on the other side.

Belleruth Naparstek, A.M., L.I.S.W., is the author of *Your Sixth Sense: Unlocking the Power of Your Intuition*. A clinical social worker and psychotherapist who has practiced for more than three decades, she is a nationally recognized pioneer in the applications of guided imagery for healing and nutrition and the creator of the popular, 24-title Time-Warner CD series *Health Journeys*. Ms. Naparstek lives in Cleveland, Ohio, where she writes, lectures, consults, and runs www.HealthJourneys.com.

Trademarks

All terms mentioned in this book that are known to be or are suspected of being trademarks or service marks have been appropriately capitalized. Alpha Books and Penguin Group (USA) Inc. cannot attest to the accuracy of this information. Use of a term in this book should not be regarded as affecting the validity of any trademark or service mark.

What Does It Mean to Have Psychic Intuition?

When you hear the word "psychic," do you picture a peasant woman sitting behind a crystal ball? In your mind's eye, does she look up and say, "I was expecting you!"? Well, times have changed. If you want to see what a real psychic looks like, look in your mirror—because you yourself are already psychic.

You're probably still wondering just what that means. This part offers an overview of all matters "psychic." We'll look at psychic phenomena and psychics from the points of view of science and psychology. Also, we show you how your psychic abilities work in the real world by looking at your dominant means of psychic communication. First, let's start with what you want to know most: How do you know you're really psychic?

Are You Psychic?

In This Chapter

- It's true: you're psychic!
- Mysterious words for everyday events
- Discovering your source of psychic power
- Honing your psychic gift

Let's clarify what you already intuit: everyone is psychic. And that includes you! In this book, we'll show you how to mine your special powers and use them in exciting and constructive ways.

Your psychic ability has been with you since the day you were born (or perhaps for centuries before you were born, but we'll talk more about that later). We all enter the world with an innate ability to sense information that seems to come from outside, or beyond, ourselves. This ability manifests itself in many forms (almost as many as there are individuals). It provides insight and information as general as a gut feeling and as specific as the details of a future event.

Most likely, at least one of the following has happened to you. Each is an example of a psychic phenomenon:

- You anticipate when your phone's going to ring, and you know who's calling without a distinctive ring or checking your Caller ID.

- You constantly find yourself in the right place at the right time. For example, the person sitting next to you in the jury pool happens to be a piano teacher—and you've just inherited a piano!

- You buy a gift for a friend, only to discover that your friend has been looking for that item for some time without success and hasn't told you (or anyone else) about it.

- You dream about a place you've never been before and discover, upon visiting it, that it looks just like you dreamed it.

- You're teamed up with a new business associate with whom you feel instantly comfortable. Before the end of your first meeting, you're finishing each other's sentences.

But if being psychic is so common, why don't we talk about it more often? For one thing, people in our Western culture aren't encouraged to acknowledge and train their intuitive skills. As schoolchildren, we focus on mastering our ABCs and 123s. Most of us have never been required to take an emotional or psychic IQ test! Yet, according to a Pew Research Center survey, more than 60 percent of Americans believe in some form of psychic phenomenon. For now, rest assured that you are indeed psychic—and that what you now need is the confidence to get started on developing this wonderful gift.

Psychic, Intuitive, or Just Plain Crazy?

Perhaps the vocabulary of psychic intuition is another thing that makes discussing "psychic stuff" difficult. Throughout this book, you'll encounter some words that will be familiar and many that may not be. We'll introduce you to telepathy, clairsentience, extrasensory perception (ESP), psychometry, psychokinesis, remote viewing, channeling, precognition, the paranormal, and more. We'll also look at the study of psychic phenomena, called *parapsychology*.

 DEFINITION

Parapsychology is a branch of psychology that studies psychic experiences. The term came into use in the late 1920s, when the field's founder, J. B. Rhine, created the first institute for psychic research: The Rhine Research Center, situated near Duke University in Durham, North Carolina.

These days, the term "psychic" means many things to many people. It's a word that has been around the block a few times, so it's carrying some extra baggage. For one thing, "psychic" can refer either to the ability to transcend concrete knowledge or to a person who has this ability. For some people, the word "psychic" has a negative connotation. It's not unusual for people to fear something that has no rational explanation.

When you're "being psychic," you're accessing knowledge without understanding how or why that knowledge is given to you. You just know it! Being psychic is all about trust—trusting that your source of information is more powerful than your own imagination and trusting that it's there for your greatest good.

In the field of medicine today, we're seeing doctors embrace the power of the connection between our bodies and our minds to heal and nurture us. While high-tech computer and biomedical advances are changing the face of medicine, these breakthroughs coexist with a new respect for alternative medicine techniques such as acupuncture, chiropractic, and biofeedback.

Disciplines that combine mental and physical well-being (such as yoga, meditation, and massage) are enjoying a renaissance—and some medical schools are conducting scientific studies into the documented healing effects of prayer. Doctors and scientists agree that there's a lot they need to explore about how the health of the psyche and the soul influences one's mental and physical health. So let your fear of "psychic stuff" and/or the fear that others might not understand—or worse, that they might think you are crazy—become a thing of the past!

Sure, some psychic experiences can sound strange, but that's often because they are hard to describe. One reason is because they occur in a nonphysical realm, which means that they aren't concrete. You can't touch them or take them home to show your mom. And it can be very difficult to prove them. One of the key lessons you'll learn from this book is to have faith in yourself. The foundation of improving your psychic power is trusting yourself. As the saying goes, "Trust your intuition."

In fact, Lynn believes the words "psychic" and "intuition" are interchangeable. In her practice, for instance, she refers to herself as an intuitive consultant. The word "intuitive" sheds new light on being psychic because it focuses on discerning truth through a direct—albeit unexplained—source of knowledge (as compared to receiving information from a supernatural force). "Intuitive" suggests that the information sent or received finds its origin inside one's self. So if you work on developing your ability to think and feel intuitively, you're being psychic.

How's Your Psi These Days?

Psi (pronounced "sigh") is the study of psychic phenomena from a psychological perspective. It's another term created in an attempt to talk about the abstract concept of being psychic. The *Journal of Parapsychology* defines psi as "a general term to identify a person's extrasensorimotor communication with the environment." The *Journal* was created by a group of researchers who were trying to prove the existence of *extrasensory perception (ESP)*.

DEFINITION

Scientists who study psychic phenomena created the term **psi** as a neutral (that is, a more scientific) way to refer to psychic experiences and abilities. Psi is a letter of the Greek alphabet and the first letter of the Greek word *psyche*, which literally means "breath" in Greek and refers to the human soul. Having **extrasensory perception (ESP)** means that you are able to perceive someone's thoughts, situation, or issues in life without using one of your five "ordinary" senses.

In general, psi isn't a word used everyday—but it's sure the buzzword within the psychic community! You might want to save it for an impressive opening line at a party. But we want you to avoid getting too attached to any specific terms for the psychic experience so that your mind will have more freedom to welcome and explore the many intuitive messages that come your way every day.

Do You Have It?

Like many people, you've secretly wished you could read someone's mind, see what was happening with a loved one on the other side of the country (without the use of the phone or email), or receive guidance and insight into matters of your healing and spiritual growth. Although most people, especially those without any training, are not open to experiencing these types of mental feats, everyone does have a psychic sense (including you!).

Lynn once asked a physicist whether he believed in psychic intuition. His answer (the short one!) was "No." His long answer, however, reveals something interesting. This physicist postulates that psychic awareness relies on an accumulation of knowledge and the ability to predict outcomes successfully based on that knowledge. It's a little bit like playing the odds—the more inside information you have, the more accurate your choices and the greater chance you have of beating those odds. So according to our physicist friend, if you have intuition, you're consciously applying knowledge you've accessed and processed in an unconscious, unexplainable manner that science has yet to catch up with.

Ever Had a Psychic Experience?

Because you're reading this book, we'll assume that you are among the 60 percent of Americans who believe in psychic phenomena. But maybe you're in doubt about whether you're psychic yourself. Consider the following questions:

- Do you get hunches about things coming up in your life?

- Do you sense what is going on with other people's feelings?

- Have you ever known about future events before they happened?

- Do you feel physical sensations (knots in your stomach or an all-over heaviness, for example) that alert you when you're making a decision that's wrong for you? Do you honor those physical clues?

- Do you feel physical sensations (tingling or lightness, for example) that alert you when you're making a good decision? Do you honor those sensations?

- Are you aware of how your intuition speaks to you?

- Do you receive information through kinesthetic (physical) sensations, through more cerebral hunches, or through feelings and emotions?

- Do you check in often with your intuition when you need information?

Did you answer "Yes" to any of these questions? If so, this confirms the answer to the question you've been asking yourself all along: "Am I really psychic?" Doubt no more! The answer is "Yes."

In future chapters, we'll talk about why you answered "Yes" to some questions and how you can use each question to develop your psychic intuition. Everybody has a unique way of getting in touch with his or her own psychic abilities. Throughout this book, we'll help you discover the best ways to tap into yours. We'll give you insight into the various forms of psychic ability and help you understand where your special talents fit into this awesome, yet undeniably real, range of powers.

When first getting in touch with your personal psychic skills and strengths, be aware that there is a wide range of possible ways to receive information. Some people might feel a physical sensation in the body, others might experience an emotional change, and still others might hear a voice or see an image. The possibilities are infinite because they are all unique to each individual.

> **ARE YOU AWARE?**
>
> Each individual receives psychic information in his or her own way, and the way it arrives can change depending on the situation. If you're stressed, you may develop a headache as your body's way of saying, "Get some rest." If you're about to say "No" to a great career opportunity, your stomach might tighten. If you shouldn't take that walk in the park after dark, you might feel a prickly sensation at the back of your neck. If you're asking for intuitive guidance about a decision, you might get a warm feeling at the thought of a good decision.

Separating Questioning from Questing

To start learning where your psychic potential fits in on a grander scale, you need to know where you're coming from. For starters, examine your existing attitudes and beliefs toward the amazing and mysterious world of psychic stuff. Chances are you will feel a mixture of curiosity, anxiety, fear, doubt, and eager enthusiasm when thinking about being psychic. All of these feelings are normal, especially when you're exploring new territory.

Think about all the input you've received over your lifetime about the psychic realm. The popular media tends to view psychic phenomena with an equal measure of suspicion and fascination. Popular TV shows tap into the public's strong desire to investigate the nature and truth of psychic experiences and events. In movies and television, though, psychic phenomena tend to be larger than life—often with supernatural or paranormal qualities attached. (They do have to entertain, after all!) But harnessing psychic power in your own life is not so extreme, scary, or out of this world. Being psychic can be an everyday way of being—another part of who you are.

> **MIXED MESSAGES**
>
> Beware of becoming overly eager in your quest for psychic intuition. Don't let wishful thinking or personal ambition convince you that desired—but possibly inaccurate—information is meant to be a psychic blessing. Like any skill, psychic development takes practice. It might take a while for you to distinguish between intuitive insight and wishful thinking.

Traditional religions have a wide range of viewpoints on psychic matters (not all of them positive). Your own parents, depending on their religious backgrounds, probably downplayed psychic impulses or spurned them for fear of putting "silly" ideas in your head. Yet, each great religious tradition from Buddha to Mohammed to Jesus Christ has a tradition of prophecy and miracles.

How often have you stopped to think for yourself about what being psychic really means?

The Soul Connection

Perhaps the intuitive messages you receive can be looked at as gifts from the universe offering to guide you along a clearer, smoother path. Perhaps they originate from an all-seeing and all-loving God who speaks to you through these impressions. Or, perhaps they are entirely physical biochemical sensations brought on by body chemicals that scientists are only just discovering. Experts have no answers to these ponderings. Explore your beliefs so that you can resolve any possible barriers that could prevent you from opening up to something new—your own incredible psychic potential!

GUIDED INTUITION

Always know that you are in control. Although some psychics insist that the future is etched in stone, we believe that your choices and decisions matter. Intuitive information forms messages you receive from your higher self, offering guidance rather than an ultimatum. You're in control of your own destiny!

"I Know, but I Don't Know How"

A common expression among many beginners—and even masters—in the world of intuitive insight is, "I know, but I don't know how." If you've ever had this sense, you're definitely on track. But what does it mean?

You've probably had a moment when you stopped short, struck with a thought that seemingly came from nowhere. Perhaps it had no relation to any topic you had on your mind, and yet the information later proved accurate. Once you gain a little experience with receiving intuitive information, you'll be able to say, "Ah ha!" with the full confidence that the information is something that comes from a source beyond your five senses. You may never be able to describe your source, but you can get better at recognizing and using this type of knowledge.

Intuition as Life's Teacher

Your intuitive messages are your soul's instructions. They guide you to make correct decisions according to your higher purpose. The messages you receive might give you information about how to proceed in life, offering suggestions for taking your next steps (large or small). Or, they might provide insight into what lessons you should be learning from your experiences. In addition to positive growth in your personal and spiritual lives, your relationships with others can also benefit. Psychic insight can grant us greater understanding, empathy, and compassion for others. It informs us about our world in new ways, giving us a fresh perspective. I like to refer to intuitive information as "an instruction package for planet Earth." But don't worry too much about reading the entire world. When you start seeing your immediate surroundings, the larger world will come to you.

Neophyte to Master: Honing Your Talent

Remember one thing: keep an open mind! As you begin tapping into your psychic information, you'll discover it's a hit-or-miss proposition at first. It might take you some time to sort out which messages are meant for you. Eventually, you'll tune into the method of sending or receiving information that works best for you. You'll also start to get a good sense of when an intuitive message is truly coming to you loudly and clearly.

Here's an image to help illustrate it. Envision your intuitive powers as radio signals. The power is always there; you just need to know how to tune in. For some, this tuning-in involves a concerted learning effort; others might just hit the best position on the dial right off the bat. With a little effort, anyone can soon gain access to a usable frequency. You just need a few lessons on how to fine-tune your psychic receptors.

Everyone Has the "Gift"

Everyone is born with some degree of psychic ability. It's not a sacred gift intended only for a few select geniuses. Just like studying piano or training as a soccer player, anyone can do it. As with any other skill or talent, the more you use your psychic abilities, the better you'll get. (If you dread the thought of practicing anything, here's some consolation: practicing your psychic powers is much simpler than lugging a tuba to lessons or getting dressed for a hockey game.) As you become more confident and in control of your intuitive abilities, the better able you'll be to trust your psychic insights when making major life decisions.

Although you may not be able to locate your neighbor's missing dog or predict tomorrow's lottery jackpot numbers, with effort and concentration you'll soon find yourself accessing your own powers of psychic intuition. Over time, you'll gain confidence in what you "know" and will learn more about where and how that knowledge comes uniquely to you!

Intuition Exercise: Practice, Practice, Practice

Now that you're convinced you have this tremendous gift, get ready to use it. In the upcoming chapters, we include exercises to help you find the right psychic path for you. We focus on the many aspects of psychic ability. Somewhere in there, you'll come upon a method(s) of being psychic that works for you. Try to be aware and open to this connection to your own psychic talent. We'll help you tune in to your intuitive side. And don't forget: practice makes perfect.

ARE YOU AWARE?

Does psychic intuition run in your family? Just as musical virtuosity and athletic finesse tend to be genetic, psychic talent also appears to have a genetic component. Indeed, research indicates that it seems to skip a generation. My family is proof: my grandfather contacted my mother late in life (he hadn't been in touch with her since she was 12) and revealed that he was a professional psychic. (To test this out yourself, give Granny a call and ask her if she has always had uncanny insight into people and their situations.)

Let's start now with a relaxation exercise that will help you open to your intuitive guidance. Sit quietly and comfortably in a straight-backed chair with your hands resting on the tops of your thighs, palms facing down, and your feet flat on the floor. Close your eyes. Breathe in deeply, letting the air fill your abdomen. Breathe out slowly. Repeat this for five deep, full breaths. Quiet and center your concentration on the breath flowing into and out of your body; feel your heart beating. Remember that in Greek, *psyche* or soul is literally "breath."

Imagine a ball of your favorite color. In your mind's eye, see this ball of color floating over your head. With each inhale, see the ball of color move closer to you. See the ball of color sliding down and filling your head. As the color fills your head, it relaxes your nerves and your muscles. Feel the color relaxing your scalp, your forehead, your brain, your ears, your cheeks, and your tongue. Feel the color filling and relaxing your neck and your throat.

The color moves down into your shoulders and relaxes them. It fills and softens your arms, elbows, forearms, and wrists. The color flows into your chest, relaxing it. Your rib cage, lungs, and heart relax. The color flows into your abdomen and down your back. Your spine relaxes, and your stomach relaxes. The color fills your pelvis and hips, relaxing them. It flows down your legs and relaxes your thighs, knees, calves, and ankles. The color fills and relaxes your feet and your toes. You are completely filled with your favorite color, and you are completely relaxed and focused.

Stay like this and feel the peacefulness in your body and your mind for as long as you like. When you are ready, breathe in—and then, as you begin to exhale, imagine the color starting to fade. Let the color fade slowly with each exhale, leaving you both relaxed and energized. When you are done, open your eyes.

You can use this exercise any time to help you relax and focus. Remember that an open, clear mind is a psychic mind.

The Least You Need to Know

- Everyone—including you—is psychic.
- The words "psychic" and "intuitive" can be used interchangeably.
- Each individual has a unique way of tuning into his or her own psychic abilities.
- Our intuitive talents can provide guidance in every aspect of our lives.
- Although developing psychic power is not difficult, the more you practice, the more accessible it becomes.

What Science and Psychology Say About Being Psychic

In This Chapter

- Studying psi phenomena as a science
- What we're learning about the brain and psi
- Who's researching and how
- Psychology and spiritual emergence

Artists, prophets, and philosophers have been talking about psychic phenomena for ages. Indeed, the sacred Vedas, written in India thousands of years ago, state that it is an illusion that individual minds are separate from each other—but in fact, our minds can cross boundaries of time and space to access information. In this sense, people are not only all psychic but all psychic *together*. Perhaps the first psychoanalyst to suggest that everyone's unconscious mind shares certain thoughts or images was Carl Gustav Jung (1875–1961). Jung proposed that the unconscious mind expresses an awareness that is shared by people with similar cultural traditions. Jung called this shared level of common symbols and knowledge the "collective unconscious." The "Gaia hypothesis," proposed by James Lovelock in the 1940s, also supports the idea that many minds are connected. According to the Gaia theory, the earth is actually an enormous biological system that makes up a single living organism. This idea infers that the earth and all beings on it share one mind. So people's individual minds may respond to the earth's needs in a unified way.

Today, the hard sciences are finally catching on to—and trying to catch up with—ideas of the collective mind. In both the hard sciences and social sciences, researchers have been focused on proving that psi exists and then defining exactly what it is. In this chapter, we take a look at how science and psychology regard psychic phenomena.

The Science of Parapsychology

When professional researchers of psychic phenomena refer to what they are studying, they use the word "psi," which we introduced in Chapter 1. The scientific study of psi includes areas such as telepathy, precognition, clairvoyance, and psychokinesis.

Modern science's early attempts to study psychic phenomena actually began more than a century ago. In response to the highly popular Spiritualist movement, various scientists organized investigations. In 1882, scholars from Cambridge University in England founded the first such organization, the Society for Psychical Research—which still exists and functions in London. This organization focuses on examining—and whenever possible, debunking—the most famous mediums of the day. It established certain research standards and keeps copious records.

ARE YOU AWARE?

Among the world's earliest scientific researchers of psychic ability was Upton Sinclair, author of *The Jungle* (1906) and a Pulitzer Prize winner for his conscientious critique of social ills. Yet, in 1930, he broke from his usual realistic subject matter to publish *Mental Radio*, a book that documented hundreds of experiments that confirmed his wife's ability to see telepathically. The investigative methods and their results were so impressive that Sinclair's friend, Albert Einstein, wrote the book's preface in praise of their scientific validity.

Its counterpart, the American Society for Psychical Research, was formed in 1885 and remains America's longest standing organization with documented reports of psi research. It has an exhaustive library of information on almost every experiment conducted on just about every type of paranormal phenomena. You can visit them in New York City or look them up on the web at www.aspr.com.

Your Brain: Psychic Central

The obvious place to look for information about intuition is the source of all thinking: the mind. Sounds simple enough until you start asking what "mind" really means. Is it simply the brain, or does it include the thoughts that make up, and possibly transcend, the actual physical boundaries of the brain? Where does psi live? What is it in a physical sense?

Questions such as these are enticing medical specialists, psychiatrists, psychologists, and psi scientists as well. These experts have begun studying all aspects of what is called the mind, including the brain, the subconscious and unconscious minds, and the joining of many people's minds. It's possible that psi is another aspect of brain function—an additional perceptive sense that is somehow based in your physical brain. It's also possible that psi is a bridge that connects your physical brain to a larger, universal mind.

Psychology, in particular, can gain many new inroads through the continued study of psi. Because psychic ability is associated with the mind, the brain is a logical place to start studying what may be going on.

The Split-Brain Theories (Ouch!)

In recent decades, one of the most profound discoveries in medicine won the Nobel Prize in 1981 for Roger Sperry. This brain researcher went beyond the conventional wisdom that the left hemisphere of the *neocortex*, responsible for reason and analytical thinking, reigned supreme in the brain. He revealed that the right hemisphere makes an equally important contribution, providing the power of intuition as well as imagination, artistic creativity, and free association.

A more recent theory, put forth by Paul Maclean (a brain researcher at the National Institutes of Health), is that the brain can be divided into three sections—each with a unique function, starting from the bottom up. He found that the basic brain, at the bottom, is the oldest (in terms of evolution) section of our brain and is associated with basic animal instincts such as the fight-or-flight reflex. The second section is the limbic system, which is responsible for feelings and emotional attachments. Above that is the *neocortex*, the newest section of the brain, which Maclean and others credit with higher thought.

DEFINITION

The **neocortex** is the uppermost region of the brain, which is responsible for rational and higher thought.

Opinions differ on what part of the brain houses the intuitive abilities. Some people say that they are situated in the basic brain, which is linked with instinctual responses. Recent research suggests that intuition, with its ability to see in visual, symbolic images, is positioned in the neocortex.

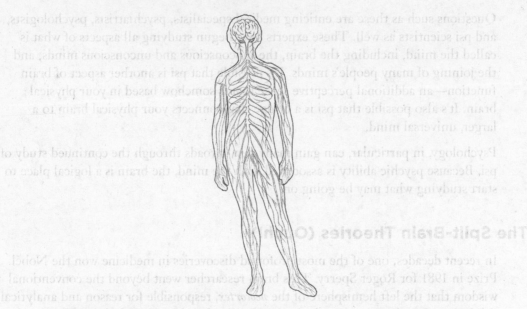

The human brain and central nervous system is as complex as any communication system in creation. It's no wonder that some scientists believe that our hidden powers of psychic ability lie within this labyrinth.

An important theory about left and right brain hemispheres acknowledges that the interaction between the two creates the ideal mental state. To use our brain's abilities to their fullest, input from both hemispheres should be balanced to create an equal input of logical and intuitive thinking.

Although we tend to focus on the rational functions carried out by our left brain, we can help to increase our right brain's input by participating in creative activities and meditation. This may explain why meditation helps us access our intuition ... or maybe there's more to it than that.

Surfing the (Brain) Waves

Our brains constantly produce electrical impulses. These currents of electricity are called brainwaves, and there are four types: beta, alpha, theta, and delta. To make it simple (and highly oversimplified), here's a table of what they do.

Name of Brainwave	Where It Occurs Most	What It Does
Beta	Normal waking states	Maintains rational, concrete thinking
Alpha	Daydreams, fantasies, and visualization	Bridge to subconscious; improves memory and creative insight
Theta	Subconscious; dreaming sleep	Repository of creativity, inspiration, and memory
Delta	Unconscious mind; deep sleep	Gives restorative sleep; may access intuition and empathy

Although this looks fairly simple, our brains are always combining these waves. For example, our theta waves are the strongest—and the most helpful—during meditation, yet they benefit us even more when they interact with delta waves. Some scientists suggest that this blending of various brainwaves actually creates a new type of brainwave. Some followers of Eastern philosophies propose that the awakened mind, wherein a person is more fully aware of his or her spiritual existence, combines all four forms of brainwaves at once. The Silva Method, a self-help program that has been around since the 1940s, uses brainwave science to aid people in accessing their intuition and spirituality.

The Study of Psychic Phenomena

A number of individuals and institutions are keeping their eyes on psi for a number of very different reasons. From U.S. intelligence agencies and the advertising industry to religious leaders and hardened skeptics, what's going on in the scientific world of psi is getting some widespread attention.

Parapsychology Research Labs

The Rhine Research Center, the first American research facility devoted to the scientific study of psychic phenomena, was founded in 1927. Situated next to Duke University in Durham, North Carolina, it remains greatly respected for its high standards; its publication, the *Journal of Parapsychology*; state-of-the-art research techniques; and remarkable results.

Following in the footsteps of the Rhine Research Center, several newer psi research labs have formed over the last few decades. Here's a list of other leading psi research facilities:

- Anomalistic Psychology Research Unit, Goldsmiths College, University of London, England
- Australian Institute of Parapsychological Research, Sydney, Australia
- Boundary Institute, Los Altos, California
- Center for Consciousness Studies, Tucson, Arizona
- Cognitive Sciences Laboratory, Palo Alto, California
- Division of Psychiatry, University of Virginia, Charlottesville, Virginia
- Mind-Matter Unification Project, Cambridge University, United Kingdom
- Koestler Parapsychology Unit, University of Edinburgh, Scotland
- Institute of Noetic Sciences, Petaluma, California
- Institut für Grenzgebiete der Psychologie und Psychohygiene, Freiburg, Germany
- Institut Metapsychique International, Paris, France

As you can see, scientific research on psi is not limited to a specific region or country.

GUIDED INTUITION

If you look on the web, you'll find lots of information on state-of-the art psi research—much of it provided directly by the research facilities themselves. For details, check out the list of websites in Appendix B.

The Physics of Psi

The verdict is still out on what's really going on in the world of physics in relation to psi. Of course, scientists always strive to create a theory to explain what makes everything tick and how it all fits together. Some skeptics think this puzzle about how the universe works may never be solved, whereas some scientists believe psi may be able to help solve it.

One of the more popular theories today relies on the principles of quantum mechanics. The idea is that all matter is made up of tiny bits of energy called *quanta*. These bits come together to form atoms that, in turn, vibrate at a unique level for every person and every thing. This level of energy vibration, called a frequency, is like a fingerprint that leaves its mark anywhere you've been. Anything that is part of you or closely associated with you (perhaps even your thoughts) also contains this mark. In that sense, your presence can spread much more broadly than your physical body.

Another modern theory, posed by the British physicist David Bohm, combines relativity and quantum theory. The idea is that everything is made of energy that runs throughout the entire universe simultaneously. This energy contains a deep level of consciousness that interconnects everything, including an implicate (unseen) and explicate (physical) order. This underlying, conscious energy permeates and affects everything all at once. It is able to manifest itself in both the material and energetic realms via a means of holographic movement.

ARE YOU AWARE?

One scientist who is raising a lot of questions about the implications of psi in traditional science and its experiments is Rupert Sheldrake. His book, *Seven Experiments That Could Change the World: A Do-It-Yourself Guide to Revolutionary Science* (Park Street Press, 2002), explains his views. You can learn more about him and his most recent books at his website: www.sheldrake.org.

Bohm's idea challenges the long-held belief that existence occurs on a linear plane, in only one place at only one point in time. Using mathematics, Bohm theorized that time and space do not really exist—except as constructs on which people agree. In essence, everyone and everything is part of a *nonlocal reality*, meaning that events that are far from your awareness can, nevertheless, have an effect on you. This principle allows for the possibility that psi works by transcending the boundaries of space and time, creating the interconnectedness that yogis and philosophers described 5,000 years ago.

DEFINITION

Nonlocal reality refers to the scientific concept that events distant from someone can affect him or her. The term "nonlocal mind" is often used in psi circles to refer to accessing a vast, eternal mind that transcends space and time.

One thing that physicists and psi scientists agree on is that physics and psi probably follow the same set of natural laws. Of course, within the realm of physics, no one school of thought is agreed upon as describing the truth. In general, even most psi researchers aren't ready to proclaim that psi has all the answers. Rather, they suggest that psi may lead them to ask the best questions to gain deeper understanding.

Field Consciousness Effects

Modern physics supports the idea that everything exists as waves, rather than as specific points in time and space. Another way of referring to these waves is "fields," which include time, space, and gravity. Recently, certain scientists suggested that consciousness itself is a field. Like gravity, the field of consciousness has certain properties, including a force comparable to that of gravity. It could be that this force is similar to Jung's idea of the collective unconscious. Researchers in *field consciousness* are testing the theory that when many minds focus on a single topic, this focus produces a measurable effect. Author and researcher Lynne McTaggart has written about this topic for a popular audience, and so has Dean Radin.

DEFINITION

Field consciousness expresses the idea that mental awareness comes from a source other than the internal physical cells contained in our brains. Just as modern physics supports the concept that matter and time exist as fields, consciousness might also fit into this category.

This information about coordinated thoughts and consciousness may increasingly be put to use by advertisers, governmental leaders, and even casino owners. The potential power of this unity of thought adds a scientific basis to social activists' hopeful efforts to create change by raising consciousness. It also suggests that prayer may provide a powerful source of healing.

What Inquiring Scientific Minds Want to Know

Psi is fascinating to study because it calls so many basic beliefs—scientific and otherwise—into question. Just when you think you have it all figured out, some strange synchronicity or flash of insight gets you thinking about the nature of reality all over again. Many scientists feel much the same way: psi isn't possible to explain, but it's definitely out there. They can't just ignore it, so what can they do to make sense of it?

Psi researchers typically divide psychic phenomena into several primary areas and then pick one area on which to focus. Those primary areas include:

- Telepathy, which involves the study of direct mind-to-mind communication

- Precognition, or studying the transfer of information about future events that could not be inferred through any known way

- Clairvoyance, or studying the transfer of information about faraway places without using the normal senses

- Psychokinesis, which involves the study of mental interaction with material items, whether animate or inanimate

- Biological psychokinesis, which involves the study of mental interaction with living systems (for example, healing from a distance)

All these areas call traditional knowledge and assumptions into question. For physicists, these psi topics might lead to a new understanding about space and time and how energy and information travel. For biologists, these subjects raise questions about what possible senses people may have that they aren't even aware of yet. Psychologists might work to reexamine the ways that the mind, memory, and perception work.

ARE YOU AWARE?

Over a period of 16 years, a majority of Nobel Prize–winning scientists acknowledged that they tapped into their intuition when making their discoveries. According to a 1995 article in *Intuition Magazine*, 82 of the 93 winners said they believed in scientific intuition, whereas only 11 denied, or expressed doubts about, its existence. But during the interviews, even the skeptical scientists recounted experiences that could only be described as intuitive.

Common Experiments to Test Psychic Ability

Over the years, researchers have focused on certain experiments to help them detect and prove psi. They continually revise the experiments in an effort to weed out any possibility of getting false or biased results. We'll describe three main types of experiments here:

- *Ganzfeld* experiments
- *Remote-viewing* experiments
- *Random number generator (RNG)* experiments

DEFINITION

Ganzfeld is a German word meaning "whole field." It refers to opening the inner mind by shutting out external data, such as light and sound. When these distractions are eliminated, the mind is more susceptible to picking up psychic signals. **Remote viewing** is the ability to use the mind to see a person, place, or object that's located some distance away and beyond the physical range of sight. This ability also enables one to witness events at a remote site without using the known senses. A **random number generator (RNG)** refers to a machine that creates random sequences of electronic bits that are equivalent to "heads" and "tails." The patterns respond to changes in thought patterns by becoming less random.

One of the better-known techniques used to research psychic ability in individuals is the ganzfeld experiment. During these experiments, the subject is placed in an environment without sound, light, or other sensory input. The subject's eyes are covered with half-spheres that look like (and sometimes are) Ping-Pong balls. They wear microphones that enable them to constantly describe their impressions to the tester, although they are not given any feedback.

When all external distractions are eliminated, the subject is sent information through psychic means. Usually another person gazes at a photo and telepathically sends the subject that same image while the subject continues to describe any images or feelings he or she picks up. By describing the image he or she is receiving, the subject enables the sender to improve his or her technique of sending information. When the sending part of the session is over, the subject is shown four images, including what the sender was looking at and sending. The subject chooses the image closest to what he or she saw in his or her mind. Success is measured on whether the subject chooses the correct image.

Pure chance predicts that the correct image will be chosen 1 time out of 4, creating a 25 percent success rate. But the actual results of more than 700 ganzfeld sessions, carried out by various labs, averages about 34 percent. This may not sound like a high number to you, but remember that it's a strong percentage above chance. Clearly, some sort of telepathy occurs among some of the subjects and senders.

Scientists use remote-viewing experiments to measure whether subjects can obtain information without having a sender transmit it. One remote-viewing experiment begins with someone who has no contact with the subject selecting a photograph from a group of hundreds and setting it aside in a separate location. No one involved in the test sees this photo, but the subject then tries to describe its contents. This process may be repeated several times with various subjects and different photos during the experiment. At the end, a group of judges matches up the subjects' descriptions with the available photos to see how closely they meet the mark.

This test has been tried thousands of times at different laboratories over the last two decades, and the cumulative results indicate that sensitive subjects can perceive remote images even without a sender involved. To add an interesting twist, some researchers have used a version of this experiment to have subjects describe photos that would be selected in the future—and they were right on target! You can read about remote viewing in greater detail (and even try a remote-viewing exercise) in Chapter 5.

Another popular research tool is the random number generator (RNG). These machines combine electronic and computer technology to measure whether the mind has an effect on the machine. Basically, the machine spits out a series of zeros and ones in random patterns. The experiment aims to measure whether psychokinesis (using the mind to affect matter) occurs.

In one type of RNG experiment, a subject focuses his or her thoughts on trying to change the random distribution of the numbers. This is sort of like a high-tech coin toss, where you expect to get a 50:50 ratio of heads and tails. Using a completely computerized testing system eliminates the possibility that someone could somehow cheat by flipping the coin in a controlled way. Researchers have found that intense mental focus does appear to affect the machines: RNGs in these experiments consistently spit out a higher ratio of a single number.

Many labs across the world have used RNG to study group mental focus. Dean Radin, PhD, a senior scientist at the Institute of Noetic Sciences (IONS) and adjunct faculty in the Department of Psychology at Sonoma State University, has both conducted studies and gathered data from many other studies to show the effects of field consciousness. Events that have been measured show surprising evidence that something occurs when many individuals simultaneously focus on the same event. In other words, the experiments show that thought alone, without any physical action, can create a certain degree of order from chaos.

Are You Psychic—or Crazy?

Why is it that when a child has an imaginary friend, he or she is called cute—but when an adult has one, that person is called crazy? One of the world's most famous experts on mental health had regular conversations with his imaginary friend—as an adult. His name was Carl Jung, who readily revealed that his imaginary friend was named Philemon.

Until recent decades, many psychologists and psychiatrists viewed psi with skepticism and confusion. Today, people are more open to psi. Some experts even suggest that psi should be treated as an ordinary aspect of the mind, such as consciousness or learning. Indeed, understanding psi may help explain how we perceive and process information on all levels.

In some individuals, this ability to communicate with beings beyond their visible world extends into the spirit realm. Mediums can do this, as do people who communicate with spirit guides or angels. And who are we to say that these unseen beings aren't real? So how can we differentiate between being psychic and being mentally ill? A common symptom of *pathological* and *schizophrenic* individuals is their inability to combine their impressions into a healthy, whole image of reality. For example, an individual who has multiple personalities perceives and reflects the existence of only one character at a time. Such a person does not recall that he or she has another personality aside from the one he or she is experiencing in a given moment. A similar situation occurs with schizophrenics who hear voices: they cannot distinguish what they hear in their mind from the facts they see in the material world. In contrast, a healthy person has a solid center and realizes the difference between the material world and the unseen world.

DEFINITION

Pathological refers to a deviation from a healthy, normal condition.
Schizophrenic refers to a severe mental disorder marked by emotional withdrawal, intellectual deterioration, bizarre speech and behavior, hallucinations, and delusions.

The Least You Need to Know

- Many top-notch, international academic institutions have psi labs.
- Scientists are putting together theories on the interconnectedness of all minds.
- The same natural laws that apply to physics and other hard sciences also apply to psi.
- Psi might actually be a type of mental process or state, such as memory, learning, or consciousness.

Building Your Psychic Intuition

Part 2

Hearing about someone who has highly developed psychic senses is pretty fascinating. We know that you wonder how that person got from where you are now to where he or she is today. This part tells you how to develop your own psychic abilities.

A major hint is to be aware. Your intuition is sending you information all the time; you just need to pay attention. First, we'll help you ascertain your current skill level. We'll show you how to open up to greater psychic receptivity and tune your psychic equipment so you can read your own psychic messages loudly and clearly.

How Do You Receive Psychic Information?

In This Chapter

- Different ways of receiving psychic information
- Your compatibility with each psychic mode
- Exploring your own psychic niche
- Discovering which mode works best for you

An important first step to building your intuition is paying attention to how you as an individual best receive information. We each have a dominant mode or combination of ways to receive psychic impressions, and understanding what works for you is the key to opening your intuitive insight.

If you're a beginner, think of the ways that you normally relate to the information that you receive through your five senses. Do you usually find yourself thinking in images? If so, your psychic skills probably work through the same channel. The same principle applies for those of you who have a keen sense of hearing. Your psychic information will probably come to you via your ears, and likewise for physical touch and even smell. Even taste can make an appearance on the psychic scene.

This chapter will help you focus on where your special abilities lie. Becoming aware of your natural inclinations will help you tap into an easy psychic source for yourself. If you want to explore more than one pathway, that's fine, too. You certainly should take some time to follow your curiosity. But starting with the easiest way first will be more direct and productive and may help you get to other modes faster in the long run.

Clairvoyance: Your Inner Vision

Clairvoyance comes from French, meaning "clear-seeing." It refers to the power to see an event or image that appears in the past, present, or future. This type of sight usually does not occur with your physical eyes but instead with your inner eye.

> **DEFINITION**
>
> **Clairvoyance,** from the French meaning "clear-seeing," is the ability to perceive things that cannot be seen with the physical eye. It also refers to keen perception and insight.

For example, Lynn was preparing to give a reading for a new client named Esther. When she closed her eyes, an image of a huge umbrella immediately popped into her mind. She saw it quite distinctly. In her mind's eye, the umbrella stood in the corner of the room, tipping over. Although she often receives symbolic, intuitive messages, she couldn't make any sense of this falling umbrella. Not knowing what else to say or do, she simply told Esther what she'd seen.

To her surprise, Esther shrieked, "Oh no! That can't happen!" She then explained that she owned an event-management business and intended to put on a huge promotional function—held under a tent—for her largest client the following week. All of the buffet tables were to be decorated with umbrellas! "They can't fall over. It would ruin everything!" explained Esther.

Because Lynn doesn't believe that everything is predestined, she suggested that Esther tie down the umbrellas securely—and, while she was at it, secure the tent itself with extra rope and fasteners. Esther called a week later to say she'd arrived at the event early in the morning and "battened down her hatches." When she returned a few hours later, all of the other tents had blown over in a sudden windstorm. Esther's was the only one left standing!

Sometimes the images received through clairvoyance are literal images, such as the umbrella blowing over. Oddly enough, this image was so literal that only Esther herself could understand it. On the other hand, many images are symbolic and need to be interpreted by the person who personally receives them. Whether the images are literal or symbolic, they usually do not appear outside the intuitive's own mind or inner eye.

Many people think of the term "inner eye" as a figure of speech, but the yogic tradition also uses the term "third eye." According to the Eastern tradition of *chakras*, wherein certain areas of the body influence energy flow in specific aspects of our lives, the third eye is the seat of clairvoyance. Located in the center of the forehead, it is the screen that receives visualizations, whether in the form of visions or imagery. Although a person might not feel that a picture literally appears in his or her third eye, the concept provides a slightly more concrete way of thinking about clairvoyance.

DEFINITION

Chakras are centers of energy located between the base of the spine and the top of the head. They are described as vortices or funnels of energy. Chakras serve as a place of interconnection between the body and the spirit. For more about chakras, check out Anodea Judith's website, www.sacredcenters.com, or read *The Complete Idiot's Guide to Chakras* (Alpha Books, 2009).

Some people, through the use of their psychic vision, are able to look beyond the world of concrete forms and see pure energy. Among the various types of psychic vision is auric sight, which describes the ability to see auras. We call the energy emitted by every object, living and otherwise, an aura. The aura of every thing or being has its own coloration and characteristics. Certain people have the ability to see these auras, which we'll talk more about in Chapter 7.

When the process of clear seeing occurs inside one's mind, it's called subjective clairvoyance. But clairvoyance may reach beyond sheer visualization as well. In some instances, intuitives report seeing physical manifestations, which they call objective clairvoyance. (If you aren't up for any visits from unexpected guests, don't worry. You have to work hard to develop this ability, and even for people who are able, this type of experience is rare.)

Clairaudience: Your Inner Voice

Simply put, *clairaudience* is "clear hearing." *Webster's New World Dictionary* defines clairaudience as "the act or the power of hearing something not present to the ear but regarded as having objective reality." Clairaudience can include hearing sounds, such as music or ringing, as well as voices. Like clairvoyance, clairaudience can be divided into two types: objective clairaudience, which occurs in the real world so that anyone can hear it; and subjective clairaudience, which occurs only in one's mind.

DEFINITION

Clairaudience is the ability to hear sounds that aren't accessible to the physical ear but seem to have objective reality.

When people hear voices, they can get confused about this form of intuitive information because it often sounds like their own, inner voice (which is sometimes referred to as self-talk). Through practice, you can discern whether you're hearing psychic information, self-talk, simple wishful thinking, or an expression of something you're afraid may happen. One helpful hint for distinguishing the source is that, generally, intuitive impressions come through to you in a very kind, loving, and helpful manner—something your self-talk may not do.

MIXED MESSAGES

Certain types of schizophrenics also report hearing voices, and if you start hearing voices out of the blue, your first stop should be your doctor's office. We also recommend that you make sure you're truly hearing psychic information before acting on what you hear. And whatever you do, don't try anything dangerous because you think it's based on your intuition!

Lynn once experienced this form of intuition while giving a reading to a young woman we'll call Cathy. Lynn and Cathy had been discussing her difficult relationships with men, which had been quite emotionally painful to her. Cathy feared that she would always make bad choices where men were concerned and felt quite hopeless about this.

As Lynn tried to gain some insight into this issue, she heard a very insistent voice in her head saying, "Read her the quote! Read her the quote!" As Lynn heard this voice, she also saw an image of a page of inspirational quotes that she keeps in a file cabinet. Because the quotes didn't really have anything to do with the reading (or so Lynn thought), she was a little confused. However, the impression was so insistent that after apologizing to Cathy for the odd interruption, she did what her intuition suggested. Feeling drawn to the third quote on the page, Lynn read it to Cathy along with the author's name.

When Lynn looked up, Cathy was crying. Because the piece wasn't particularly moving, Lynn was surprised at Cathy's response. After a moment, Cathy said, "The man who wrote that ... I lived with him for eight years." She went on to explain that their relationship hadn't been all bad, and that relationships could have positive aspects after all. Although she didn't go off in search of this long-lost love, Cathy renewed her sense that relationships didn't have to be hopeless and decided to take a more optimistic look at future possibilities.

Those psychics who receive information in this auditory way claim that they have a particular "psychic ear," meaning that either the left or right ear is the dominant one for receiving their psychic auditory impressions. Clearly, they are hearing a sound, rather than sensing a thought (as we discuss next).

Clairsentience: Your Inner Sensing

Clairsentience is commonly considered "clear thinking" or "clear knowing." Webster's defines it as the "ability to perceive things out of the range of ordinary perception." This is the type of information that makes us say, "I know, but I don't know how I know." It may come to you as an "ah-ha" moment or as new information that makes such perfect sense that you feel like you've always known it (and you probably have).

Although clairsentience does not fit the mold in that it isn't directly related to one of the other five senses, it is the most common way that people receive psychic information. That is, most people receive information in this way, whether they know it or not. They may have described it simply as a hunch—not connecting it with the psychic aspect at all.

As mentioned earlier in the chapter, this clear-knowing is Lynn's predominant mode of receiving information. For instance, one of her clients recently had some trouble with his boss and needed advice about how to work with her more effectively. To help focus on the person in question, Lynn asked her first name.

DEFINITION

Clairsentience is the ability to perceive information out of the range of ordinary perception. It's translated as "clear-thinking" or "clear-knowing."

Lynn closed her eyes and said the woman's name to herself, then immediately sensed someone very angry and controlling. Lynn also received a symbolic, visual impression of this woman coming toward her with an ax—the term "battle ax" immediately leapt to mind! When Lynn related all this to her client, he started laughing. The boss was apparently known in the office, not so affectionately, as the Battle Ax Boss. Lynn then went on to describe some effective strategies for dealing with her.

Trusting Your Gut: Your Physical Knowing

Although there isn't an official word for clear touching, the kinesthetic or physical mode of receiving information definitely exists. It doesn't refer to an external physical touch, as much as your own internal physical responses when sensing information. For example, if your stomach is in knots after you make a decision, you're probably receiving intuitive information through your body that your decision was wrong. In fact, this experience is probably where the expression "following your gut instinct" comes from. Sometimes, feelings come from touching an object—and by doing so, tapping into its past—a technique called *psychometry*, which we'll discuss in Chapter 4.

Other types of physical knowing also occur. Husbands of pregnant women experience sympathy pains, and some medical intuitives feel someone else's pain in the same spot in their own body. Headaches may also express psychic information, warning that you are overstressed and need to slow down.

> **DEFINITION**
>
> **Psychometry** is one type of intuition that involves psychic feeling going beyond the inner world to the outer, physical one. This sense involves the ability to touch an object and thereby tap into its past and its owner's past. It works when you pick up the vibrations that accompany the object's past.

So Close You Can Taste—or Smell—It

Some people also receive intuitive information from tastes and smells. They may get a bad taste in their mouths when facing an uncomfortable situation or when something doesn't seem right. Or, they may smell smoke as a warning signal for impending trouble.

Some people know when they receive a psychic insight because the insight is accompanied by the scent of roses. Other people find they smell something familiar and specific—like their grandmother's perfume—when receiving intuition.

Finding Your Niche

You may also hear the term claircognizance, meaning "clear knowing." For most people, their claircognizance is accessed through the psychic senses we have defined in this chapter—clairvoyance, clairaudience, clairsentience, kinesthetically, or through taste or smell. Sometimes, though, a psychic thought will come to you as a thought. It just pops into your head. When that happens, you're experiencing claircognizance.

Now that you have a better idea of what types of intuition are out there, here are some clues about where to start finding yours. But you need to do the legwork by answering the questions in the following exercises. Take your time and be thoughtful. Feel free to come back to these questions and revisit your answers if you feel so moved.

Intuition Exercise: Information Gathering

Here's an exercise to help you figure out your dominant mode of receiving information. It may seem a little open-ended, but that's how this exercise works. For that reason, you should consider this an information-gathering exercise, not a final, definitive statement about your abilities. You may want to come back to these questions over the course of a week or more. Then, you can add any new information that has come to you during that time.

Get out your notebook and a pen. Take a few moments to center yourself by focusing on your breath. If it helps you to relax, put on a piece of calming music. Or, light a candle or some incense to create a special, psychically aware mood.

Remember a time when you had an accurate intuition about something. Describe that experience in your notebook.

Did you just "know"? Describe your perceptions. Did you receive a flash of insight? Write about that perception.

Did you have a physical sense in your body? If so, where in your body? Describe that experience.

What did the experience (no matter how it presented itself) feel like? Describe that feeling.

Did you interpret it as a positive or negative impression? Describe that perception.

Did you hear a voice or have an auditory impression? Describe what happened.

What did it sound like? Describe that perception.

Was it your voice? How did you differentiate it from your normal self-talk? Describe your experience.

Did an image come to your mind? If so, what was it? Write about what you saw.

Did you get a symbolic representation of your answer? Describe what you perceived.

Was there a smell associated with your insight? Describe your perception.

As we mentioned at the beginning of this exercise, it is intended to be open-ended. We want you to start thinking about how you access your intuitive insights. Now that you've answered these questions, what do you think is your main mode of receiving intuitive information?

Intuition Exercise: Meditation and Your Intuition

Although not impossible, it's unlikely that you'll be open to psychic impressions when you're busy—physically or mentally—with other things, especially at the start. You'll be most open if you're relaxed, which you may be best able to achieve through quiet meditation. Before you begin this meditation, think of a question you would like some intuitive information about. Phrase the question so that it evokes more than a "yes" or "no" answer. The following are some examples:

- What could I do to enhance my psychic abilities?

- What could I do to improve my relationship with (name)?

- What are some ways that I could increase my income?

When you feel comfortable with how your question is worded, find some quiet time just for you. Create a relaxed atmosphere for yourself. Why not lower the lights, light a candle or some incense, and put on some soothing music? When you feel ready, try the following technique:

1. Close your eyes. Take a deep breath and relax.

2. Visualize the sun over your head, warm and glowing radiantly.

3. Imagine the light from the sun flowing through your body, filling your head, down through your neck, across your shoulders, down into your arms, through your hands, and then into your fingers. The light fills your chest, back, belly, and hips and flows down into your legs, feet, and toes.

4. Imagine the light is bathing every cell with healing and calming energy. The light also brings knowledge and wisdom.

5. Now, visualize this light flowing down through your physical body and out around your body. Feel it soothing and relaxing you.

6. Take a deep breath in and slowly let it out as you say the word "relax." Begin to slowly count from 10 down to 1. As you do, imagine you are becoming more and more relaxed.

7. When you arrive at the number one and you're in a deeply relaxed state, ask your question. Allow yourself to be open to any information that comes. Pay attention to your feelings, symbolic impressions, and any physical sensation or words that come to mind.

GUIDED INTUITION

Take your time when it comes to receiving intuitive information. Many people in Lynn's classes find that answers come to them after—sometimes hours after—they come out of this meditation. Don't be discouraged if you don't get an immediate response.

As you begin practicing these exercises, you'll start to notice that information comes to you more often—even when you aren't expecting it. You'll also build confidence and that good old trust in yourself that we keep talking about.

Intuition Exercise: Daily Observation

Here is an exercise to help you get in touch with that "everyday-occurrence" type of intuition. Even when you don't take time to sit and meditate, this exercise can help you become more aware of the amazing intuitive stuff going on around you.

1. Pay close attention to what your intuition is telling you as you go about your day. Check in with it often. If you find it difficult to remember to do this, set a soft chime on your watch or phone to remind you to stop, breathe, and check in.

2. Ask your intuition questions, such as, "What should I do in this situation?" "What do I need to know about this?" (Remember that you may get the answers from a variety of sources, including feelings, words, images, body sensations, and so on.)

3. Act on the information you receive. For example, is there a person you feel guided to talk to? If so, go and do it. Or perhaps there is a class you want to take or a book you've been itching to read. If using your intuition is new for you, try using it in low-risk situations first.

4. If you don't understand something, ask for clarification. You may not receive information immediately. Remember that developing this skill, like any other, is about practicing. You may not be perfect at first.

5. If the information doesn't feel right or you aren't ready to act on it, don't!

6. Write down the guidance you receive. It's helpful to look back at what you've experienced from time to time to see how accurate your guidance is.

We'll talk more about keeping a psychic journal in Chapter 4. For now, remember that your intuition is always there to guide you and provide you with encouragement and information. Learn to trust it!

Intuition Exercise: Let Your Intuition Decide

Whenever you have a decision to make this week, stop, take a breath, close your eyes for a moment—if that helps you—and tune into your intuition. This can work for the smallest matters as well as the grandest. For now, focus on a larger type of decision that you need to make this week, but try to apply these steps to smaller ones, too, as you go along.

What decision do you need to make? Describe it in your journal.

Write down all the impressions you receive about this decision.

First, describe your emotional/feeling impression(s). Describe your physical impression(s). Describe your auditory impression(s). Describe any other impression(s). What does this information tell you about the decision you hope to make? What does it tell you about how you go about making such decisions? Are you beginning to trust your instincts?

Intuition Exercise: Assessment

After completing these exercises, we're certain that you're much more aware of your recent decisions and the process you followed in making them. But did this process change the outcome of your decisions? Think back on that a little more.

How did your decision turn out? Describe the results in your journal.

Which of your impressions were most accurate or most helpful?

What is the dominant mode in which you received this information?

Can you isolate anything that helped you separate a true psychic insight from a false one?

Is there anything else that you noticed about this decision-making exercise?

We hope you feel comfortable with how your decision turned out. If you feel good about your decision, what helped confirm your comfort level? That's something you'll want to focus on when you're looking for future intuitive insights.

Now that you have a sense of how you receive information, you'll want to gain a better sense of where you're at right now. The next chapter contains a great-big "You Are Here" sign. As you continue your quest to get in touch with your psychic side, knowing where you're at now helps you become more centered on the psychic path.

The Least You Need to Know

- Understanding how you receive intuitive messages is a first step toward building your psychic awareness.
- We all receive intuition uniquely. No one way of receiving information is better than another.
- Finding the form of intuition that works best for you may help you tap into your abilities more easily.
- Pay attention to how you normally take in information. You may receive psychic insight through the same sense.
- Don't pressure yourself to attune to a specific method or form of intuitive insight. Let nature take its course.

How Psychic Are You Right Now?

In This Chapter

- How intuitive are you?
- Exercises for added psychic insight
- Tune in to what's really going on
- Document your journey with a psychic journal

Well, now that you know you're psychic and understand a bit better how you receive psychic information, the question is: How psychic are you? Your present level of psychic awareness is an individual and personal matter. There's certainly no contest going on here, but seeing where you are now will help you know in which areas you need practice. And, as we all know, practice makes perfect!

In this chapter, we offer guidance in measuring where you are in relation to your intuition. We also include several exercises that allow you to try different types of psychic skills.

Determining Your Psychic Personality Profile

Just as people have certain personality traits, they also have traits in their psychic lives. You might carry on a relationship with your intuition that seems to come from outside yourself (for example, through clairvoyance or clairaudience). Or, you might feel that your psychic information comes through highly internal processes (such as clairsentience or simply knowing). How you react to the information you receive also reflects your psychic profile. Whether you remain silent about your psi sense or talk about it openly, the way you sense and respond to psychic information is individual and unique to you.

Your First Psychic Steps

Getting a handle on your psychic self doesn't have to be difficult. Many methods exist for helping you delve into your intuitive side. Before you drop into your intuition, though, you need to concentrate on clearing your mind. Try the four-step exercise that follows.

Intuition Exercise: Clear and Focused

These four steps seem to work for many people (and they should remind you of the meditation exercise you performed in Chapter 3):

- Choose a calm place and begin to breathe deeply.

- Focus on the spot just between and above your eyes, which is the location of your third eye.

- Acknowledge to the universe (or to your chosen higher power) that you are open to receiving information and are willing to wait for it.

- When you feel peaceful and open, you can simply wait for information to come to you, or you can direct your focus toward whatever exercise interests you, such as one that follows.

If you feel a lot of emotions bubble up when you sit down to meditate, don't worry. Many people, especially those who are busy all the time, experience the same thing. Sometimes the process of taking a moment to check in with yourself can feel moving. Some people say that it feels as if they have just made contact with someone they miss a great deal. Who is that person? Themselves! If you have this type of experience, just keep breathing and keep practicing meditation! It will do you good. After some time and with practice, the feelings will become less intense, and it will be easier for you to sit still, be with yourself, and just breathe.

Once your mind is clear and focused, you'll want to try the following exercises.

Intuition Exercise: What's Your Dominant Psychic Sense?

Record yourself reading the paragraphs that follow. Then, listen to the text and allow yourself to feel with all your senses. (Or, get a trusted friend to read the text to you.) Close your eyes, take a few deep breaths, and relax. Imagine that you are on a beach.

It's a beautiful, warm summer day. You hear seagulls calling in the distance. You hear the waves breaking gently on the shore. See the water and the sand in your mind, and hear the waves and the gulls. Feel the healing rays of the sun on your skin. A breeze floats salty sea air around you. Take off your shoes and experience the warm sand on your feet. Take a few steps toward the water and feel the wet, cool ocean on your feet. You hear children laughing behind you and look to see a little boy and girl building a sandcastle.

You're calm and relaxed as you stroll along the beach. You're getting thirsty, and you see a lemonade stand a short distance away. You approach it and smell the sweet-tart scent of lemons. You buy a cup of ice-cold lemonade and take a sip. Taste the lemonade and feel it slide down your throat.

Now, open your eyes and record your results in your notebook.

- Could you see the sandcastle, lemonade stand, and the ocean?
- Could you use your sense of touch to feel the sand, the ocean water, and the cup of cold lemonade?
- Could you smell the sea air and the scent of lemons?
- Could you taste the lemonade?
- Could you hear the sounds of the child or the gulls calling?
- What emotions did you feel as you walked along the beach?
- Was one or more of your senses easier to access than another? Which sense do you think was dominant for you?

As you explore, be aware that your strengths are likely to lie along the lines of your dominant sense as you defined it in Chapter 3. Trust the information that comes to you along that pathway.

Intuition Exercise: Can You Feel It?

We mentioned psychometry in Chapter 3. The term is derived from the Greek words *psyche*, meaning "soul," and *metron*, meaning "to measure." The concept of "measuring soul" refers to the idea that every object possesses certain vibrations that reflect its inner essence, which you can read if you are open to it.

This type of intuition is often referred to as "seeing with the fingers." It enables you to pick up information about an object's history through holding or touching it.

Many psychics consider psychometry a form of clairsentience, which is perhaps the most common form through which most people receive psychic information (see Chapter 3). For this reason, teachers often recommend that beginners focus on developing psychometry as a first step. This ability can be mastered within several months and is a great first step toward learning more challenging skills.

So here's a psychometry exercise to get you started. Choose a few objects that you'd like to read psychically. Good choices are a handwritten letter; a piece of jewelry; a metal object such as a key; or an older object, such as an antique vase. We recommend you try this with an object that has some history, so you'll want something that has been held and used. For example, you won't get much information from a form letter from your insurance company, but a letter from your grandmother will have an energy that you can pick up on. Note that a piece of clothing or fabric will work only if it hasn't been cleaned.

Choose objects that a friend or relative can give you factual information about after you've practiced the exercise. Their knowledge allows you to get some verification of your accuracy when you're finished.

Arrange the objects on a table in front of you. Sit in a comfortable position and close your eyes. Take a few relaxing deep breaths. Choose an object and hold it in your hand. Concentrate fully on this object. Don't rush. Pay attention to images that come to your mind. You may receive fragments of information. They may come in words, feelings, symbolic impressions, or a physical sensation. If you get a strong impression that is upsetting to you, try to shift your perspective to be an observer of the information and not an absorber of it. Your purpose is to pick up on the vibrations of the object and to receive a description of its owner.

MIXED MESSAGES

When first trying out your psychometric skills, keep it simple. You'll want to narrow down the amount of information you get so you won't be overwhelmed. For this reason, stick with reading personal objects that have always belonged to one individual.

If you're doing this exercise with a friend, verbalize any information you receive. If you're doing it on your own, jot down your impression or record your voice. Don't try to intellectualize or remain rational at this point. You might even feel like you're making things up. Don't worry about that. The time to analyze the content is after you're through. Stay open. You might want to hold the object in your other hand to see whether the information you receive is any different. Record any and all information you receive. Repeat this process with all the objects you have chosen.

When you're through, you may want to shake or wash your hands to release any of the vibrational impressions that came from the objects you were holding. After you've done that, check your psychic information against the known facts about each object. How did you do?

You'll probably be surprised that you actually perceived some of the information correctly. But you don't have to be! Many intuitives believe that this information—and much more—is always there for you, just waiting for you to tap into it. And every time you practice psychometric exercises, you will be able to tap into this ability more easily.

Remote Viewing

Remote viewing, which we first mentioned in Chapter 2, was pioneered by a group of scientists in a government-sponsored program at SRI (Stanford Research Institute) International in California. Participants were taught to enter an altered state of consciousness, then trained to view places, situations, and people at a geographic distance in order to gather information. The government used this data to gain intelligence information on everything from distant military activities to descriptions of weapons stockpiles. In other words, the government practiced psychic spying!

One insider from the operation, David A. Morehouse, has written a book describing how he learned remote viewing and how you can learn, too! It's called *Remote Viewing: The Complete User's Manual for Coordinated Remote Viewing* (Sounds True, 2011). Morehouse was initially a commander of a Ranger Company, an elite combat unit. In 1987, he was shot in the head during duty—and though he recovered physically, his injury brought a disturbing psychic wound. He had recurrent dreams telling him that he had chosen the wrong path—that he should have been on a path of peace.

He kept these dreams secret; exposing them would have ended his career. Several years later, he was recruited for a top-secret unit requiring that he undergo a battery of psychological tests. During these tests, he confessed to both the dreams and his disturbing out-of-body experiences. He expected to be given his walking papers, but to his surprise he was shown a file marked "Top Secret/Grill Flame." The folder contained references to "viewers" and "monitors" who seemed to be seeing or visiting a site in nonphysical form.

Morehouse was given more information about the psychic espionage program, learning that it had been in existence for 24 years. It was known by the names of Scanate, Grill Flame, Center Lane, and Stargate, to name a few. He joined the program and began a 10-month training session.

He learned to enter an altered state of consciousness and to take mental journeys to other places. He was trained to write down information about what he saw, tape record his impressions, and sketch them according to strict guidelines. He was discouraged from interpreting what he saw or using his imagination to elaborate further. Eventually, he reached what he calls a "philosophical impasse with the unit." He believes that remote reviewing is a gift to be used to further humankind, not to be used as an espionage tool.

A number of other government-trained remote viewers have popular books out as well. Look for titles by Russell Targ and Joseph McMoneagle. On the internet, you can also read Ingo Swann's memoir of his experiences with remote viewing: www.biomindsuperpowers.com. Swann, who is also a visual artist, is credited by many as being the father of remote viewing, having demonstrated his abilities in this area as early as 1972. Be sure to check out the website of the International Remote Viewing Association (IRVA) at www.irva.org, where you will find instructions for how to do a remote-viewing session yourself. Founded in 1999, the IRVA is a nonprofit group that promotes scientifically sound research in the field of remote viewing, proposes ethical standards and means of testing, and provides accurate information about remote viewing to the public.

Today, several laboratories as well as independent consultants are continuing to research remote viewing. Its use certainly transcends espionage. In fact, you can try it right now by following the instructions in this simple exercise.

Intuition Exercise: A Remote-Viewing Visit

For this exercise, choose a target place that you wish to visit. This should be a place that you don't know.

If you're by yourself, choose a place you can visit in the near future to confirm your accuracy. Make sure to record your remote-viewing experiences.

If you're with a friend, try to remote-view a place familiar to your friend but not to you. This might be your friend's office or a relative's home. Your friend can ask you questions about the remote-viewing site, and you can relay the impressions out loud as you experience them. Ask your friend not to comment on your accuracy or inaccuracy until after the exercise is completed. Have your friend take notes during the exercise so you'll both remember points to discuss later.

After choosing the target place you wish to visit, get into a comfortable, relaxed position and close your eyes. Take several deep breaths and exhale each one slowly. Imagine that you are floating gently out of your body and moving to the site you have chosen. Begin to notice and describe the details of what you see around you. Here are a few things to look for:

- What buildings do you see? Are they brick, concrete, or painted? Is there a street? Is it paved? Is it busy?

- Is there a park or a body of water? Are there people around?

- If you're in a building, what does it look like? What color is it? What do the furnishings look like? Are there any unusual objects that catch your attention? Are there windows? What shape are they?

Take your time. Move slowly. Stay aware of your surroundings. When you've finished with one area, you may want to move on or go back to an area you've already looked at. Depending on the site you have chosen, your questions may vary.

After you finish your exploration, move back to your physical body. Take some deep breaths, wiggle your toes and fingers, stretch, and mentally come back into the room.

If you're working alone, write down all the impressions you received so you can check on their accuracy later. If you're working with a friend, ask for his or her feedback on your remote-viewing data.

Keep in mind that with many of these practice exercises, you are learning new skills. Many people feel that they are making things up and are then surprised to find they were highly accurate. Be willing to take a risk, even if it means being wrong. Don't expect to be perfect. (Even the experts aren't!) Keep practicing.

ARE YOU AWARE?

The George Clooney movie *The Men Who Stare at Goats* (2009) is fiction, but the book of the same title upon which the movie is based (Simon & Schuster, 2009) is true. The book was written by Welsh journalist Jon Ronson, who has also worked for BBC radio, wrote a number of other investigative books, and made documentary films.

How Perceptive Are You?

Picking up on intuitive information has a lot to do with being open to it and aware of it when it comes. Dr. Daniel Cappon, a Scottish-born psychiatrist, environmental expert, and author, has identified 20 skills that naturally intuitive people have. He divides these skills into two categories: input skills and output skills.

Based on his list of skills, Dr. Cappon has devised an IQ test that measures intuitive ability. It's much too long to include all of it here, but we thought a small sampling would offer some insight. The input skills include 10 skills involving the ability to take in information quickly. Among these skills are:

- Quick visual perception (the ability to spot danger in the blink of an eye)
- Quick visual location (the ability to spot things quickly, such as a familiar face in a group photo)
- Accurate estimation of time, dimensions, or weight
- Quickly taking in an entire scene and remembering the details

The 10 output skills involve acting on information quickly, even with a minimum of background information. Among these skills are:

- Knowing the best time to intervene in a situation (such as when to play the stock market and when to quit)
- Having hunches that often prove accurate
- Describing what has already happened without having any outside source of information (finding out after you've described something that it *did* occur as you saw it)

If you're interested in a fun way to assess where you're at, Dr. Cappon has devised several exercises for testing your own intuitive ability at home. Here are two of Dr. Cappon's homegrown tests. Try them yourself:

- Ask a friend to draw an image on a paper and then cut it into six or seven pieces, sort of like a puzzle (but with straighter edges). Make sure that your friend doesn't let you know what he or she drew ahead of time! Then, ask your friend to scatter the pieces in a random arrangement on a table. As soon as you look at the pieces, ask your friend to time you—but you're allowed only seven seconds! If you can identify the image in seven seconds or less, consider the experiment a success!

• Ask a friend to select several sets of photos that you haven't seen. Each set should include photos that show a sequential event (for example, a building before and after it is torn down). Your friend should time you, allowing you to look at each photo for just seven seconds. The catch is that you will try to predict what the second picture will show after seeing only the first one. If you can do that, consider the test a success!

Learning to Focus

Focus can mean many things and can be applied on many levels. But the key to understanding—and doing it—is making a mental effort to be aware. To put this into context, consider the psychometric exercise we talked about earlier. If you hold a watch in your hand, you can definitely focus on its physical traits. But after you've done that, allow your attention to move to a level beyond what you can sense in the physical realm.

DEFINITION

Webster's has nine entries to define **focus,** but the most relevant for our purposes is "a central point, as of attraction, attention, or activity." Another entry says merely "to concentrate."

Just as you can focus your thoughts on the material world, you can also focus on a less-tangible one. Following are a few ways you can become more attuned to the psychic experiences that are constantly occurring around you. When you are open to noticing them, you'll begin to see how abundant they are.

Paying Attention to the Subtle Message

Messages from your intuition are often faint or indistinct at first. Because we're so used to hearing our negative self-talk, we often drown out our own intuition. It's not called your still, quiet inner voice for nothing!

When you're just beginning to tap into your intuitive cues, you may have difficulty differentiating between your intellect and your intuition. One way to tell the difference is to note whether you are experiencing any fearful or anxious thoughts. When information comes from your intellect or negative self-talk, it's often based on thoughts of guilt, feelings of fear, or a need to protect yourself from a perceived threat. Guidance from your higher self tends to come through in a way that makes you feel peaceful and balanced; it is always encouraging and positive. Think of it this way: your intuition "speaks softly"; it's your intellect that carries "a big stick."

Synchronicity

A common saying is, "Synchronicity is God's way of remaining anonymous." Carl Jung coined the term *synchronicity* to describe "a causal connecting principle" that links mind and matter. He believed that an underlying connectedness draws everything together and that meaningful coincidences cannot be explained by cause and effect. Rather, synchronicity seems to draw everything together with a sense that something bigger is happening out there—and it seems to have everyone's best interests at heart.

> **DEFINITION**
>
> **Synchronicity** is a coincidence of events that seem to be meaningfully related.

Many times, your inner knowing helps you arrive at the right place at the right time. Indeed, events come together with such precision that you might feel launched on some predestined course. When you are in the benevolent flow of synchronicity, you know you're trusting your intuition. Here are a few samples that many people can relate to:

- You've just applied for a job in a company where you really want to work— and a long-lost colleague calls and tells you she was recently hired there.

- You have a dream about a favorite uncle. In the morning, you receive a call to tell you he died the previous evening.

- You pick up the phone to call your sister and discover she's already on the line, having called you at the same time.

Many people may brush these experiences aside as mere coincidences, but there's nothing mere about them. They are all examples of synchronicity. Whether we know it or not, they happen for a reason.

My friend Elena is a seamstress who received a suit for alteration from a client. After the client left the shop, Elena reached for a pair of scissors and accidentally knocked a soft drink onto her client's suit, staining it irreparably. Elena was horrified. She prides herself on her professionalism and integrity and always takes great care with her client's clothes.

She decided that she would have to find the same fabric and remake the suit. She went to four fabric stores. She found the fabric in several places, but it was always the wrong color or shade. Finally she went to a fifth store in a very out-of-the-way place and again had no success.

She was about to resign herself to having to confess to her client when she instead decided to pray and ask for guidance. She went into a corner of the store and said, "Okay, God. Listen to me. If you want me to remake this suit, you're going to have to show me where to get this fabric!" A few seconds later, the bolts of fabric she had been leaning against toppled over. Guess what? The fabric she had been seeking was right there. Her client was thrilled with the beauty of her "re-tailored" suit and was none the wiser.

GUIDED INTUITION

If you find that you're good at predicting business trends, you may find yourself in a new career. This intuitive skill, called business forecasting, is highly sought after.

Did You Get It?

As you increase your awareness, you'll improve your ability to hear your "still, small voice" and recognize the signs of synchronicity. But until you gain confidence in your ability to pick up on these subtle cues, here are a few exercises to help clue you in. Remember that practice really does make perfect, so use these exercises regularly. Remember to breathe while you do them. Soon, your reception of psi information will be an everyday event.

Intuition Exercise: Tuning In, Times Six

In each of the following exercises, pay attention to how you receive your psychic input. It's just as important to pay attention when you're wrong as when you are right. And try to enjoy practicing these psychic skills just for fun!

- Next time you're at a bank of elevators, see whether you can intuit which one is going to arrive next.

- As you're coming out of a sleep state in the morning, see whether you can get any impressions about the day's news.

- Try to name who's on the phone when it rings. (And distinctive rings and Caller ID don't count!)

- Try to see whether you can intuit some of the headlines for the next week, month, or year. And keep a list in your journal (which we'll talk about next).

- Pay attention to what you intuit about the business trends or stock-market performance in your industry this year.

- Play a guessing game with your radio or streaming music. "Name that tune" before you turn on the music. You might be surprised at how often you get it right!

Any time you find yourself getting one of these everyday occurrences right, give yourself a pat on the back for tuning in on target. You're getting there!

Your Psi Practice Journal

How did you do with these exercises? If you're like most people, you'll find that you get better and better at tuning in and recognizing your psychic ability the more you use it.

To keep track of your progress, as well as record all the interesting experiences you're bound to have, we suggest you start keeping a psi practice journal. Purchase a small notebook that you can carry with you to record all that you learn. Record any of your own thoughts or impressions as well as the topics we suggest.

This book contains a lot of fun exercises, quizzes, and games to help you become more psychic. Many times, we'll ask you to explore your attitudes and beliefs as well as write down your psychic impressions. By writing in your journal each day, you'll begin to see how often you receive intuitive information. (In fact, you may want to revisit some of the earlier chapters, particularly Chapter 3, and write down some of the results of the exercises described there.)

Here are a few tips to help you get started on your psychic journal. We want to help you keep accurate notes while charting your progress. You'll be amazed someday when you look back at how far you've come! You can also use your psychic journal to exercise and get in touch with your intuition. If you like, light a candle or some incense before you sit down to write, or put on some relaxing music to help you get into a psychic mood.

- Record synchronicities and coincidences. Sometimes the information you record will not seem immediately important. In retrospect, you may see that you had a clairvoyant experience about the future.

- Don't edit or censor the information you receive. You learn as much from your mistakes as you do from your successes. Also, time might tell you that you were more right than you could ever imagine.

- Feel free to draw pictures of any images you receive or to write down any dreams that come to you.

- To access your intuition, try writing in your journal using your non-dominant hand. (If you are right-handed, use your left hand, and if you're left-handed, use your right.)

- Practice automatic writing. To do this, place your pen on the paper but don't look at it. Allow your hand and the pen to move and keep moving for 10 minutes. Even if it is hard to read, what you write using this technique might surprise you!

Remember: when you write in your journal, always note the date. This offers an entirely new way of understanding the information when you look back at it someday.

As you pay attention to the amazing psychic events surrounding you, your mind will begin to open and realize an ever-expanding consciousness. To help you get in touch with this, the next chapter sets you on a path toward your inner journey. It's a lifelong journey that takes as much energy as you are willing to put into it—and transforms that energy into your ever-growing self.

The Least You Need to Know

- Simple psychic experiments can get you started on a path toward discovering your true intuitive skills.
- Focusing your mind is an essential part of getting in touch with your intuition.
- Don't underestimate the power of your intuition. If you suspect it's there, it is.
- An important way to acknowledge and learn from your intuition is to keep a psychic journal.

Opening Up to Your Psychic Self

In This Chapter

- Be true to yourself
- Discover the basic keys to meditation
- Make contact with your special guide
- Open your mind to new types of messages

Whether already deeply in tune with our intuitive sides or just starting out on our journeys, we all pause occasionally to wonder where our psychic ability comes from. Does it come from a divine source that resides outside ourselves? Or, is it our own inner awareness rising up from the hidden depths of our unconsciousness? Every intuitive will answer this question in a slightly different way according to his or her own unique experience.

What each of us perceives as the source of our psychic gifts is based on our own personal beliefs. And just as personal is our journey to explore this source. In this chapter, we'll focus on your inner journey—the one that leads you closer to discovering who you are and how you'll relate to the unseen world.

The Psychic Journey Within

Every one of us must face our unseen world and its new lessons on our own terms. It's extremely unlikely that a fully materialized ghost, like Jacob Marley who visits Ebenezer Scrooge in Charles Dickens's *A Christmas Carol*, will tap us on the back and tell us to clean up our act. Rather, we receive only lessons and insights that we're prepared to take in.

One way to let the universe know you're ready to receive, and to affirm that fact yourself, is to prepare your mind. Getting your mind to slow down and then focus on staying empty is no easy feat. In fact, the challenge is so great that many spiritual leaders have devoted their lives to mastering this ability. A few examples of those who searched long and hard for a quiet mind are Buddha, Yogananda, and the Dalai Lama.

The Dalai Lama once said, "Tibetan Buddhism considers sleep to be a form of nourishment, like food, that restores and refreshes the body. Another type of nourishment is samadhi, or meditative concentration. If one becomes advanced enough in the practice of meditative concentration, then this itself sustains and nourishes the body." Medical science also sees a relationship between sleep and a meditative state. Both sleep and meditation are thought to occur in four cycles of increasing depth. In addition, the brain waves of meditating people can also resemble those of the sleeping.

GUIDED INTUITION

Physical exercise helps prepare and quiet your mind for meditation by allowing you to let off steam and release blockages of stress and anxiety that interfere with clear thoughts. So why not try meditating after your workout? That's what yogis do—stretch and sweat first, then sit and breathe afterward.

So why, you might ask, have humans evolved such a high level of intelligence only to have to empty our minds to achieve a higher level of consciousness? Well, to step up to that higher level, we need to step outside our individual, ego-oriented ways of perceiving things, which brings us right back to our psychic sense. To understand more about the unseen world, we need to keep our minds open to receiving information in ways that transcend the physical world.

The true masters of the open mind—Buddha and the Dalai Lama, for example—recommend a few practices that have stood the test of time. These include meditation, mantras, mandalas, and the classic wisdom "Know thyself." This is a phrase that resounds throughout many schools of philosophical thought. It is often credited to Plato, who included it in his writing. But it actually made its debut on the architrave (the section of a façade in classical architecture, which is above the pillars and below the decorative frieze) of the temple of Apollo at Delphi—that favorite hot spot for oracular insight.

Honoring Your Inner Voice

The intuitive journey is exciting on many levels. Not only does it introduce you to the possibility that entire worlds exist that you hadn't previously imagined, it also gets you in touch with your inner self. Getting to know your thoughts and understand your feelings is a gift in itself. But sorting through this personal information also helps you distinguish what comes from your intellect and feelings and what is really intuition. All these levels come together to make up what you call "yourself." You must learn to recognize which part of yourself is taking control when you're seeking information or trying to make a decision.

To access your higher consciousness, you may first need to get to the bottom of how you're feeling emotionally. If you begin to meditate and a certain thought keeps tugging at your mind, maybe you need to deal with that first. This could actually be both your emotional and intuitive sides telling you that you need to address the issue. However, if you've taken care of the big and little stuff and annoying preoccupations keep needling their way in, then you'll appreciate meditation and other mental tools for helping you focus.

Using your tools for inner guidance will get you to a place where you can hear what your inner voice wants to say. When you ask for direction and get a clear sense (if not a strong verbal message) about what you should do, then follow it. That's what understanding your intuition—and honoring your inner voice—is all about! Trust your intuition, and it will take care of you.

Mantras

Sound can also be a way to approach a higher plane of consciousness. One such method uses a mantra during meditation. Repeating a particular word or phrase, which usually has a sacred connotation, throughout the meditation helps to keep the mind focused.

A common Sanskrit mantra is *om nama shivaya*, which roughly translates to "I honor the Self in all." The Hebrew word *shalom* (meaning peace) is commonly used as a mantra. Other frequently used words are "love," "beauty," "peace," and "God." Any word that is sacred to you or evokes a special feeling of a quality you seek to develop is a good word to try.

Meditation

As discussed in previous chapters, meditation helps you receive intuitive guidance because it puts you in a state where your mind is relaxed and less distracted by everyday details. Over time, a daily meditation practice of 15 to 20 minutes will work wonders to replenish your body, mind, and spirit.

Many people talk about how great meditation is. But if you haven't tried it, you might be inclined to ask, "What's the big deal?" In fact, in today's busy world, taking time to do nothing is a big deal. But when you meditate, you aren't really "doing nothing." Meditation can:

- Open you to a higher energy source and recharge you.

- Reduce stress and anxiety (you'll gain a calmer and more peaceful approach to daily life).

- Improve your health and general well-being.

- Help you tap into a source of spiritual guidance that can direct you in your daily life.

- Assist you in finding a source of creative ideas to help with decision-making.

GUIDED INTUITION

If you're uncomfortable with the term "meditation," try thinking of this as a time for stillness, quiet time, or even prayer. William Wordsworth called meditation "a happy stillness of mind." It really doesn't matter what you call it—just do it!

Most people find it easiest to meditate before they begin their day. Others like to practice at the end of the day. Try different times to see what works best for you. Despite how busy you are, make time for at least 15 minutes a day. Choose a time when you're most likely to be undisturbed, and remember to turn your phone ringer off and your answering machine on so you won't be interrupted or worried about missing anything.

Keep in mind that meditation is a learned skill. You're training your mind to be still—and that takes effort, because your mind usually likes to jump around in a manner that many meditation teachers have described as a "drunken monkey" (or "monkey mind").

Intuition Exercise: Lynn's Meditation Method

Here's the meditation that Lynn uses when she wants to connect with her intuition:

1. Sit in a chair with your back straight and your shoulders relaxed. Your feet can be on the floor or you may sit cross-legged, whichever is more comfortable for you. Fold your hands in your lap and close your eyes.

2. Take three slow, deep breaths. Inhale and exhale slowly.

3. In your mind, hold a picture of a beautiful, light-filled scene. Imagine that your entire body is filling up with this white light. Pause. Picture every cell being bathed in white light, filling you with peace. This light holds all the wisdom and love from the universe.

4. See the light completely filling you and surrounding you. You may even imagine it filling the room you're in.

5. For 10 to 20 minutes, simply pay attention to your breathing. Watch your breath in your mind's eye, going in and out of your body. If your mind wanders, gently bring it back to watching the breath. Continue to feel the light growing radiant and warm around you. Imagine its connection to a higher source.

6. You might find a mantra helpful to use during this meditation. You can simply say, "Peace," "Om," or "God." Do whatever feels right for you if it helps you with the meditation and your focus.

7. When you are nearing the end of the meditation, ask your intuition whether there is a message for you, and listen for an answer.

8. You also may say a prayer for a person or situation or simply ask for continuing guidance on an issue about which you may need insight.

9. End your meditation by visualizing the light being sent to a person or situation that could use its help.

Some people also like to say "thank you" or "amen" at the end of meditation. Whether you choose to do that, or follow this meditation to a T, or pursue your own path, don't worry—there's no right or wrong way to meditate. It's a very personal practice, and whatever works for you is fantastic!

Making Time for Peace and Joy

One of the ways that your intuition speaks to you is by directing you to joy and peace. Writer Brenda Ueland has coined a term she calls "moodling." She defines it as "long, inefficient, happy idling, dawdling, and puttering." We rarely give ourselves time like this and may even think of it as laziness.

When we're our most busy selves, bustling around complaining about the direction our life is taking, we're most in need of moodling. Such preoccupation prevents our intuition from breaking through the mini-dramas we've created. We need to slow down to hear the still, small, quiet inner voice again. That voice will show us how to bring our lives back into harmony.

The following exercise gives you three steps to help you realign your awareness of inner joy. First, recall what has worked for you in the past, then open yourself to where you're at in the present—and then see what amazing changes can come along.

Intuition Exercise: Expand Your Inner Joy

1. Think of three times in your life when you experienced inner peace. Describe them in your journal.

2. Close your eyes, take a deep breath, and relax. Ask your inner self what would bring about greater joy and serenity in your life. Pay attention to any images, feelings, and body impressions you receive. Write about the guidance you receive.

3. Based on the above information, what steps could you take in your life right now to bring about more joy and harmony? Be certain to take time every so often to simply "kick back and smell the roses." But if you think you need a "quick fix," come back to this exercise. It will help you come back to yourself.

Opening Up to Your Guides

Lynn believes that we all are born with a guide who is with us throughout our lives. Some people have additional guides who come to help them in a specific lesson they need to learn or with a certain project they want to accomplish.

More and more people report having guides, and some feel confident that they have more than one guide at a time. There are many different kinds of guides. They are here to help people and are available when people ask for help. People can perceive their guides in various ways. Some people describe their guides as angels. Others experience their guides as an energy or a light or even a warm, loving feeling. They don't always hear words or see a vision but get a feeling.

Guides are your friends. They are here to love, support, and encourage you. They are wise teachers, and they often give you information through your intuition. At first, guide-provided intuition doesn't feel much different from other types of information you receive. But once you learn to recognize it, you can easily see when you're receiving extra-special insight. In addition to offering information for spiritual growth and healing, guides provide information about your creative endeavors, such as music, art, and even writing.

MIXED MESSAGES

Keep your guides close! Although there's no rule that you can't talk to other people about your psychic experience, limit your sharing to those who are understanding and respectful. In case someone isn't kind, you could find yourself feeling defensive about a positive, very personal experience. When you have a sense that you have made a connection with your spirit guide, cherish the impression.

When Lynn was a small child, she discovered her guide sitting at the foot of her bed one night. The guide seemed very real to Lynn, and it puzzled her that other people didn't see the guide as she did—as a beautiful woman in a white robe. At her young age, Lynn simply referred to her guide as "the lady." She was always very comforting. Lynn felt, and feels, profound peace whenever the lady is with her. Lynn didn't so much hear her talk as she felt her presence—and still does. Lynn frequently asks her for insight about clients as she does readings and for information about projects that she's working on.

Not everyone will experience their relationship with their guide in the same way that Lynn does. Indeed, "guides" might be just one way that some people conceptualize the intuitive information they receive. Everyone who does so reports a common trait: the presence of one's guide creates a sense of being filled with love and light. If you do not sense the presence of a guide, do not bemoan the fact; it might not be the ideal path for you. However, if you're interested, we provide exercises to help you explore the possibility that you, too, have a guide to help you receive and interpret intuitive information.

> **GUIDED INTUITION**
>
> Using guided imagery tapes, instead of reading a meditation out of a book, frees you to relax, close your eyes, and focus on the words and the images evoked. If you would like to try one of Lynn's meditations, go to http://lynnrobinson.com/category/meditations-prayers.

Creating an Inner Sanctuary to Meet Your Guide

Your inner sanctuary is a place you can go in your imagination to receive psychic guidance and assistance. You might perceive this information as coming from your own intuition or from a spirit guide outside yourself. Some people have what they think of as an inner guide who is connected to their intuition. Whatever way you experience the information is okay. For now, picture that it comes to you in a safe haven in your mind's eye. But how do you get there?

Lynn has designed the following meditation to help you take a psychic journey to meet your special guide. The easiest way to perform this exercise may be to have someone read it to you slowly or to read it yourself into a tape recorder and then play it back. Otherwise, you might be distracted by the act of reading as you attempt to meditate.

Intuition Exercise: Meet Your Guide

1. Close your eyes and allow your physical body to become relaxed and comfortable. Allow your conscious mind to drop any cares of the day. Inhale deeply through your nose until your abdomen rises. Hold your breath for a moment, then exhale slowly through your nose. Continue breathing in this way for a few moments. Focus your attention on your breathing. Feel your breath coming in. Rest. Feel it go out.

2. Let yourself begin to feel relaxed and open.

3. Allow yourself to enjoy these feelings. Let your breathing move to a comfortable, relaxed rhythm. Tell your feet to relax. Say in your mind, "I am relaxing my feet." Feel the muscles become loose and relaxed. Relax your ankles. Say in your mind, "I am relaxing my ankles." Relax your lower legs. Relax your knees ... your thighs ... your pelvic area. Take a deep breath and imagine that breath flowing into your abdomen and relaxing that area. Now, imagine it flowing into your chest ... your back. Your neck is relaxing ... your shoulders. Feel the relaxation flowing into your arms and down into your wrists, hands,

and fingers. Now, relax your jaw. Let it drop. Relax the muscles around your mouth, your tongue, your eyes, your forehead, and your scalp. Take another deep breath and relax still further.

4. Count from 10 slowly down to 1. As you do, feel yourself moving into a more and more relaxed yet alert and open state of mind. Let yourself enjoy a feeling of floating and moving weightlessly through space. Feel yourself traveling toward an illuminated, light-filled area. In your mind's eye, find yourself in a beautiful natural scene filled with the sights, sounds, and smells of a lovely day. The sun is warm on your skin, and you have a feeling of relaxed safety, comfort, and peacefulness. This might be a setting in the mountains, at the seashore, by a lake or stream, or in a meadow. Accept whatever scene feels most peaceful to you and go there.

5. When you find your special place, you might want to imagine a house, a small cottage, or some other form of shelter there. You might want to place crystals, incense, plants, or flowers around your sanctuary. An altar of your own devising might feel appropriate. Create and arrange things there for your convenience and enjoyment. You may even want to have a high-tech sanctuary and imagine a computer where you receive guidance or a large screen upon which your guide appears. Do whatever works for you. You can change and refine your sanctuary as you practice this exercise in the future. Your sanctuary is a place in your mind that you can return to at any time to receive intuition information for yourself and others.

6. Explore your environment. Allow your awareness to encompass the colors, textures, shapes, and spaces of your sanctuary. Notice any sounds you hear, and notice the general feeling of this sacred place you have created. Be aware of any feelings or impressions you receive.

7. Take another minute to explore your environment.

8. Now, beside your sanctuary is a path. You might not have noticed it before. As you see it, your attention is drawn to a being surrounded by light that is approaching you. As it approaches, you feel your heart opening and you are filled and surrounded by a wonderful feeling of love and acceptance. This is your guide. Your guide steps toward you and greets you warmly. Your guide has been waiting for you. Allow this guide to be whatever it will. Allow it to emerge into your awareness without any assistance from you. Become aware of its qualities, form, and appearance. You might experience the particular essence of your guide as a scent, a feeling, or even a light being. Your guide may be male or female or may be perceived without gender or form.

9. Find a comfortable place for both of you to sit. Ask your guide for a name. Your guide responds: "My name is ...."

10. Ask your guide whether there is a message for you, and listen for the answer.

11. Ask your guide the following questions:

    a) How can I work with you to develop my intuition?

    b) What is my life purpose?

    c) What steps can I take right now to enhance my life?

    d) [Your own question.]

12. When you feel you have completed your aim, bid goodbye to your guide. Know that you will easily be able to connect with your guide any time you want.

13. When you feel ready, open your eyes and return to your normal consciousness. Wiggle your toes, flex your legs, and stretch your limbs.

To evaluate your experience, take out your journal and respond to the following questions:

- What did you experience during this exercise?

- Describe your sanctuary. (Many people like to draw or paint a picture.)

- What was your guide like? Did you receive a name? (Don't worry if you didn't. It may come later.)

Look back at the questions you asked in step 11. What information did you receive? You may get more information as you write down your answers.

You might not have received answers immediately, and you probably don't know yet whether they are right for you or not. But keep your eyes peeled, because you're sure to be getting some answers soon—and probably in some unexpected ways!

A Willingness to Be Wrong

Whether you're a total beginner at developing your psychic awareness or an experienced pro, you probably already know that there's always something new to learn. And anything new always involves a certain amount of risk. When opening up your psychic insight, the risk might feel greater because there's nothing tangible or visible to confirm your impressions. But that doesn't mean you're alone.

In Lynn's "Developing Your Intuition" workshops, she uses this exercise to help people discover how much they really know. Each person sits with a partner he or she doesn't know. They look at each other and then use their psychic abilities to access information about each other. Part of this partner exercise is to see what you receive psychically about your partner's career and interests.

After Lynn introduces the exercise, she always hears at least one person in class moan, "I can't do this. Everyone else can. I can't! I don't know how." She asks them to be willing to be wrong. If they feel like they are making up the information, so be it. This is intended to be a practice exercise to help them develop a skill. Sometimes people can gain just as much knowledge from how they received wrong information as they can from receiving correct information.

One student started complaining that she "wasn't getting anything" about her partner. Lynn asked her to make something up, to just pretend to be psychic. She exclaimed, "Bees! Bees! I just get bees!" Her partner sat there quietly with his mouth agape. He stared at her and finally stammered, "I run an apiary." Another even stranger story started the same way with a similarly recalcitrant student. She seemed quite agitated because her psychic information about the partner's career didn't make any sense. Lynn explained that many times intuition works because we know some-thing but we don't know *what* we know or *how* we know it and encouraged her to be willing to be wrong and to tell her partner what impression she received. Reluctantly, she said, "I see a head being cut open and love being poured in." Are you ready for her partner's answer? He was a neurosurgeon who practiced psychic healing!

Taking a risk is part of learning, and being willing to be wrong can even be the key to being right!

Psychic Energy Protection

Often, people feel awestruck or even afraid of their newfound insights on the amaz-ing power associated with psychic ability. Fear is a tool that many people rely on as a defensive strategy for facing anything new and difficult to understand. Part of your inner journey is coming to terms with this fear, sorting out why you're afraid, and learning ways to help yourself adapt.

When you begin to develop your psychic ability, you might feel that you are much more sensitive to the energy around you. Have you ever walked into a room and the tension was so strong that you could "cut it with a knife"? You might pick up intense emotions from others more easily and begin to experience them as your own.

As people open up psychically, they often find themselves in situations where they feel that things are not as they seem. At a former job, Lynn had a secretary who seemed overly pleasant and agreeable. But whenever Lynn entered her office, she began to feel impatient and irritable, when just moments before she had felt upbeat and cheerful. There was no apparent reason for feeling this way. Lynn rationalized her reaction for some weeks but couldn't shake the impression that something was wrong. Lynn later learned that the secretary had been spreading rumors in an attempt to get her fired and take her position. This is a form of *psychic attack*.

DEFINITION

A **psychic attack** occurs when someone is willfully and consciously sending you negative energy. In all likelihood, this energy does not come from someone who has developed his or her psychic skills—just a regular person who thinks negatively about you.

How can you avoid having your energy adversely affected? You can strengthen your own force field by maintaining a positive attitude. When your own thoughts are full of joy, happiness, and hope, you are less apt to feel the effects of others' negative thoughts and attitudes. Have you ever had a really bad day and everybody around you seems to just add to the awfulness of it? The theory is that "like attracts like." When you feel upbeat and full of energy, you attract a similar positive energy from others. The more loving, optimistic, and hopeful you feel, the more your "up" energy attracts others of like mind.

Even on our best days, intuitives often feel a need to separate themselves from a flood of psychic information. We want to be able to turn it off when we're ready to rest. As a way of separating herself from everyday life, Lynn practices a number of meditations before seeing clients—including the one described earlier in this chapter. Here are a few more techniques; try them and then decide what works best for you.

Intuition Exercise: Empathic Energy for the Higher Good

If you are an empath who often picks up on others' feelings and energy, try this helpful technique:

Imagine yourself enclosed in a bubble of white light. The light fills you and surrounds you with energy and peace. See this light flowing down to you from above. Say to yourself, "Only that which is good and needful may enter."

If you are feeling drained by someone close to you, try the following method of strengthening yourself:

Visualize an intense, bright blue globe of light above your head. It explodes like fireworks so that the bright blue lights shimmer around you. Feel the energy that the light draws to you. Say to yourself, "I am energized and strong. I attract only good."

If you are going into a difficult negotiation or situation, first define the outcome you would like to create. Then, try this visualization:

Imagine yourself standing under a waterfall of energy. Think about the qualities that you need to have for this difficult situation. Do you need power, strength, love, or courage? Visualize the energy in the waterfall pouring the quality you desire through your body, soaking into all your cells and then surrounding you. See your guide there to help you and add to this energy. Imagine the challenge you are going into, and see yourself successful and all parties feeling good.

GUIDED INTUITION

There are many ways to deal with feeling psychically overloaded or just plain stressed. Learning to ground yourself and your energy can really help. Practice one of the meditations in this book. Or, check the internet for a new technique. We found some good grounding exercises here: www.squidoo.com/ Grounding-Techniques. Check them out!

As in most areas of intuitive growth, there is no right or wrong way to create a sense of safety and confidence. And, like most areas, exercises that appeal to your dominant psychic sense are also those to practice for strengthening your abilities.

How Does Your Guidance Speak to You?

Learn to go within and seek the guidance of your inner self. It may speak to you through small glimmers of insight, flashes of knowing, or whispers in your thoughts. It always shows the next steps to take—a new direction in your personal and spiritual growth. Intuition does not explain but simply points the way. If you use it every day, your intuition will flourish and greatly enhance your life.

As we continue our journey, we'll show you additional ways to understand what your intuitive guidance is telling you. In Chapter 6, we'll progress from opening up your psychic self to fine-tuning your psychic tools. As part of this, you'll learn how to keep your skills in good maintenance and use them for practical purposes.

The Least You Need to Know

- Meditation is a great way to open up to your higher self.
- There are many methods and tools for meditation; choose what works best for you.
- You have a special guide to help you grow and heal, and you can take the initiative to contact your guide.
- You can learn to protect yourself from negative energy and foster the positive.

Tune Your Psychic Instrument

In This Chapter

- Refine your psychic perceptual skills
- Put your intuition to work for you
- Feel inspired—and stay that way
- Take a new view of time

Now you've amazed yourself with your own ability to tap into an awesome source of energy and information. It can be such an enlightening experience that all you want to do is sit and meditate. Or, you might have drawn a blank and are still wondering, "So what's the big deal?"

Whether you're awestruck or unimpressed, you have more to learn. You can definitely dig deeper to gain greater insight and awareness. That's what this chapter is about: helping you tune and further refine your psychic potential.

Using Your Psychic Abilities

Have you ever played an instrument? If you've played one that needs tuning, you know that before you can make music, you need to listen. Is your instrument in tune? Paying attention to your inner insight—in other words, listening—is the first step toward making sure you are properly tuned. Your first attempts might be met with sour notes. But rest assured that with practice, you can count on receiving the needed information at the right time so that you can act on its wisdom.

In psychic circles, common wisdom says that intuition is here to guide us in our spiritual healing and growth. Often, issues that affect us deeply may express themselves in other areas of our lives. For example, tremendous amounts of stress or tension might show up in the form of a headache or some other illness.

That means getting in touch with what ails you on a spiritual level can help clear up difficulty in other areas of your life. For that reason, you shouldn't judge, discredit, or ignore the psychic information that comes to you. Even when you don't understand why it's there, you would do well to accept and trust it. That information can help you in every area of your life, from work to family to friends and more.

ARE YOU AWARE?

Lynn has lots of experience using intuition in the business realm. In fact, she has written an entire book about it—*Trust Your Gut: How the Power of Intuition Can Grow Your Business* (Kaplan Business, 2006). If business interests you, you may want to check it out.

In Business

Because psychic ability is often seen as an aspect of our spiritual side, many people assume that it just doesn't blend with business. Nothing could be farther from the truth. In fact, business is a huge part of your life, so why not use every tool available—including your intuition—to make it as positive and productive as possible?

Your intuition can help you improve your business skills, including the following areas:

- Forecasting trends
- Predicting stock fluctuations
- Planning strategies
- Making decisions quickly and effectively
- Hiring the right person for the job
- Managing effectively
- Overseeing transitions
- Understanding and motivating employees

- Understanding bosses and other decision-makers
- Predicting promotions and politics
- Knowing clients' needs and how to communicate with them
- Negotiating deals and contracts
- Becoming more competitive

Any type of business can make good use of these skills. If you work in the financial arena, you can learn to trust your intuition about investment decisions. If you work in marketing or sales, you might get hunches about when to approach people and how. Researchers, engineers, and troubleshooters can gain amazing insight into technical problem-solving. Managers can gain insight into motivating their staff as well as understanding problems, both professional and personal, that may be hurting their employees' performance.

You can also use your psychic ability to make personal decisions about career paths and job changes. If you're not happy with your current job, your intuition might help you get in touch with the source of your difficulty, find out how colleagues view you, or better understand what makes your bosses and co-workers tick—all of which can help you do your job better (and thus feel better about it). Even if you're happy at your job, you can attain a keener awareness of how to appreciate what you have, improve your surroundings, and make your efforts even more fruitful.

These abilities can come to you, the psychic searcher, when you open your mind to the possibilities and express your desire to sharpen your skills and gain further insight. Your intuition may speak to you in your dreams, through a sudden flash of insight, or by means of a subtle accumulation of logical information.

In Relationships

Your intuition is the perfect tool for helping you tap into the deeper feelings associated with love, family, and friends. All people have an incredible fascination with what makes other people tick. Often, people experience a great deal of pain when someone close to them is doing something they don't understand. What Lynn does as an intuitive is step inside someone's skin (so to speak). Lynn tries to see the situation from his or her point of view. She tries to feel what he or she feels. Lynn gives a voice to the feelings, concerns, and troubles that both the client and whomever he or she is asking about is experiencing. Then, Lynn tries to present a plan of action to resolve the situation. You can undergo a similar process when you tap into your own intuition.

Take a minute to think about the types of relationships you're in, whether they're romantic, friendly, family, professional, or something else. How can your intuition help you improve these? Often, it works by helping you gain insight into the other person's way of thinking so that you can understand his or her feelings and get a sense of what motivates him or her. When you know where that person's coming from, you can take tremendous strides toward connecting and communicating with him or her.

Lynn has a client who is involved at a high level in her religious organization. Despite everyone's good intentions, her colleagues often have differences of opinion that prevent them from working well together. One day, this client asked Lynn to help her with a stubborn standoff taking place in the group. Using intuition, Lynn was able to explain the viewpoints of one of the leaders, along with his reasons for rejecting the group's plans. Lynn and her client discussed ways to show him that she empathized with his views but had suggestions for effective compromises.

Oddly, the day after this conversation, Lynn heard the leader on the radio—expounding on the very same viewpoints that she had explained to her client. If you're wondering about the outcome of their conflict, this situation didn't have an easy solution. The information Lynn provided helped everyone in the opposing group understand the other group's leader from a different perspective, which helped the lines of communication remain open for everyone. Lynn reports that they finally resolved their differences.

Your intuition also keeps you in touch with your own needs and what you can do to help yourself in relationships. A classic example of how this comes in handy is when new relationships form. Lynn has had various female clients come to her after about a year of dating new men with the sad news that they had chosen the wrong person. And yet, when they look back at their first few dates, these women can usually remember a point when their inner voice told them, "This is not a good relationship to pursue." Despite hearing these inner alarms, many people choose to ignore their intuition. Often, because they have made mistakes in the past, they have become afraid to trust their own judgment. Once you are attuned to your intuition, it can act as both a warning signal and a confirmation sign that your own judgment is intact.

One simple area where Lynn always applies her intuition is in choosing the professionals who will work for her, such as doctors, dentists, and even car mechanics. Many parents rely on intuition when it comes to choosing the best schools or teachers for their children. By understanding how two people will get along and how they will motivate each other, you can better decide the direction to follow for a long-term decision. In addition, you can understand how to present information about new transitions to others so that change can be much easier for you and everyone else involved.

Many intuitive people believe that each person we come in contact with is there to teach us something specific. For example, a child is teaching his or her parent patience while the parent is teaching his or her child discipline. Even an angry boss can teach us something, whether it's the importance of being on time or learning to stay calm when your boss is freaking out.

Decision-Making

Many of us panic when faced with making a significant decision (and sometimes even a small one). Often, we can't seem to find a clear "yes" or "no" answer. We write endless lists of pros and cons. We discuss it with our friends and families. We often scurry about trying to gather as many facts about the situation as we can … and then we end up feeling even more confused than when we started.

When making important decisions, try following the process outlined here to take advantage of the intuitive input your psyche can give you. Intuition is not meant to replace logic and rationality; rather, intuitive input simply adds information about yourself, as well as the world around you, to your decision-making process.

The Preparation Phase

In this phase, you research your problem. For starters, write about the decision you're trying to make. Gather as much data as you can about the issue. Declare a firm intent to make your decision. Learn as much as you can about yourself and your response to the issue. This lays the groundwork for the intuitive information to come through. Frame the decision in the form of a question: "Should I take this job with XYZ Company?"

Here's an example from Lynn's experience:

Before Lynn started her psychic reading business, she was an operations manager of a software company. She gave readings for friends a few hours a month. A writer for the *Boston Globe* newspaper heard about her readings and asked whether she could book a session with Lynn. Several months later, she wrote about her experience. The article produced such a response for Lynn's services that her phone was ringing off the hook, and she had to hire an administrative assistant.

Lynn's questions for her intuition were:

- Should I stay in my job and forget the readings?
- Should I leave my job to start a psychic reading business?
- Should I attempt to do my job *and* the readings?

Lynn did as much research as she could during this phase. She found out about renting an office, setting up a business, getting insurance, and finding secretarial help. Lynn spoke with other psychics in the area. She also spoke with her boss about the job, the future of the company, and how he saw her role in it. Lynn gathered data.

Want to hear what happened next? Read on through the transition phase.

The Transition Phase

This is the toughest part for most people. It's the stage during which you're waiting. It often feels like you're doing nothing, but it's a time for letting the solution to your dilemma percolate. If you're a believer in guides, angels, and other helpers of the universe, you may want to think of this as a time when they are gathering resources, connections, and synchronicities to bring about your answer.

Try to enjoy a little downtime. Take care of yourself. Get a massage. Take the day off. Meditate or do yoga. Relax. Sleep more. It's often difficult for your intuition to get through the usual "busy-ness" of your mind. Do anything that helps you slow down.

Now, back to Lynn's example:

Lynn is an action taker, so she hated this waiting phase. Lynn prayed about the decision and asked for dreams or any form of guidance. She meditated and wrote in her journal. She asked for a sign to indicate the direction she should take. Playing out various scenarios in her mind, Lynn tried to feel out her response. She felt scared of the risk. Would it work to have her own business? Could she do this full-time? Could she make it on her own? What about benefits and security? Lynn also felt excited by the idea of change and the possibilities it presented. Meanwhile, she continued to do her software job and give readings. She waited.

Sometimes, if you're not sure what decision to make, waiting is the best strategy. Allow time for your answer to come to you. If you feel you're in a time crunch, create a bit of quiet time away from your usual busy routine to allow a sense of inner calm to come your way.

The "Ah-Ha" Phase

If you've followed the first two steps with the clear intention of receiving intuitive input about your decision, the next step will happen all by itself. The answer may come in a dream, by a continual inner nudge toward a certain answer, or sometimes by a simple inner certainty about the right decision. The answer may come when you least expect it (and most need it). See the way it happened to Lynn:

Lynn's answer came in a dream. In her dream, she was out on a beautiful lake. As she took in this glorious scene, she noticed that she was in canoes. That isn't a typo. Lynn had one foot in one canoe and her other foot in another. The two canoes were going to opposite ends of the lake. Lynn immediately woke up and laughed. She couldn't continue to try to go in two directions! She instantly understood that she couldn't possibly hold down her software job and give her intuitive readings. The answer became clear.

Your information may come to you in a similar way or much differently. Just remember to trust it, as well as trust in your reading of it. It's a special-delivery message just for you, so don't take it for granted or feel afraid to act on it.

The "I Know I Made the Right Decision" Phase

When you've made the right decision, you usually feel relieved, excited, and maybe even calm and peaceful. Often, events start to click into place for you. This is part of the synchronicity we talked about in Chapter 4. You find yourself wanting to move into action. You may receive more nudges from your intuition about what to do next as the new path unfolds for you. Pay attention to the feelings of excitement or positive anticipation that usually come with this phase.

To finish the story:

Lynn was amazed at the coincidences and synchronicities that followed her decision. A friend had an office that she was thinking about subletting, and Lynn took it. Another acquaintance had just come back from several years abroad and needed a temporary job. She became Lynn's receptionist for awhile. Everything clicked into place as more clients called and referred their friends. That was 25 years ago, and Lynn has never regretted her decision.

It's important to separate the fact that you made the right decision from the normal amount of anxiety that the actual change may bring about in your life. Most of us feel a little anxious when we make a change. We might have to move, leave a job and friends, or undergo some other unsettling event. Remember that there's always a learning curve in any new situation, but someday you can look back and say, "Piece of cake."

If you'd like to try a decision-making exercise, take a look at Chapter 18.

Using Your Personal Psychic Symbols

When you're waiting to receive intuitive information, don't overlook what might be right in front of you—literally! These messages can come in many forms, such as dreams, natural events, unusual statements coming from individuals, or a phrase or passage of text that jumps out at you.

Your life is filled with messages that appear at every turn, yet you often don't even recognize them. Or, if you do realize that they're intuitive signs, you don't always know what they're trying to tell you. For that reason, you'd be wise to sort out what symbols you associate with certain words or concepts.

Some psychics use the different varieties of flowers as symbols. They might associate visions of a certain flower with a specific feeling or occasion. When Lynn teaches, she uses an exercise in which she asks her students to pair up and imagine their class partners as flowers. If a student psychically sees an image of a flower separate from all the others, that student might extrapolate that his or her class partner is alone or lonely. If a student sees an image of a flower towering over other flowers, that student might make an interpretation that his or her partner is a leader. Lynn had a person in her class who saw a weak-looking flower as a symbol of her class partner. She exclaimed, "I think you need fertilizer!" It turned out her partner was trying to get pregnant.

> **GUIDED INTUITION**
>
> Here's a fun way to get an answer when you feel stuck. Describe the details of your problem in writing, as if you were asking for help from an advice columnist. Take a deep breath, then give out your best advice. To help you do that, ask yourself: "What would a wise person do?" Before you know it, the solution to your problem will materialize.

Here's an example of how you can use symbols to gather intuitive information. Suppose you are meditating and ask for guidance by saying, "What should I do to have more energy?" The symbol for a change in career pops into your mind. You realize that your work has gotten stale of late, and you decide to seek the advice of a career counselor.

You've been bothered by the fact that you've been having difficulty with a co-worker with whom you used to get along. You wonder whether you have done anything to offend her. You ask for guidance, saying, "What is going on with my co-worker, and how can I fix the relationship?" You receive a symbol of a broken heart. You recognize this as your symbol for a love relationship that has ended. Suddenly, you understand what might have happened to your co-worker and decide to be more compassionate toward her. Here's an exercise to help you define your personal symbols.

Intuition Exercise: Discover Your Psychic Symbols

Get out your notebook, then write down the circumstances surrounding the situation you want to understand. Then, go down the list of psychic symbol words that follows and write down the first response that comes to mind. If images come to you instead of words, feel free to draw your symbols instead.

- Work
- Education
- Marriage
- Money
- Home
- Health
- Travel
- Friends
- Divorce
- Career in healing
- Change in career
- Musical ability
- Change in location

- Vacation
- Someone who is shy
- Someone who is controlling
- Teacher
- New situation/change
- Fall
- Spring
- Spirituality
- Ambition
- Family
- Love
- Nature
- Power

After you've completed this list, meditate upon what you've written to discover intuitive insights. You might also want to add other symbols that come to you in the future, whether they're new categories or revisions of old ones. Just don't cross out any records of previous associations, because one concept can have more than one symbol. You might soon have an extensive guide to much of what's going on in your mind.

MIXED MESSAGES

If you feel continually stuck in fear or anxiety, especially when you need to make a decision, check out one of Susan J. Jeffers's books. She wrote *Feel the Fear and Do It Anyway* (Ballantine Books, 2006), which is now in a twentieth-anniversary edition. Or, look for *If the Buddha Got Stuck: A Handbook for Change on a Spiritual Path* (Penguin, 2005) by Charlotte Sophia Kasl. Don't let yourself stay stuck!

What to Do When You're Stuck

What if you're keeping your eyes open and you still can't see any sign of psychic guidance? We've given you a lot of exercises to work with (and will give you a lot more!). Remember that not all the ideas and concepts will work for you. Everyone responds differently, but keep practicing, take small steps, and have fun.

Make sure that you're taking care of the small stuff, too. Do your research on any decision you need to make. Write thank-you notes to people who've helped you. Make sure you exercise so that your thoughts and energy flow. Go on a walk around your neighborhood so you see a different view of a reality that surrounds you. Dance, jump, or punch a pillow. Stop taking yourself so seriously! Remember the saying, "Angels can fly because they take themselves lightly."

When You Don't Get Information Right Away

Keep in mind that you're still learning, and learning patience—with yourself, as well as your circumstance—may be a big part of your current lesson. Remember that everything takes time.

Many facts and forces might need to come into play before the path becomes clear. For example, you might be waiting to hear about one job possibility because another—even better!—job is about to become available somewhere else ... maybe at a level or company that you never dreamed you'd have a shot at. This takes us back to that old adage that we keep sending your way: trust your intuition.

But if you're really restless, here's something you can do to get some answers about what you think, feel, dream, and imagine.

Intuition Exercise: Not Your Typical Coin Toss

1. Think about the decision you're trying to make. Form it in your mind as a "yes" or "no" question. "Should I take the job with XYZ Corporation?" "Should I apply to graduate school now?" "Should I stop dating John?"

2. Take a coin and flip it. Heads indicates yes. Tails indicates no. Okay, what was the answer?

3. Think about how you felt about the answer. Were you disappointed? Relieved? Did you get a thrill of excitement through your body or a knot of fear in your stomach? Admit it, did you immediately want to flip the coin two more times and try for best two out of three? (Or have you actually done that already?)

Any of these responses is an example of your intuition speaking to you. Your response gave you information about the answer to your decision. So often we expect our intuition to be a booming voice saying, "Lynn, take that job at XYZ Corporation—now! Go girl!"

Your intuition is more likely to speak through subtle feelings, inner nudges, or physical sensations. When you learn to pay attention and act on these responses, they can be just as loud and clear as a booming voice.

When it comes to your intuition, practice includes many of the techniques we talked about in Chapter 5. Meditation works for many people, and exercise, praying, *chanting*, and *contemplation* help others. But in order to keep practicing, you need to stay or get motivated. If you're unclear about your goal or feel fuzzy about what you like, need, and want, check out the exercise called "Why Am I Here?" in Chapter 18.

 DEFINITION

Chanting is the singing of a short, simple melody or even a few monotonous notes. It often involves repetition of the same words or sounds in order to attain a spiritual state. **Contemplation** involves deep thought or reflection as a type of meditation or prayer. For example, you focus your thoughts on a single concept, such as peace, as a way of reaching a more spiritual state.

Getting in touch with why you're blocked and what you need to do to remain motivated can help you immensely. You can learn much about yourself to understand why you aren't moving forward. Remember, your intuition is always giving you an opportunity to learn.

Take Time for Inner Guidance

Life doesn't always go in a straight line—even when we're doing everything right. Just as nature has seasons, ebbs, and flows, so do our lives. Our task as spiritual human beings is to learn how to love and forgive, experience peace within ourselves, be of service, and have compassion for others. The universe has many ways to help us learn those lessons in our schoolroom called Earth.

Our problem with time isn't that we don't have enough of it, it's that time doesn't exist—but we still don't understand that it doesn't exist. Sound crazy? Well, some people actually believe that the commonly accepted idea that time moves in a straight line is nonsense. Where's Einstein when you need him? His relativity theory is what got a lot of people thinking about this. Basically, modern physics is showing us that time is not fixed, and many psychics, including those who lived long before Einstein, know this.

How to Speed Up an Event You Want to Create

"The greatest discovery of my generation is that human beings, by changing the inner attitudes of their minds, can change the outer aspects of their lives," proclaimed psychologist and philosopher William James (1842–1910). This certainly presents a good argument for free will. It also shows us the power of our minds.

Creative visualization is built on James's type of thinking. If you think about what you'd like to achieve in your life, you can do just that. For example, if you want to own a brand new car, picture yourself in that car, happily driving off the lot and waving to your friends. Be aware that using this technique works best when you place yourself in the picture. If you just picture a beautiful car that's empty, it will stay that way—and so will your driveway.

DEFINITION

Creative visualization is a process in which you create an image of the outcome you desire. This image is often called to mind during meditation or deep relaxation.

Lynn has found that clients who are clearest about what they want to create achieve their goals much more quickly. Those who feel unsure of their goals, feel they don't deserve them, or believe they might be unattainable slow down or even halt the process of manifesting their desires.

Painting a picture of what you want to achieve works in various ways. For one thing, visualization sends a signal to your intuitive side about what you want. Then, your intuition can begin to put the moves in motion that will make your desires become real. But don't expect your intuition to do it all alone. That's where the second part, taking action, comes in.

Your tasks are to focus on your goals and then act on your intuitive impulses. Pay attention to any clues from your intuition that may help you achieve your goal. You might have a sudden impulse to call a friend. Call! You might feel drawn to read a certain book. Read it! You might have a sudden impulse to speak to the person standing next to you in line. Talk! Action and intuition work off each other to accomplish your goal. Your intuitive "higher mind" can see the overview of what it needs to do to pull all the events together to help you get what you want.

Similar to visualization are *affirmations*. These positive verbal expressions also send a message to your mind indicating what you want to achieve. When you choose a positive affirmation, always use the present tense so that your changes can take place *now*, rather than some time in the far-off future. For example, say, "I am open to my intuition and easily act on its wisdom," instead of, "I will be open to my intuition ...."

Lynn used affirmations and visualizations to help start her business. Her positive affirmation was, "I have a successful, full-time psychic reading business." Lynn's visualization included a full appointment book, her answering machine with a lot of calls from clients, and an image of a beautiful office with a smiling client. It all happened!

DEFINITION

Affirmations are statements that create a reality or truth through frequent repetition. We often hear about positive affirmations, which people repeat to improve their situation—but negative thoughts that we repeat often also work on us (and in a bad way!).

Slow Down the Pace of Your Life

You probably know people in your life who always appear confident, organized, and serene. These people never appear frazzled—they never seem to be overwhelmed if their computers break down when they're on a deadline or the carpools don't pick up their children in time for school. Their desks don't look like they require an archeological dig to find a piece of paper. What's their secret?

The key to remaining calm is being aware of what's going on in the big picture around and beyond you. In a crisis or period of frustrating feelings, stop panicking and ask yourself: "What am I learning? What could I have done—and what can I do in the future—to prevent this situation from happening?" Your answers might include the following:

> • Learn to say no to things that drain you.
>
> • Focus on bringing the things that make you happy into your life.
>
> • Reevaluate what you really need to do and have.

Here's an exercise to help you slow down the pace of your life. Why not unplug the phone, step away from the television, and try it now?

Intuition Exercise: Go Slow

Get out some paper or use your psychic journal. Without thinking too much, quickly write a list of five experiences that you have often that drain you and leave you depleted of energy. Then, quickly make a list of five ordinary things or experiences that make you happy, give you energy, and help you feel centered. Choose one thing on the "happy list" that you'd like to expand on. We'd like to help you be even happier by doing this exercise. Imagine how this thing or experience will impact you. Envision all the details of what it would be like to have even more of this happiness in your life.

Now, write about this happy experience. If you feel more comfortable with drawing than writing, feel free to draw your answers. Use as many different colors as you like, and include images from magazines or photographs that you have collected if you feel so moved.

When you are done describing your positive experience, take a breath. Tell yourself that you are allowed to have what you want. Make a commitment to yourself that this month you will take steps toward having more of this type of happy event in your life.

Now, look back over your list of things and experiences that leave you drained and off-balance. Pick one and cross it out. If you like, make an entire drawing that shows you eliminating this source of stress from your life. Learning to say no and setting limits can be an important part of coming into your psychic power. If you think about it, you probably already know what experience you have on a regular basis that leaves you feeling frazzled. You probably also know that you could avoid it. Now, make a commitment to yourself that you will protect yourself from this particular source of stress.

Whew! Don't you feel calmer and more centered already?

Staying balanced and centered helps you live in the moment and be open and aware of all the messages that are coming your way. We admit, it does sound a bit contradictory! We suggest you stay centered in the present and also envision your future happiness. At the very least, you'll learn to get your priorities straight. At best, you'll attain a level of awareness that can connect you directly to the force that keeps us all living and loving. Stay tuned for more on how intuition works with our life force in Chapter 9.

The Least You Need to Know

- You can use intuitive information to help you in every aspect of your life.
- Learn to understand your own set of psychic symbols.
- Getting in tune with your intuition is a process. Be patient.
- Changing your view of time helps you gain control.

Intuitive Intelligence

After you've experienced your body-mind connection, you'll be ready to gain a deeper awareness of how to transcend the everyday. In this part, we'll start by looking at the amazing healing power within your own body and soul. Then, we'll describe more advanced steps you can take to train your mind to access your esoteric psychic self.

We'll help you understand the importance of altered states of consciousness, from hypnosis to dreaming to telepathy and beyond. We also offer insight into the finer points of trusting your intuition and believing in yourself.

Healing Power of the Body Psychic

In This Chapter

- Emphasize the positive
- What scientists think of prayer
- See your life-force energy
- Stress and your psychic health
- Heal the world

We all have access to an awesome universal energy source. Psychics who have a strong sense of this energy are able to work with it in many ways, on many levels. They see that it exists for everyone in body, mind, and spirit. With a little guidance, you can sense this energy and learn to balance it in yourself, as well. You can begin to improve your flow of energy, soothe your inner self, and create harmony in all that surrounds you—and in the world at large.

The Power of Positive Thinking

As you've probably recognized from your own life, healing the body doesn't happen easily if the mind is unhealthy or full of doubt. This body-mind connection can exert a powerful influence over almost all aspects of your life. Worry and doubt are easy. Creating change requires courage from you—both to let go of your skepticism and to take steps toward wellness and wholeness.

You can use strong verbal messages and visual images to direct your mind. These symbols penetrate your unconscious to become embedded in your brain and create new pathways of thought and action. They provide your intuition with new avenues for insight and opportunity and express your openness to receiving all the exciting changes that your intuition has to offer. But how do you find the right words and images for you?

Intuition Exercise: Tell a New Story About Your Life

If you tend to indulge in negative self-talk, this exercise is for you. Consider it a thought experiment.

First, you'll want to pay attention to what you are saying to yourself. In other words, notice your negative self-talk.

Then, stop! Don't say the negative thing.

Now, choose a new thought.

Pick one from the list that follows:

> I am open to new possibilities.
>
> I am beginning to enjoy myself.
>
> I choose to be more optimistic.
>
> More and more, I am listening to my intuition.
>
> My life is becoming easier.
>
> I welcome wonderful, fun, and new adventures.
>
> I invite abundance and prosperity in all forms.
>
> I am available to more good than I've ever experienced before.
>
> Wonderful, new opportunities are beginning to come my way.
>
> Things have a way of working out for me.
>
> I'm beginning to do what I dream.
>
> More and more positive things are happening to me.
>
> I'm becoming luckier.

I'm beginning to work less and play more.

I invite and welcome good health and vibrant well-being.

I am beginning to notice all the wonderful things I already have in my life.

I am becoming more confident.

I am looking forward to ...

I used to (overeat, smoke, feel insecure, and so on), but now I ...

What if the things I want and desire also want me?

Wouldn't it be great if ...

I am becoming more aware of my inner guidance and act on it daily.

I am beginning to attract wonderful new opportunities.

How can I make this fun?

This is just a temporary bad period. I'm moving toward better things.

It's normal to feel a little scared (lack confidence). I'll get better at this.

Commit to using one of these new thoughts for a week. After the week has passed, check in with yourself. Do you notice any tiny changes? If you are so inclined, keep working with the thought you chose or pick a new one.

Creative Visualization

When you visualize, you form a mental image of what you want to create. You can use positive mental images of yourself and your life to create a better self-image and to improve your personal experiences. For example, if you want to lose weight, you can hold an image in your mind's eye of how you want to look. If you want to develop your psychic awareness, imagine yourself being psychic. Fill in all the details of your experience—how it feels to recognize and trust your intuition and how secure it is to know and trust your guides. You can use your ability to visualize to conjure the images and feelings of yourself as a psychically aware human being. Your intuition will probably help!

Creative visualization is the umbrella term for the ability to imagine your desired future. When it is focused in a way that helps the mind and body work together to create healing, it is called guided imagery. Much attention has been paid to guided imagery as a form of healing—or at least slowing—serious illness. In fact, *guided imagery* was developed for that very purpose.

> **DEFINITION**
>
> **Guided imagery** is a technique in which you use your imagination and all of your senses to imagine a desired outcome. Seeing and feeling this outcome in your mind will aid you in achieving it in real life.

Guided Imagery: The Mind as Healer

"Our emotions and words let the body know what we expect of it, and by visualizing certain changes we can help the body bring them about," says best-selling author Bernie Siegel in his book, *Love, Medicine, and Miracles* (William Morrow, 1990). In his more recent book, *Faith, Hope and Healing: Inspiring Lessons Learned from People Living with Cancer* (Wiley, 2009), Siegel brings together stories about the way that visualization and positive thinking have impacted the lives of real people. Research shows that guided imagery can help lower blood pressure; reduce anxiety, depression, and physical pain; bolster the immune system; ease nausea during chemotherapy; lower allergic responses; and speed recovery from cuts, burns, fractures, and surgery. It also improves performance in sports and even certain types of mental activities.

When guided imagery is most effective, it encourages you to imagine with all your senses. In addition to using images and thoughts, guided imagery involves imagining how things sound, feel, taste, and smell. Because sensory input is how the mind and imagination tend to take in information, guided imagery can go straight to the unconscious mind—bypassing all those words that can get in the way of direct communication between mind and body.

Another reason why guided imagery seems to be so effective is because it involves the emotions. In fact, guided imagery seems to work best when using images that strongly affect emotions. Similar to how images and other sensory input bypass reason and travel directly to the unconscious mind, emotions also go directly to the unconscious mind. In addition, emotions carry a history with them that interacts with the body's systems. For example, if you imagine spending a happy, sunny day with someone you love, your body also re-experiences the same joyful, relaxed, and ecstatic physical responses.

Prayer and Science

Tapping into this all-powerful source of spiritual healing can have many names, including prayer. The relationship between prayer (and religion or faith) and science has changed greatly in the last few decades—ever since Einstein pointed out that there's not much difference between energy and matter. Until then, scientists pretty much agreed that what you see is what you get. The material world reigned.

Today, more scientists and doctors acknowledge the power of the mind to affect the material world. Although the scientific community isn't quite sure what to call this ability, many in the spiritual community call it God, or universal energy, or chi. Many religions call the effort to direct this force "prayer." And more scientists and medical professionals are looking at this force as a form of distant healing.

Medicine and Science on Prayer and Healing

One physician who is famous for looking into healing prayer is Larry Dossey, MD. In his book, *Healing Words: The Power of Prayer and the Practice of Medicine* (HarperOne, 1995), Dossey describes his scientific quest to discover the relationship between healing and consciousness and his exploration of the connections between medicine, mysticism, religion, and physics. Recently, psi scientists have investigated the distinction made between directed and nondirected prayer. When you pray in a directed manner, you have a specific goal or outcome in mind, as in, "I want my husband's Parkinson's Disease to go away." In this case, you're attempting to steer the outcome in a certain direction, such as curing Parkinson's. In nondirected prayer, you ask God for the highest good for all concerned.

Spindrift, a Salem, Oregon, organization concentrating on prayer research, conducted studies to see which prayer technique was more effective. The Spindrift researchers looked at the impact that prayer had on plant life (because it is easier to measure the results on simple biological systems than it is on humans). One such study follows how prayer practitioners can affect the development and metabolism of yeast cultures and the sprouting of bean and wheat seeds. In both exercises, they discovered that prayer helped trigger growth. Perhaps surprisingly, the nondirected technique was quantifiably more effective than the directed prayer technique, yielding double the results.

GUIDED INTUITION

You can try your own prayer experiment at home. Buy two plants in the same condition at the same time. Put them in places of comparable light and "comfort," and give them the same amount of water. Indeed, the only difference is that you "pray" for one plant and not the other. Just be sure to put them far enough apart that your prayers don't "spread."

The results of the Spindrift studies suggest that when you heal or pray, it's most helpful if you keep your mind free of specific goals. In other words, simply pray for what's best for the individual. "May the best of all outcomes happen for this individual" appears to be the most effective form of prayer. Although this approach worked best in the Spindrift studies, it has not been tested widely with people—and the jury is still out on the best way for you to pray for your own or someone else's healing and growth.

Are You a Doubter or a Doer?

Although you needn't believe in a specific god called by a certain name, faith and a true desire for wellness are important ingredients in many types of healing. Many people pray expecting that God will simply grant their requests. But it doesn't usually work that way. Prayer, with its built-in positive thinking, is a partnership. If you're always afraid to believe that it may work, you'll never even have a chance of knowing that it can.

Think of it this way: the odds of "winning" are better if you try to step beyond doubt. If you are in doubt and remain there, nothing can change. But taking action—even when you still have a few reservations—is the first step toward conquering doubt. Taking action requires at least a tiny bit of faith in the ability to improve and create change.

You're provided with many tools, but you have to use them. These tools include a strong intellect with which to choose your goals and visions. You have your imagination to envision the kind of life and health you want so that you can begin to create them. You also have been given the gifts of decision-making, intuition, and your individual talents. You can use these gifts to create joy and happiness for yourself and others, or you can ignore these gifts and run the risk of never seeing changes occur. The choice is yours.

MIXED MESSAGES

If anyone suggests that you rely on prayer alone for healing, don't neglect to check into other options as well. Prayer is a tremendous gift. However, the healing power of prayer might also guide you to an appropriate method of treatment, such as a skilled doctor. Answers to prayers come in many forms; healers who are in touch with that fact humbly recognize it and don't insist that theirs is the only way.

Energy for Life

When your vital life-force energy is flowing smoothly, all is well. But when it's not, your life can become out of balance. Understanding this energy and its flow is a big step toward creating a balanced, harmonious life. Many alternative healers, some of whom are called energy healers, work with life-force energy. Some can feel it (as a form of clairsentience), and others can see it (as a form of clairvoyance). The field of energy that surrounds each living organism is referred to as an *aura*.

DEFINITION

An **aura** is the field of electromagnetic energy that permeates and surrounds every person and thing, both living and not living. The word comes from the Greek *avra*, which means breeze.

What's an Aura?

Webster's dictionary defines an aura as "a subtly pervasive quality or atmosphere seen as emanating from a person, place, or thing." In intuitive-speak, the aura is a vibrating field of energy (often perceived as light) that pulses around and through your body at all times. In religious renditions of sacred events, you've seen them painted as halos around holy heads.

The aura is a luminous atmosphere that surrounds all living things. Many people believe that this field around the body is an electromagnetic field, which might even conduct electricity through the water contained in the body. While surrounding the body, this field protects you and also helps you sense others' feelings and allows others to perceive your true self. The aura can be perceived through feeling, "sensing," or seeing. Barbara Y. Martin, a clairvoyant, aura specialist, and a pioneer in the field of metaphysics, has written a book about auras—*The Healing Power of Your Aura: How to Use Spiritual Energy for Physical Health and Well-Being* (Spiritual Arts Institute, 2006). In this book, she details her theory on what causes illness and what you can do to attract healing energy and cleanse your aura. Martin sees the aura as your spiritual support system. She says that your aura will show you where you are in your consciousness and that to create change in your life, you must first change your aura. You can read more about Martin's work here: http://spiritualarts.org/DiscoverYourAura.aspx.

About now, we are guessing that you'd really like to see an aura. It turns out some people are wired to see auras more easily, whereas others can feel or sense them. Even people who don't seem to have a natural inclination for seeing auras can learn how with practice. Here's an exercise to get you started.

Intuition Exercise: How to See an Aura

1. Get into a relaxed position in a dark room. Leave the lights out, but don't worry about a little light coming in through the blinds or under the door.

2. Hold your palms up about eight inches in front of your face. Hold them facing each other, about one to five inches apart. Look at the wall behind your hands; avoid focusing directly on your hands. Move your hands in toward each other and back out (as though clapping), increasing the space, and then decreasing the space. Do you notice an energy building up between your hands? You might see a light or feel a pulsing or tingling sensation. This is your auric, or energy, field.

3. Now, outstretch one arm at chest level and turn your palm up as though carrying a tray. Place the opposite hand about 10 inches above your forearm, with your palm facing down. Slowly move your hand closer to your arm. Pay attention to the feeling or sensation in your hand. Does it change as you get closer to your arm?

When you're seeing your aura, you'll realize that it is made up of various colors. Most people emit certain colors that predominate in their auras, yet these colors can change with their moods. For example, a person who has a happy disposition might tend to have a bright-yellow aura, but it could momentarily change to red if the person becomes angry. Someone else might have a red aura, suggesting that the person is often angry. If someone's aura has dark spots in a specific area, it might show that the person has an energy block in that area. An energy block may originate from a negative thinking pattern, repressed emotions, or even a physical issue such as tight muscles.

> **GUIDED INTUITION**
>
> Barbara Brennan is a teacher, physicist, psychotherapist, author, and leading authority on healing. If you'd like to continue learning about auras, check out her classic book *Hands of Light: A Guide to Healing Through the Human Energy Field* (Bantam, 1988). Or, look for Donna Eden and David Feinstein's *Energy Medicine: Balancing Your Body's Energies for Optimal Health, Joy, and Vitality* (Tarcher, 2008).

What the Colors Mean

Within the body are seven major energy centers that correspond to the chakras. Each center is said to be like a wheel of vibrating, spinning energy. Auras penetrate and radiate from these energies. Expert energy healers such as Barbara Brennan perceive the aura as having a particular structure that corresponds to the shape and size of the body. She can see frequency bands, in the form of color, that radiate through and out from the body in seven levels, which correspond to the chakras.

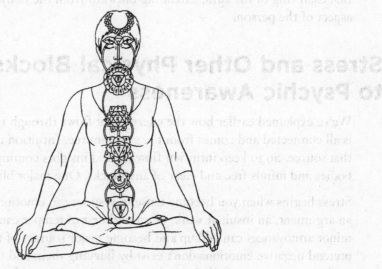

Yoga's seven chakras are energy centers.

Energy healers believe that each of the aura's seven energy levels also corresponds to one aspect of life. The following table offers a brief summary of the auric colors, where they originate, and the life aspects they represent.

Auric Color	Chakra/Center	Life Aspect Corresponding to Color
Red	Base of the spine	Physical sensation, survival, and strength
Orange	Sacral	Personal emotions: sexuality, creativity, and healing
Yellow	Solar plexus	Mental state: personal thoughts of power, anger, or hostility
Green	Heart	Interaction with others: love and harmony
Blue	Throat	Communication, expression, and judgment
Indigo	Forehead	Inner vision, wisdom, and perception
Violet	Crown of the head	Divine purpose: destiny

Although these colors match up with the seven main chakras and life issues related to them, the aura is not seen as a row of horizontal stripes that starts at the top of the head and moves down to the feet. Rather, the layers surround your body in concentric rings, similar to the layers of an onion. When reading an aura, some experts believe that each ring of the aura, extending outward from the body, expresses a different aspect of the person.

Stress and Other Physical Blocks to Psychic Awareness

We've explained earlier how the energy that flows through the body, mind, and spirit is all connected and comes from the same source. Intuition is one manifestation of that source. So to keep intuition flowing and insights coming, people must keep their bodies and minds free and clear of any blocks. One major block is stress.

Stress begins when you become tense in response to emotional upsets. Certainly an argument, an insult at work, or an outburst of temper can cause stress. But even minor annoyances can add up and become major sources of tension. Trying to pretend negative emotions don't exist by burying them and then acting happy doesn't work, because you usually bury them somewhere in your body. And this accumulated dumpsite later becomes the place where an illness takes shape.

In addition to stress (or in response to it), other problems can interfere with your healthy flow of life energy and intuitive information. Alcohol and other mind-altering drugs can become an escape route for many people who don't want to face the discomfort of emotional hurt. Other people pursue relationships with others as a form of distraction, even when the relationship may not be a healthy one. Anything—even TV—can be an unhealthy escape route if relied upon to avoid issues that need to be faced.

One problem with cutting yourself off from your feelings—physical or otherwise—is that you also cut yourself off from other areas of your life. For example, you might ignore tension in your neck that is telling you to slow down in your life before you become ill. Or, you might avoid communicating with someone because of uncomfortable feelings, which gradually cause the relationship to weaken and possibly end. Something similar can apply with intuition. If you cut yourself off from feelings, you're likely to cut off your intuitive input as well.

Psychic Health

To keep energy flowing through you in a healthy way, you must release all this built-up, pent-up, and negative energy and stress. Each of us needs to discover our own ways to clear these blocks.

Here's a list of simple, everyday things that you can do if you're feeling stressed or psychically blocked to help you release negativity and get hooked into the great flow of life energy again:

- Work out.
- Take the dog for a walk.
- Take yourself for a walk.
- Drink a glass of water.
- Play with your cat or dog.
- Practice yoga.
- Write, draw, or dance in response to your feelings.
- Take a bath or shower, or go for a swim.
- Breathe.

Or, why not try a psychic cleansing bath to help you relax and tune into your body? Here's a commonly used recipe:

> 3 parts Epsom salts
>
> 2 parts baking soda
>
> 1 part table, kosher, or sea salt
>
> A few drops of your favorite essential oil

Mix all the ingredients together in a large bowl. Run your bath and dissolve ½ to 1 cup in the water. Turn off the phone. Step into the tub and spend some time soaking and allowing your mind and body to drift. When you're done, your skin and your psyche will both feel great.

All these activities will help you feel more in your body—more connected to your own energy and to the energy of the universe. And when you feel connected to the universe, you feel more alive and psychically in tune. In addition, many people explore alternative health areas, such as acupuncture, Reiki, and massage to help themselves relax and open up. And everyone needs to develop regular healthy habits for handling emotional issues and daily stresses as they occur.

Fostering Compassion and Empathy

Helping heal the world around you may actually be simpler than you think. Begin by paying attention to where help is needed. Once you start to really look at the people and things around you with an open mind, you'll be able to see what you can do. You might notice a man walking with his shoulders slumped, as if he's carrying a heavy burden. He probably is. Someone whose face looks tired, tight, and stressed is probably thinking about something that concerns him or her greatly—physical pain, grief, or maybe hurt feelings.

When you start to really see what's going on in the world around you, don't be afraid to acknowledge and feel it. Accept that you have a gift—the gift of intuitive understanding. Many call it empathy, and what you do with this gift can be called compassion. It is not always necessary to run in, shouting and waving a flag that screams, "I care." Indeed, overt expressions are not always appropriate. Rather, take a deep breath and ask for guidance.

The ideal way for you to help people may not appear to you when you first realize their needs. Perhaps you'll have an opportunity to talk with them at some future date. They might want to pour out their hearts, and it's your job to just listen. Or, you might never know exactly what troubles them, but perhaps what you offer can be as simple as a smile or a silent prayer. Any offering of compassion can be a form of healing.

At the same time, you'll come to realize that you are healing yourself as well, because each moment of awareness and empathy you share with another—and every blessing you offer that person—helps you appreciate all that you have and are.

Take a moment right now to appreciate yourself. Go ahead—you deserve it! Exhale and let any anxiety or tension flow out of your body. Inhale and feel your life energy. Let yourself revel in the energy and the way it feels. Spend a few moments appreciating your unique energy and your body. As you inhale, allow the life energy you draw in to travel within you to any place of hurt or "dis-ease" and soothe the trouble. Listen to any messages from your body and from your body's wisdom that will help you heal and continue to develop and refine your psychic awareness.

The Least You Need to Know

- Doctors and scientists are showing increased interest in the healing effects of prayer.
- Whether you call it prayer or not, you can direct your thoughts to change your health and life for the better.
- You can learn to direct energy to help heal yourself and others.
- Truly looking at others is a simple way to learn compassion.

Hypnosis and Altered States of Consciousness

In This Chapter

- Opening to an altered state
- The power of suggestion
- Divine dictation
- You're in the driver's seat

For thousands of years, philosophers and scientists alike have recognized that thoughts can affect both behavior and bodily functions. But during the last century or so, great efforts have been made to learn whether it's possible to actually direct these thoughts to influence the physical world. So far, the evidence indicates that the best way to do so is by reaching a state beyond normal, everyday consciousness.

Franz Mesmer (1734–1815), a doctor who pioneered the use of the hypnotic state as a part of treatment, employed hypnosis to help his patients deal with pain during a procedure and help them relax if they suffered from anxiety. When Freud came along with his theory of the subconscious mind, the plot thickened. By the beginning of the twentieth century, the pieces were in place for people to invent ways to direct the subconscious mind to control thoughts (and hence, behavior). In this chapter, we'll show you how you can tap into that power yourself.

> **GUIDED INTUITION**
>
> If you would like to delve even deeper into altering consciousness to induce intuition, check out Belleruth Naparstek's *Your Sixth Sense* (HarperOne, 2009). Her chapter on "Imagery to Access Psi" examines the components of intuition and replicates them with specific guided-imagery exercises to alter consciousness and activate your psi. Or, check out the Personal Development section of Kelly Howell's audio store at www.brainsync.com.

Going into a Trance

People have used *trances* for millennia to help them access their intuition and gain spiritual insight. A trance, like meditation, is a safe and natural state of altered consciousness that you can learn to enter. When in a trance state, the barriers that the conscious mind creates can soften, allowing you easier access to your intuition. Trances can be induced in a number of ways. Listening to a steady drum beat over a period of time can create a trance state for some people. Another way to enter a trance is to hypnotize yourself.

> **DEFINITION**
>
> A **trance** is an altered state of consciousness marked by a heightened but narrowed focus of attention, and of quieting the mind. It is also described as a state of complete mental absorption.

Several steps are integral to achieving a trance state, including the following:

1. Relaxing
2. Concentrating
3. Turning inward
4. Focusing on specific sounds, words, or images
5. Choosing to change one's conscious state

You can enter into a trance using any number of techniques, including meditation, communion, prayer, spiritual transcendence, and the best-known form of trance: *hypnosis*.

Going Deeper, Deeper ...

Through the entertainment media, you've no doubt been introduced to hypnosis as a technique that reduces or eliminates people's inhibitions and makes them do silly, embarrassing things. But hypnosis is not a parlor trick; it is a medical and psychic tool used by health professionals around the world. At its heart, hypnosis is simply a state of intense concentration. When you're hypnotized, you're more alert and receptive to new ideas or suggestions.

Perhaps the biggest myth about hypnosis is that the person undergoing hypnosis gives up control of his or her own mind and is subject to the control of someone else (namely, the hypnotist). This myth has given hypnosis a bad rap. In fact, experts in the field of hypnosis propose that, although they make suggestions, all hypnosis is self-hypnosis and that its power lies in the mind of the person being hypnotized.

Hypnosis is actually achieved when you reach such an intense level of concentration that you block out any mental interference that distracts you from your focus. When hypnotized, your brain waves slow down measurably, from conscious beta waves to subconscious alpha waves or perhaps even theta waves, which mark the dream state. (If you'd like a refresher on brain waves, revisit Chapter 2.)

In a sense, hypnosis is like guided meditation. You pass through a series of steps to go deeper into the unconscious but actually hear every word during the process. Whether you enter a light trance or a deep one determines whether you experience other effects as well. A light trance might give you a feeling of being very relaxed or perhaps weightless, but otherwise you might not feel all that different from the concentrated frame of mind you achieve when reading a good book. Free from the rational constraints of the conscious mind, you'll be able to heighten certain innate abilities, including your imagination, your memory, your creative tendencies, and your suggestibility. All of these abilities are closely linked to the intuitive side of your brain, which helps explain why hypnosis is such an effective tool for psychics and others seeking intuitive insight.

Don't experiment with hypnotizing your friends unless you've had professional training. Guiding the process effectively is more complicated than it sounds. And that goes for someone who wants to use you as a guinea pig. Tell him or her to seek appropriate training first.

Hypnosis and Intuitive Insight

Hypnosis can work with intuition in many ways. You can use it to improve your physical health and self-image, to resolve emotional conflicts, and to increase spiritual insight. Hypnosis makes these changes easier because it allows you to overcome your conscious mind's resistance to new ideas and its attachment to old beliefs. For example, if you smoke cigarettes especially when you're nervous, you could ask a hypnotist to suggest that you no longer crave nicotine when under stress. After hypnotizing you and explaining why smoking is harmful, the hypnotherapist might then suggest drinking cool, fresh water instead of smoking when the craving comes on strongly.

In the case of improving your physical health and mental attitudes, a hypnotist can help by replacing old thought patterns with new ones. This can apply to overcoming problems such as stress, insomnia, nervous habits, allergies, phobias, and more. For instance, a hypnotist with a client who wanted to quit biting her nails would access his or her client's unconscious mind. The hypnotist would then review the benefits of giving up the habit before suggesting a new behavior to replace the old one. When the unconscious mind was convinced of the wisdom of not chewing on fingernails, it would lend its support to the conscious decision to quit. Hypnotism can also help you improve in areas in which you're already strong, such as sports performance, public speaking, test-taking, study skills, and more.

However, to overcome bad habits or achieve new goals, you often must resolve long-standing emotional issues—and doing so usually requires working with a hypnotherapist. Such professionals are trained to help you get to the underlying cause of problems, which can be deeply imbedded.

One technique employed by some hypnotherapists to investigate the source of deeply buried emotional problems is *age regression*. Age regression involves guiding a patient's memory back to an early time in his or her life—or even before he or she was born—to uncover painful events or examine unpleasant emotions. Some people claim to remember experiences from past lives, another facet of psychic phenomena. (If this topic interests you, stay tuned; we'll talk more about past lives in Chapter 12.)

DEFINITION

Age regression is an application of hypnosis in which the client regresses to a younger age with the guidance of a hypnotherapist trained in this technique.

On a simpler spiritual level, hypnosis can help you quiet the defenses of your conscious mind and open your senses to new sources of information. This information about personal and spiritual growth may be so wise and wonderful that you sense it must come from a source beyond yourself.

Intuition Exercise: Self-Hypnosis

Why not learn more about hypnosis by trying it yourself? Self-hypnosis is a great tool you can use to help you achieve your goals in any area. Follow these simple steps:

1. Find some quiet time and space. Turn off your phone and put it away. Step away from the computer and take off your watch (if you wear one). When you are ready, sit or lie down and make yourself comfortable.

2. Close your eyes. Take a few deep breaths. Tell yourself that you are relaxed and that you are going into a trance.

3. Deepen your trance by imagining yourself at the top of a set of stairs. There are 10 steps in front of you. As you step down the first step, feel yourself relax still further. Slowly continue down the stairs. With each step, feel yourself grow more and more relaxed. Feel yourself going deeper and deeper into your trance.

4. When you are in a deep state of relaxation, say to yourself the following:
   "I am becoming more intuitive every day.
   I listen to and act on my inner guidance.
   My life is becoming more balanced and filled with joy."

5. Spend about a minute in your trance. Then tell yourself, "At the count of 10, I am fully awake, open to my intuition, and feeling great." Count from 1 up to 10. When you reach 10, say, "My eyes are open, and I am fully awake," and open your eyes.

GUIDED INTUITION

If you want to learn more about hypnosis, check out *The Complete Idiot's Guide to Hypnosis, Second Edition* (Alpha Books, 2004) by Roberta Temes, a psychotherapist, hypnotist, and an assistant professor of psychiatry.

Try recording yourself reading this script. Then, you can relax and listen to your very own self-hypnosis induction any time. If you practice this exercise every day, you will become more in tune with your own intuitive insights and will get better at self-hypnosis, too.

Muse or Myth?

We've all heard the ancient tales about creatures called muses who plant lyrics in the minds of great poets and otherwise inspire artists, musicians, and singers. Most of us view such a concept as pure myth or the superstitious belief of ignorant ancients. And yet, many modern psychics believe that their intuitive power comes from a source higher than their own conscious minds. For example, the British medium Rosemary Brown (1916–2001) was visited by the spirits of dead composers such as Bach, Beethoven, Debussy, Chopin, Liszt, and Rachmaninoff—all dictating new compositions to her. Was the source of her new music the unconscious imagination or inspired guidance from a muse?

Even among intuitives, opinions vary about the source of the extraordinary information that comes to them, especially in creative areas. Some say that the source is the person's own higher consciousness or higher mind; others say that the person's higher mind acts as a bridge to spirit guides who provide inspiration. Reaching a conclusive answer to this question is probably impossible—and also unimportant—because each person has his or her own way of perceiving knowledge, relaying it, and describing it.

The important point to focus on is finding your own way to receive information. When you reach an altered state of consciousness, whether through hypnosis or meditation, your mind is wide open and ready to learn. You can take in several types of information in several different ways. You might sense that you're gaining insight into your own personal and spiritual growth, receiving messages from spirits with specific advice for you or someone else, or even seeing images that can change the course of art, science, or the state of the world.

There are at least two ways to directly receive this type of information: *spontaneous drawing* and *automatic writing*. These skills are different than feeling highly focused and productive in your work. They require your mind to step aside and let your hands do the work. The less you think about it—or anything at all—the better. That's why an altered state of consciousness, which sidesteps the rational mind, is so crucial.

> **DEFINITION**
>
> **Spontaneous drawing** and **automatic writing** are forms of creative expression thought to occur during an altered state of consciousness, when the rational mind is shut off and the unconscious mind steps in and takes control. Spontaneous drawing involves the creation of visual images or pictures, whereas automatic writing involves writing words.

Spontaneous Drawing

If you put yourself into the right frame of mind—an altered state of consciousness—you can experience spontaneous drawing. When your mind is free from rational explanations and judgmental demands (such as, "My artwork must be beautiful"), you'll be better able to get to the true message that your intuition is ready to reveal.

Before putting yourself in this frame of mind, prepare yourself for the artistic process. Get your pencils, chalk, or paints—or even clay if you're interested in sculpting—ready. Then, meditate or reach a trance state and focus on a question or topic about which you want to receive insight. Keep your mind clear and wait. When your hands begin to move, let them work independently of any rational efforts to control them. For example, if you feel a line looks out of proportion, don't worry about fixing it. In fact, if at all possible, try to avoid even looking at your artwork until your hands stop moving.

The point of this process is to let the unconscious creative side of your mind act freely. By doing so, you're likely to receive a symbol or image that gives you insight into an issue that's troubling you or a specific question that you've asked. In addition, some trained artists intentionally seek inspiration using this method to help them produce beautiful pieces of artwork. If that's your aim and you've been trained in a fine art, you might find that this method allows your skill to flow through your hands and into your work without requiring conscious thought. Whether you're an amateur or a fine artist, the point is to be spontaneous and have fun!

Automatic Writing

Automatic writing involves a process similar to spontaneous drawing. Although pen and paper have been the tools of choice in the past, some modern mediums find that a keyboard works just as well. The important part is freeing your hands (and your mind) from conscious mental control, which might be difficult for people who insist on using proper grammar and punctuation. You've certainly got to let that sense of mastery go if you want to tap into your unconscious mind with any success.

Automatic writing comes in various forms. As we've mentioned, grammar and punctuation are not important. In addition, you might find that the words often run together and you might not be able to recognize the handwriting as your own. Many experts advise not to look at your hands at all—except to occasionally check that they're still writing on the paper.

When you've finished writing, take time to review your work carefully. The writing might begin as loops and curlicues that eventually take shape and form letters and words. They might come as phrases that stand out from other, unclear text or as symbolic words or images (more likely in the case of spontaneous drawing). Most messages tend to be private, offering you suggestions for personal improvement. These messages also tend to be direct, factual, and wise.

In many cases, automatic writing doesn't feel otherworldly at all. You might approach it just as you would any type of informal writing. Sit down with your pen and paper, relax, and clear your mind. In fact, this is the perfect time to focus on that favorite project we've talked about before: your psychic journal.

Keeping and Interpreting Your Journal

Our higher mind or spirit guides can communicate with us in myriad ways. The previous chapters have outlined many of these methods. Automatic writing and drawing are other ways your intuition can communicate through you.

The main thing Lynn tries to get across to her students when they perform psychic exercises is that they will feel like they're making it up. Does it surprise you that—whether she's giving readings or practicing automatic writing—Lynn still feels this way; that her messages do not come from a higher spirit or even from her own intuition, but that she's making them up out of thin air? The only explanation Lynn has is that psychic information seems to reside in a place in our brains that also holds our imagination; therefore, we often confuse the two.

This potential for confusion is why keeping a journal is so important when you're learning to receive intuition or communicate with your guide. The journal provides a way for you to evaluate the insight and inspiration you receive over a period of time. (It can even help you confirm that your unique insights were right all along!)

Here's an exercise that can help you get in touch with this ability when you're ready to write in your journal. Before you start, you may want to prepare some questions to ask. Or, you can simply see what your intuition wants to communicate to you without any prompting.

GUIDED INTUITION

Choose a quiet time, when you're feeling relaxed, to practice contacting your spirit guide. Blocking out all outside stimulation will aid your communication.

Intuition Exercise: Open to Intuitive Guidance

1. Sit quietly. Do any exercise from this book you find most helpful for centering and quieting yourself (meditation, hypnosis, or guided imagery, for example).

2. Feel the light. Surround yourself and fill yourself with light, and ask that only the highest wisdom be present with you as you do this exercise. You could say the following prayer:

   "I fill and surround myself with the white light of the divine consciousness and of God so that only that which is good and needful may enter. I ask that God's wisdom be in my mind, on my lips, and in my heart."

3. Breathe. Sit and relax. Feel yourself becoming open. It's not necessary to meditate. Imagine that you are serene and receptive.

4. Listen. A message from your guide (or guides) might come to you in a block of information or through a whisper. You might receive information through a series of images in your mind. You might have an impression of being loved or a feeling of physical warmth. Ask your guide(s) to communicate to you in words so that you can write down the information.

5. Write. You might hear just a few words. It will seem like your own thoughts, but that's how guides communicate with you. I repeat: you will feel like you are making it up. With practice, you will be able to differentiate between your own thinking and messages from your guide(s). Don't force the words. You might have long pauses at first. Don't worry about making sense of anything as you write. This isn't the time to evaluate. Sometimes you'll hear

entire sentences or receive a flood of information in thought impressions. Some people just get a few words at first. Stay in an open, receptive state and just listen. You might have the experience of knowing what you're going to write before you write it.

6. Ask questions. You can have a two-way communication with your guide. Ask your guide questions in response to the information he or she gives you. You don't have to write the question unless you want to. Just form the question in your mind, and ask your guide telepathically. You might want to ask your guide's name and how you can best work with him or her.

7. Evaluate. As you practice your automatic writing and write the responses in your journal, it's important to evaluate your guide's information. Has it been helpful? How accurate is it? When you've acted on the guidance you received, have you felt better, calmer, more peaceful, and/or less stressed? You might want to ask for information from your guide that you can objectively evaluate. You might say, "I'd like information about my trip next month." "I'd like information about how to help my child with his or her schoolwork." "What steps can I take to improve my relationship?"

Lynn believes that everyone has a guide for this lifetime. Sometimes a guide works with you for a specific purpose. It might be to help you with parenting skills or to assist you in a special project. You might have several guides, each with a different role in helping you. Expect that your guides may have different personalities, interests, or energies. Some guides are funny; others are stern taskmasters; still others bring a profound feeling of love and wisdom. Guides are there for every need. Don't be afraid to ask a guide to help you in a certain area of your life. Your guides like to be of service in whatever way they can be.

Whether you feel your source of insight and inspiration is your spirit guide or your own imagination, don't hesitate to tap into this incredible power that comes through your creative process. But whatever you decide to call the source of this power, you're the one who's in control!

MIXED MESSAGES

Avoid alcohol and mind-altering drugs when you're attempting to get in touch with your psychic side. By nature, these substances involve a loss of control, which is one reason why many psychics avoid them. They recognize that altering your state of consciousness is serious business, requiring concentration, responsibility, and free will. In addition, alcohol dulls and blocks energy and overloads the body with toxins that also interfere with psi.

Who's in Control?

Whether you're working with a hypnotist or channeling your spirit guides yourself, you can choose to become fully conscious at any time during your trance. If you find you aren't comfortable with the suggestions that are coming your way, you can make the choice to come out of the trance. Remember that in these states, you won't be unaware of what's happening to you. In fact, you'll be hyper-aware, which is why these states open us to our intuition. If you want to reassure yourself of the presence of your free will, simply stop the process and return to normal consciousness.

In the next chapter, we'll talk about another altered state of consciousness in which we spend a large portion of our time: sleep! Just as you can control other altered states, you can control this one, too, after you learn how. Read on for more information about mastering this amazing pathway toward your intuition.

The Least You Need to Know

- Trances and altered mental states provide easy access to your intuitive mind.
- Hypnosis is an easy and direct way to connect to your unconscious mind and redirect your thoughts and actions.
- You can use self-hypnosis to deepen your psychic awareness or to help you move toward your other goals.
- Altered states can improve imagination and enhance creativity.

A Vision in a Dream

In This Chapter

- The stuff of dreams
- The psychic side of dreams
- Controlling your dreams
- Understanding your dreams

Dreams have captured the imagination and attention of philosophers, scientists, rulers, and average citizens since history began. Writers and artists from every culture have documented dreams, and today scientists are doing the same thing. Some investigate dreams as a function of the brain; others explore them as psychic phenomena. One fact remains: the more they learn, the more they want to know.

Are you the same? Do you want to know what your dreams mean? Could they really be windows into your psychic world? We'll explore these issues in this chapter.

What Are Dreams?

Dreams remain an awesome mystery. They can be trite or serendipitous, frightening and portentous, structured and calming, or all of these at once! Are they visions of an inescapable future, insights into your emotional state, warnings of possible disasters, or discarded thoughts that your brain no longer has room to store?

Researchers are investigating all these possibilities and responding with many different theories. Some say that no evidence exists to prove that dreams have any point at all. But most people find it hard to believe that we dream for no reason. They offer other possible purposes for dreaming, including (but not limited to) the following:

- Dealing with stress

- Preserving your mental and physical health

- Storing new skills and information

- Getting rid of superfluous information

- Leading you toward spiritual growth

- Receiving intuitive messages

ARE YOU AWARE?

For a long time, people thought that only a few dreams occurred in color and that these dreams were superior to the rest. Not true! All dreams contain color, but many appear in a dim half-light (similar to moonlight). So if you can't recall colorful dreams, don't just assume they're dull. Any dream has some sort of information to offer. Just spend a little time to delve deeper, and you're likely to find a wealth of insight ready for you to reveal.

Before coming up with an answer to why people dream, researchers need to understand the processes involved in dreaming. The logical place to start is with what happens in the body and brain during sleep. By using electrodes to monitor brain waves, eye movements, muscle tension, and other physiological data, researchers can tell when people are dreaming—and then wake them up and ask them what was going on!

By monitoring sleep patterns, researchers have identified when most dreams take place. Most people follow the same sleep patterns every night, falling asleep and going deeper and deeper into a relaxed state for about the first 90 minutes. At that point, they enter a phase called *REM sleep*, which is marked by rapidly moving eyelids and dreaming. When researchers wake up their subjects during REM sleep, the subjects almost always report that they've been dreaming—and these dreams are often quite vivid. Most people undergo REM sleep 3 or 4 times a night, following a 90-minute cycle.

But what do dreams do? Freud called dreams "the royal road to the unconscious." He believed that dreams represent our hidden desires, using symbols that combine a person's longstanding wishes with their previous day's activities.

Another more modern take on dreams views them in functional terms. A recent theory postulates that while the body's at rest, the mind sorts through and processes all the information that it has encountered that day, and this process results in dreaming—either to store information or to discard it. And then, there are those dreams that transcend the everyday. Certain dreams, in fact, appear to hold keys to the past, present, and future, and when they do, we call them psychic dreams.

DEFINITION

REM sleep stands for "rapid eye movement" sleep. This phase of sleep, when the eyelids twitch constantly, is most closely linked to the dreaming state.

Psychic Dreams

What exactly is a psychic dream? That's a difficult question to answer, mainly because almost all dreams have a bizarre or ethereal quality that seems psychic even if the content is not particularly meaningful.

In addition, it's often difficult to identify and document psychic dreams when they occur. For instance, some people—although they can't recall the dream itself—are certain that they've had a psychic revelation when they awake. They might recall some specific words or simply have that sense of knowing that accompanies clairsentience. Unfortunately, by their very nature, these dreams are impossible to document or explore further.

Another sort of psychic dream involves perceiving information about another place or time that you can't validate until a later date. In this case, your dream might seem like a normal dream, except that it includes information that only later proves to have been predictive. And then, there's the possibility that you might have psychic dreams of events that occurred in the distant past, and you simply aren't aware that you've gained a unique—and accurate—glimpse into history. From just these few examples, you can see how difficult it is to try to pin down what a psychic dream really is and what it may mean. Let's explore this rich world a little further.

Visions, Visitations, and Portents

Dreams that offer information about the future clearly appear to be psychic dreams, because this is information that you could not obtain without the aid of your intuition. A psychic dream that offers information about the future is called a *prophetic dream.*

If you believe you've had a prophetic dream, you must write it down or otherwise document it—including the date you dreamed it—before the actual, predicted event occurs. By doing so, you can later prove that the information came to you as a foresight into the future. Having a written record also helps you keep track of how accurate your dream messages turn out to be.

There are three basic types of prophetic dreams, each requiring a different standard of proof, so to speak. Categories of prophetic dreams include the following:

- True precognitive dreams
- Foreshadowing dreams
- Dreams with subliminal awareness

Although prophetic dreams in general are more common than most people think, true precognitive dreams are rare. In addition to being documented, they must exactly match what actually happens in the relatively near future. Other types of prophetic dreams occur more often. A foreshadowing dream is less demanding in terms of proof: you must also have a record of date, time, and content of the dream, but the event predicted can resemble the dream in a less-specific way and occur not immediately but within a reasonable amount of time. A dream with subliminal awareness must be recorded but might include just one or two elements that come true within a relatively short amount of time.

DEFINITION

Prophetic dreams are those that pertain to sensing or predicting the future.

Beyond Prophetic Dreams

A dream that predicts some clear-cut future event is easy to label "psychic" because it is clearly prophetic. However, most dreams offer messages that are not so easily defined. Rather, they offer hints of deeper meanings but leave the job of interpretation up to you. These dreams can be divided into general categories, including literal, displacement, and symbolic.

Literal dreams present information in actual images. This information might come in the form of a visual image or verbal phrase that stands out and thereby helps you recall the dream.

For example, you might dream that a woman wearing a red Santa suit runs up to you saying, "I've lost it." You would be tempted to think this was a symbolic dream telling you to slow down your Christmas shopping efforts—until you're at the mall one day and the event actually occurs. Even if only one aspect of the dream later transpires in real life, such as seeing a woman in a Santa suit or hearing someone say, "I've lost it," this dream still qualifies as a literal dream. You actually see or hear something in your waking life that you had dreamed earlier.

In a displacement dream, a literal image appears but in a different setting than it would be in real life. For example, you might dream that your mother gets a flat tire and has to walk home from the grocery store alone. After the dream you call her, concerned. She's fine, but she tells you about her neighbor who had a flat and had to walk home from the grocery store. The event did occur, but the lead character was displaced—fortunately for your mother!

 GUIDED INTUITION

If you'd like to explore more about the dream world, check out www.dreamtree. com. This website has a lot of fun and fascinating information that might help you get better connected to the dreamier side of your unconscious. Or, to look up specific dream meanings in a book you could keep under your pillow (or on your bedside table), take a look at *The Complete Idiot's Guide Dream Dictionary* (Alpha Books, 2007).

Still another type of psychic dream is the symbolic dream. Although all dreams seem symbolic, these dreams gain added significance once the passage of time reveals their insightful images. For example, you could be searching for the best way to treat your back pain, which doesn't seem to be getting any better. You might dream of seven lights shining, accompanied by a voice that says, "Look at the seven lights." Upon awakening, it seems like an odd dream holding no particular meaning. But a few days later, you read in a book about the seven light-filled centers associated with the body's main chakras and decide that you'll try energy healing as a way of treating your back pain. Only then does it occur to you how insightful your symbolic dream really was.

Researchers at the Maimonedes Dream Laboratory in New York have done much in recent decades to hone in on psychic dreaming specifically. Montague Ullman and Stanley Krippner devised methods for testing ESP during dreaming and showed high success rates. Their results suggest that dream telepathy is not that unusual or hard to do.

In various experiments, they had an awake "sender" look at a piece of artwork that contained a striking scene and then send this image to a dreamer. When awakened during REM sleep and questioned about their dreams, the dreamers frequently reported the image, or aspects of it, that the sender had relayed to them. According to expectations, the hit rate due to chance would be 50 percent. But the cumulated results of these experiments showed a higher success rate of 68 percent. (Subjects had 102 hits versus 48 misses.)

The Maimonedes experiments inspired others to look at dream telepathy. For instance, in the late 1990s Kathy Dalton and two associates at the University of Edinburgh in Scotland showed significant results in a clairvoyance dream experiment that did not involve a lot of high-tech measurement. They recorded the dreams they had each night in their own homes. The next morning, their dreams matched up with video clips that a lab computer had randomly selected and projected overnight, in a locked room. This research, although seemingly simple, suggests that dreams do access a level of information that extends beyond the dreamer's own mind.

Psychic Knowledge or a Subconscious Detective?

So if you have a dream about an event that actually comes true, how do you know whether your dream was truly psychic insight or simply a coincidence? Is it possible that your subconscious mind picked up on certain clues, processed the information, and fed it back to you in your dreams? Ask yourself questions such as these before you decide whether or not your dream was truly prophetic:

- Did I receive any warnings (from other people or from the media) before I went to sleep that might have triggered my dream?

- Could I have subconsciously incorporated external noises I heard or other information I received while dreaming?

- Have I ever dreamed of this topic before? (Dreams that have similar themes may be common for you. If so, the odds dictate that sooner or later your dreams are bound to coincide with real life.)

- Were there any unique details of the dream that identify the event in my dream as the specific event that actually occurred?

Knowing ahead of time that your dream will definitely come true is a rare occurrence. Only people who have had substantial experience with psychic dreams can say without a doubt that they have seen the future. Unless you have a special gift for prophetic dreaming, you will probably have a difficult time accurately forecasting which dreams are true and which aren't. If you notice that you quite frequently have dreams that later come true, pay attention to any patterns that accompany these dreams, such as the way you feel upon waking from the dream or how clearly you recall the dream. Also, be certain to keep dated records of the dreams as soon as they happen and share them with understanding people who can support your documentation and also help you recognize patterns.

Tapping Into Your Dream Power

The Chinese philosopher Chuang-Tzu once said, "One night I dreamed I was a butterfly, fluttering hither and thither, content with my lot. Suddenly I awoke and I was Chuang-Tzu again. Who am I in reality? A butterfly dreaming that I am Chuang-Tzu or Chuang-Tzu imagining he was a butterfly?" The philosopher made this observation in the third century B.C.E., and people are still fascinated by this puzzle today.

Where do your dreams end and you begin? While your dreams occur totally within your mind, they require your full attention and actually become more real to you than your sleeping body. Of course, you can reassure yourself that you always wake up from a dream—an especially comforting fact if you're one of the millions who experience nightmares!

But have you ever experienced waking up but you couldn't move and couldn't understand why not? For this brief period, your mind's dream state was still in control and your conscious mind (with its ability to move your voluntary muscles) was not. Is there a way to extend this period—when the conscious mind is aware but not quite in control—just long enough to let you have a closer look around dreamland? Some people can do this easily and actually have cultivated the art of dream control.

Boosting Your Dream Recall

Before you can control your dreams, you first must be able to remember them. This might sound difficult if you are unaware of your dreams or if you have never tried to recall them in a systematic way. Don't worry; everyone dreams, and everyone can learn to remember those dreams. Here are some simple steps to get you started:

- Establish and maintain your own personal dream journal. At the very least, keep paper and a pencil (or a voice recorder) by your bed so you're ready to document any dream that comes to you.

- Record any dream that you recall, including fragments and seemingly insignificant snippets. Do this as soon as you wake up!

- Before you fall asleep, tell yourself that you expect to dream and that you want to remember your dreams.

- As much as possible, try to wake up naturally (without using an alarm clock). Because awakening from internal cues usually pulls you directly from REM sleep, you increase the odds of recalling your most vivid dreams. On the other hand, some people use alarm clocks set at 90-minute intervals, with the idea that they'll wake themselves up near the end of a REM sleep period. That might or might not work, however, because the timing of sleep stages is rarely exact.

- Remain quiet and still when you awaken. Keep your eyes closed and send your mind back to what you were just dreaming about. Don't start thinking about the upcoming day's activities.

- Recall your dream backward. That is, remember the most recent parts first, then move backward in the sequence of the dream events.

- Try to remember all the dreams that you may have had. Then, take a few moments to make any associations between your dreams and real-life events.

- Pay attention to dreams. Review records of your previous dreams often. Recall usually improves with interest and involvement, so think, read, and talk about your dreams.

MIXED MESSAGES

Recalling your dreams during the day can be both good and bad. Sure, you should appreciate any opportunity that triggers dream information. But don't let your daytime recollections tempt you away from recording your dreams as soon as you can in the morning. And when you do recall dreams, note them right away—they will easily slip away as soon as you're distracted.

Of course, recording your dreams right after you wake up is crucial to remembering them. Don't say to yourself, "I'll write it down as soon as I get home from work this evening." The dream—or most of the details—will be gone. In fact, some experts estimate that the average dream is forgotten within 10 minutes of waking up.

On the other hand, after you get in the habit of writing down your dreams, you'll find that your recall increases at a tremendous rate. You'll probably record three to four dreams a week within your first two weeks and continue to record more from there. And if you start to feel that you're having too many dreams, read the advice we offered earlier—and do the opposite! For example, as you fall asleep, tell yourself that you prefer not to dream. And when you wake up, jump out of bed and blast your radio before you can remember anything. You get the idea. But it's hard to imagine anyone who would not want to know his or her dreams, because they offer an open door to one's own soul. We recommend that you actively value and accept each one.

GUIDED INTUITION

Listen to your recurring dreams with special attention. They tend to focus on personal issues, and if you fail to understand the lesson of the dream well and continue unwanted behavior, the dream keeps repeating the message.

Ask Your Dreams for Guidance

You can cultivate a sacred sense of your dreams by acknowledging each one as a gift from your intuition. Even when a dream does not seem to present earth-shattering insights, it can offer you a quick glimpse of some aspect of your life that you might want to look at more closely. Even when you're not certain what your dream means, the possibilities you merely guess at can provide you with enormous intuitive insight.

With practice, you can even control the content of your dreams by giving your mind a specific task just before you fall asleep. You'll be suggesting what you'd like to dream about and asking your mind to give you information in specific areas of your life. Here are some steps to help you ask your dreams for guidance:

1. Before you go to bed, get your pen and paper ready beside your bed. Write down tomorrow's date. If you've been keeping a journal, read about the last dream you wrote down.

2. When you're in bed, relax and review your day in reverse. Think about what you did just before going to bed: how you got ready for bed, what you did this evening, coming home from work, leaving work, what you did at work in the afternoon and in the morning ... and so on. Carry this through until you remember waking up and recalling the dream you had the night before. This process will help you develop a detailed ability to focus backward in time.

3. As you come closer to falling asleep, repeat to yourself continuously, "When I wake up, I will remember my dream about ...." If you have clarified what you specifically want to know, insert the question that you would like your dreaming mind to answer. Avoid asking a question with a simple "yes" or "no" response.

4. When you awake in the morning, don't move or start thinking about the day ahead. Instead, stay relaxed with your body in the same position and your eyes closed. Tell yourself that you want to recall your dream, then allow your mind to drift back to your dream.

5. As soon as you start to recall your dream, start writing. The idea is to write down whatever you remember immediately so that you're free to move on to remembering new material. If you find that you can't recall anything, be sure to write that down, too.

When you look at what you've written, be aware of how you feel and which items you respond to most clearly and strongly. Underline these points so that you can refer to them at a later date. These are the points that strike you as most relevant to your situation at this time. You might find that insights from several dreams can be put together to create a clear message for which you are waiting.

ARE YOU AWARE?

Eric Maisel, creativity consultant and author of *Sleep Thinking: The Revolutionary Program that Helps You Solve Problems, Reduce Stress, and Increase Creativity While You Sleep* (Adams Media Corporation, 2001), suggests that your brain can accomplish a tremendous amount of work during sleep—as long as you invite it to. If you clearly phrase a question that you want answered and then present it to your brain before falling asleep, your brain can give you an answer in the morning. Maisel recommends receiving this answer by writing down your thoughts on the matter first thing in the morning. For more information on Maisel's work, check out his website: www.EricMaisel.com.

Directing the Dream: Lucid Dreamers

Making suggestions for a topic you'd like to cover in a dream is a preliminary step toward actually controlling your dreams. Indeed, certain people have mastered this ability to direct the course of their dreams—referred to as *lucid dreaming*.

DEFINITION

Lucid dreaming occurs when the dreamer realizes he or she is dreaming. This awareness does not interfere with the dream's continuation but might or might not enable the dreamer to direct the dream. Lucid dreaming—controlling the course of a dream—is a skill that can be learned.

In 415 c.e., St. Augustine made what was probably the first written mention of lucid dreaming. Then, in the eighth century, the Tibetan Book of the Dead described a form of yoga that maintains full waking consciousness while in a dream state. This ancient art reveals an understanding of dreams as advanced as any proposed by today's modern researchers. The best known of these scientists is Stephen LaBerge, who founded the Lucidity Institute in 1987 to support research on lucid dreams and to teach people to dream lucidly.

A lucid dream state usually begins in the middle of a dream but can also occur when the dreamer returns to REM sleep immediately after awakening. It happens when the dreamer realizes that what he or she is experiencing is not occurring in physical reality but in a dream. This awareness might be triggered by impossible or unlikely occurrences in the dream, such as meeting someone from far away in a strange place, flying, or creating objects with the mind—although some people experience lucid dreams without a specific cue.

Levels of lucid dreaming ability can vary greatly. Higher levels of lucidity allow the dreamer to realize clearly that every aspect of the experience is a dream, whereas lower levels involve varying degrees of awareness. In a high-level experience, the dreamer is able to manipulate the dream and his or her actions within it. A dreamer's ability to imagine allows the dreamer to act out what he or she would like to do in real life or explore new possibilities.

Lucid dreaming can provide you with an important tool for achieving goals, relieving stress, rehearsing new behaviors, solving problems, finding artistic inspiration, or coming to terms with emotional difficulties. You can also direct your lucid dreams to help you access your intuition or connect to intuitive insights. Developing your skill at lucid dreaming is not all that difficult. For an introduction, why not try the following lucid-dreaming exercise?

Intuition Exercise: Toward Lucid Dreaming

The first step to learning to control your dreams is to be aware, while you are asleep, that you are in fact dreaming. To do this, start preparing during the day. Pick a common object that might appear in your dreams. You might choose a car, a flower, a cookie, a pair of shoes, a cat, or a tree. Tell yourself several times during the course of your day that when you see your chosen object, it will serve as a signal that you are dreaming. In addition, tell yourself that you will have a lucid dream during the night.

Before you go to sleep, write in your dream journal, "Seeing a cat (or whatever your object is) will let me know that I am dreaming." Picture your chosen object in your mind, and repeat to yourself that the object is a signal. Focus on your breath for a few moments, and let the image rest in your mind. When you feel ready, settle down and go to sleep.

When you wake up, write some notes about your experience. Did you see your object in your dream? Did it remind you that you were in fact dreaming? If not, try again, because practice makes perfect!

If your object did work for you as a signal, try the exercise again. This time, however, in addition to telling yourself about your signaling object, pick a topic to dream about. You might ask your dream to show you which color to paint the bathroom wall. You might ask to be shown your guides. Or, you might ask for a fun fantasy experience—why not ask to be shown how to fly?

If this topic interests you or you'd like to explore other techniques to learn lucid dreaming, look for Robert Waggoner's book *Lucid Dreaming: Gateway to the Inner Self* (Moment Point Press, 2008), or visit The Lucidity Institute's website at www. lucidity.com.

Your Dream Journal

Whether you've experienced amazing moments of lucidity in your dreams or are working toward just remembering them, writing down what you remember definitely strengthens your dream connections. Here's the format Lynn follows for recording her dreams; perhaps it will work for you, too.

Date:

Dream title:

(Leave this space blank until tomorrow morning, after you have recorded your dream or dreams. Having a dream title allows you to easily look back through your journal to access any recurring themes.)

What was your day like?

(Write three or four sentences on the key events in your day. Emphasize any emotional highlights.)

Overview of issue:

(Write a few sentences here about the nature of a problem you are facing in your life. Describe some of the possible solutions and challenges involved with this issue.)

Dream question:

(After writing your overview, summarize your concerns into a one-sentence question. Try to phrase your question so that it evokes more than a "yes" or "no" answer.)

The dream:

(Write down any dream or dream fragments that you can recall. Sometimes you might not remember the actual dream but will wake up with the sense that something is resolved. If the dream itself eludes you, write about your feelings upon awakening.)

Dream interpretation:

(What thoughts and feelings do you have about your dream? What do you think it meant? Are there any parts of your dream that seemed particularly significant?)

Interpreting Your Dreams

There must be a gazillion ways (or at least 10 or 20) to analyze what your dreams mean. One important point: keep in mind that dream symbols are highly personal. What one person sees in a flower might mean something entirely different to someone else. For example, you might dream of a flower and consider it to be a beautiful and positive sign, whereas someone who has allergies or someone who forgot to send their spouse flowers on a special occasion might consider a dream about flowers to be a nightmare.

GUIDED INTUITION

With regard to the meaning of dream symbols, consider your own associations before you consult outside sources. After you have a clear sense of what your dream means, consulting a book might help you confirm your interpretation. *The Complete Idiot's Guide to Interpreting Your Dreams, Second Edition* (Alpha Books, 2003) offers an insightful overview of dreams and their interpretations and symbols. On the internet, you may want to see what the ThinkQuest Library has to say about dreams. Check it out here: http://library.thinkquest.org/11189/nfinterp.htm.

When you see a symbol in a dream, go inside yourself to become clear about what the symbol means to you. Recall any previous associations with the image as well as your current feelings about it. Make sure to understand your feelings, and always try to write them down. Also, trust your intuition! Often, it will give you a great big pat on the back when you come upon a resonant interpretation of a dream. If you're trying to force an interpretation that's not accurate, your intuition won't let it sit right. And if you're trying to push away a message that you don't want to hear, that message will keep coming back to you until you pay attention.

Interpreting the messages in your dreams can give you an entirely new level of understanding. Reading messages from someone else's mind—via telepathy—takes an entirely new set of skills, however, and that's a subject we take up in the next chapter.

The Least You Need to Know

- Dreams are a pathway of communication between the body and mind, which become active when the conscious mind rests.

- Psychic dreams take on many forms and may reveal messages about the past, present, or future.

- Not every dream is psychic, but all your dreams contain important information about you.

- You can learn to control and direct your dreams.

- Recording your dreams strengthens recall and heightens insight.

Telepathy: You're a Mind Reader

In This Chapter

- Is telepathy mind-reading or imagination?
- Building your telepathic skills
- Focus on sending: meditate
- Measuring mind-to-mind messages

Telepathy might be one of the most common forms of intuitive experiences. For example, everyone can recall receiving a text message or email from a person he or she was just thinking about. Or, perhaps you've given a gift to someone who was about to buy that very item for himself or herself. Have you ever sensed that a loved one is ill and then called to find out it's true? Perhaps these incidents occur so often because of the close bonds shared between the people involved.

But did you know that some information can be shared between total strangers or mere acquaintances? Well, psi scientists are seeing this situation occur regularly in experiments. They're trying to understand when and why telepathy works and attempting to get to the bottom of what mind-to-mind communication really means (and what it can tell them). In the pages that follow, see for yourself what they've discovered.

Telepathy or Your Imagination?

Interestingly, the word telepathy, which comes from the Greek words for "distant" plus "experience," was first coined in 1882 by Fredric W. H. Myers, one of the founders of the Society for Psychical Research. Some people think that the term "thought-transference" more accurately describes the telepathic experience. Despite this quibble, most contemporary psychics use the more popular "telepathy" to mean the sharing of mind-to-mind experience.

We described a ganzfeld experiment, a scientific test of telepathic ability, in Chapter 2. When Charles Honorton and Marilyn Mandala Schlitz ran ganzfeld tests using students from The Juilliard School, a college-level institute of the performing arts located in New York City, they came up with some surprising results. These highly artistic telepathic receivers demonstrated an extraordinarily high success rate of 50 percent. And the music students in the group did even better. They had a 75 percent rate of accurately identifying their target image. But maybe this isn't surprising to you? We already know that creativity and intuition are closely linked. Perhaps being open to creativity, which is often described as a still, small voice, is much like being open to intuition and other psychic messages.

ARE YOU AWARE?

Ian Stevenson (1918–2007), formerly a professor of psychiatry at the University of Virginia, has collected information from various studies of telepathic communications. In his research, he found that 69.4 percent of incidents of telepathy occurred between close family members, 28.1 percent occurred between acquaintances, and 2.5 percent occurred between strangers.

The Zener card test is another well-known means to test telepathy (and clairvoyance, too). Zener cards were created by psychologist Karl Zener in the early 1930s and were first used by J. B. Rhine of the Rhine Research Center. A deck of Zener cards consists of 25 cards. Each card bears one of five images: the outline of a circle, a cross, three horizontal wavy lines, the outline of a square, and the outline of a five-pointed star. When used as a test of telepathy, the sender randomly selects a card and focuses on the card's image. The receiver uses telepathic skills to see the image being sent. Some psychics test really well, which goes to show that telepathy is not just your wild imagination.

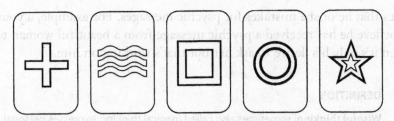

*In color, the Zener cards show a red cross, blue waves, black square, orange circle,
and green star. You can use markers and heavy paper stock to make your own
Zener cards.*

Say you have a knack for knowing what someone else is thinking. So are you a gifted mind-reader or just a good guesser? Answering this question is particularly tough when you're close to the person whose mind you're reading. For example, a mother and child who have spent many years together might recognize all sorts of unconscious clues and cues about each other's mental states and physical needs without even knowing it. So how do you sort out cogent guesswork from true psychic ability?

A few characteristics appear to mark most telepathic experiences. For one thing, a close emotional connection between the people communicating serves to foster telepathic communication.

Second, most telepathy occurs spontaneously in moments of emotional intensity. That is, most people don't sit down and say, "Let's read our minds." Rather, telepathic moments are likely to occur during times of crisis, when the sender is experiencing strong emotions or sensations.

In general, telepathy seems to work best when transferring emotions—particularly strong ones—rather than thoughts. Another aspect of telepathy worth highlighting is its simultaneous quality. Telepathics share their thoughts at exactly the moment they occur—not before. This is especially common when people sense that someone they know has died. Usually, they experience this knowledge at the person's time of death; thus, they have no opportunity to physically visit the person beforehand.

So how is imagination different from telepathy? Imagination comes from within a person's own mind and involves thoughts and motivations that never demonstrate having any basis in reality. Although imagination can seem like prescience or telepathy, you can sort imaginings into two categories: *wishful thinking* and *projection*. When someone indulges in wishful thinking, that person desires to receive psychic messages that he or she mistakes for psychic messages. For example, a young man might believe he has received a psychic message from a beautiful woman to phone her when it's only his desire to ask her out that's working on him.

DEFINITION

Wishful thinking, sometimes also called magical thinking, expresses personal inner desires but may distort the perception of reality to make the desires seem like external truth. **Projection** is a psychological term that refers to attributing one's own emotions or personality traits to someone else. This is usually done to avoid facing one's own feelings.

With projection, a person may believe that the information he very much wants to receive—but doesn't want to take responsibility for—is telepathic. For instance, an individual might feel angry at Aunt Marge for expecting him to come to Sunday dinner. But because he feels too guilty to come right out and admit those feelings, he instead "intuits" that Aunt Marge is really the one who's angry. By projecting those feelings of anger onto Aunt Marge, he can feel justified about the negative feelings toward her—and less guilty about canceling the dinner plans.

But what about information that isn't emotionally charged? How can you be sure when someone, such as a business associate, is sending a simple message for you to understand or act on? The special ability of differentiating between telepathy and imagination, like any other skill, can be learned.

GUIDED INTUITION

To test the theory that messages travel better between people who are emotionally close, practice sending telepathic messages to various people to whom you feel close. You can call them later, explain that you were conducting an experiment, and ask whether they had any thoughts about you or the contents of your message around the time that you sent it. Note whether you have a higher success rate with people to whom you feel closest.

Building Telepathic Skills

Expert psychic communicator Edgar Cayce wrote about the ability to distinguish between imagination and telepathy, often referred to as *discernment*. Cayce felt that telepathy is more than mind-to-mind contact—that it involves a spiritual force or power. So one way to know whether a message is telepathic is to determine whether it involves or improves a spiritual awareness. Also, how do you assess whether spiritual awareness is involved? By being in touch and attuned with your physical, emotional, and spiritual condition. This state requires complete honesty with one's self and benefits greatly from having a partner to work with to develop greater attunement to deeper levels of sharing and communication.

DEFINITION

Discernment in the telepathic sense refers to the ability to discriminate between personal desires, such as wishful thinking, and intuitive information.

Cayce continually emphasized the importance of spiritual development to increase intuitive abilities. He developed an exercise to help two partners develop their skills of telepathic discernment. The idea is that both partners agree ahead of time to think of each other at the same time each day. At that time, each one should write down what he or she intuits the other is doing. Later that evening, they can compare notes. They should repeat this process for 20 days, after which their skills should be fully developed.

The key to Cayce's telepathic exercise is reality testing, which allows the participants to check whether and when their responses were accurate. This requires communication and sharing. Otherwise, a person could easily fall into wishful thinking, deciding that the other person is doing whatever he or she imagines. Other intuitives, as well as recent psi researchers, have come up with additional suggestions for effective ways to relay mind-to-mind messages. But one thing seems clear: sending and receiving messages are two different processes. Performing each type of task requires your complete focus; don't try to do both at once. You'll experience sensory overload and be unable to relay clear information.

ARE YOU AWARE?

Are you fasciated by Cayce? If so, you may want to check out *The Complete Idiot's Guide to the Akashic Record* (Alpha Books, 2010) by Dr. Synthia Andrews and Colin Andrews. The authors, who have spent decades studying healing and consciousness, discuss Cayce's work and explain how you can connect to the consciousness of the universe.

Receiving Messages

To practice receiving telepathic messages, you'll want to work the way many experts recommend. That is, practice with a partner with whom you are already close. As your skills of receiving and discernment improve, you'll soon be able to apply your abilities to others you do not know as well. Also, remember to enter a relaxed or meditative state so that your rational mind is quiet and your intuitive side is open.

Think you can do it? We know you can! But if you are worried that you really cannot receive telepathic messages, that worry is going to block you from receiving them. What to do? We have an exercise for that!

Intuition Exercise: Prepare to Receive

In Chapter 7, we talked about stress as a block to your psychic awareness. And self-doubt can be stressful, right? So we're going to do some work on your self-doubt. If you like candles and incense, now would be a great time to get them out. As with a number of the other exercises in this book, you may want to record yourself reading the guided meditation, starting with step 4. Or, get a trusted friend to read it to you.

Before you begin to meditate:

1. Make sure your phone is turned off. And *really* turn it off, because you can hear it—even from across the room—when it's on vibrate. You'll also want to step away from the computer.

2. Light your candles and incense, if you are using them.

3. Make sure that you are physically comfortable. Loosen any tight clothing. Feel comfortable in your body, and allow your belly to soften.

4. Allow the words of this guided meditation to soothe you.

ARE YOU AWARE?

In J. K. Rowling's *Harry Potter* series, a number of characters are gifted telepaths. In Rowling's world, telepathy is a magical skill, and she calls it "Legilimency."

5. Close your eyes. (If you have lit a candle, face the flame with your eyes closed. Allow the light from the candle to give your eyelids a mellow glow.)

6. Take a deep breath, allowing your belly to expand. Now, slowly exhale. Pause. Inhale a big belly breath once again, and exhale slowly. Pause. Inhale deeply one more time. Inhale a little bit more, hold it at the top, and slowly let the breath go. Exhale.

7. Imagine that you are on the shore of a lake on a beautiful warm day. It's the perfect temperature, and you feel relaxed and happy. Hear the water lapping gently at the shore. Hear the soft calls of birds. Smell the water and the green plants that surround you.

8. Feel the dappled sunlight warming your toes, the arches of your feet, and your heels and ankles. As your feet and ankles are caressed by the sun, they soften and relax. The sun moves to your calves, and your calves loosen and relax. Your knees relax, soft and warm. The sun touches your thighs, and your things relax. Your hips relax. Your pelvis relaxes. The muscles of your buttocks relax. The sun travels to your belly, and your belly relaxes. Take another deep breath into your belly, allowing it to expand. Let the air out slowly. Feel all your muscles loosen some more—warm, soft, and relaxed.

9. The sun moves to your chest, warming and softening it. Your chest relaxes. Your lungs relax. Your heart relaxes. Feel the warm rays of the sun filling your heart with love and light.

10. Imagine a ray of light tinged with your favorite color. This ray comes from the sun, and it moves toward you. The ray pulses with gentle energy and love. The ray touches your heart and fills it with your favorite color. Feel the color fill you up and help you relax. Imagine that the ray carries a message. Feel that you are open to that message. Your heart is open and relaxed. You are open to receiving. You hear and feel the loving messages that are for you. Feel your openness.

11. Imagine that you are receiving a message of love from a dear friend. See an image of your friend in your mind's eye. Hear your friend's voice. Conjure any special little details about your friend, and feel that your hearts are connected. Breathe and feel the energy between you.

12. When you feel ready, let the image of your friend go. Return to the shore of the lake. Hear the water on the shore and the birds in the trees. Enjoy the peaceful atmosphere for a few moments. Tell yourself that you are open to receiving the messages that are meant for you.

13. When you feel ready, allow the lake to fade away. Imagine the room in which you are sitting. Feel your legs and buttocks supported by the surface on which you sit. Slowly open your eyes and return to the room and your normal awareness.

How was that for you? After this meditation, you should feel relaxed and open. (If you still have trouble receiving, you can practice this meditation for a few days and see whether it helps open you up.)

Now, you are ready to practice being the telepathic receiver. Our first exercise helps you receive messages that have been sent by someone using a full range of sensory information, which should strengthen the transmission. The second one has the sender focus on relaying visual images alone.

MIXED MESSAGES

Don't try too hard when it comes to receiving telepathic messages—your anxiety will only get in the way. Instead, try to relax and remain open-minded and open-hearted.

Intuition Exercise: Receiving an Object

Get your paper and pencil ready. You and your partner should then settle into a quiet, comfortable position. It's fine to be in the same room together. Remember, in this exercise you are the receiver and your partner is the sender.

1. Your partner, as the sender, should repeat several times—in his or her own mind—the name of a specific object, such as a vegetable, fruit, or flower. (Note that throughout this exercise, the sender does not need to have a real object present to look at, just his or her own mental version of it.)

2. After reciting its name silently several times, the sender should then experience the object in his or her mind. If it is a tomato, he or she should look at how red it is, smell its tart freshness, feel his or her teeth slice into it and the juice running into the mouth, and taste its particular flavor.

3. This process should take about 30 to 60 seconds. Then, you can write down the object you perceived. If you don't get a clear message, write down any information you do get, such as color, shape, or smell. As we've said about other exercises, you might feel that you are making up your impressions—but don't let that stop you. Just try to have fun with the process.

4. Don't talk to your partner about what you sensed. Just let him or her see that you've finished writing so that he or she can go on to the next object. Repeat this process about five times. You can use five different objects of one type (all fruits, for example, such as an orange, apple, pear, banana, and grape) or a variety of objects (tomato, orange, chocolate, shrimp, and coffee). Food works well because it allows the use of smell and taste. (Don't try this exercise when you're hungry, though, or your wishful-thinking mechanism may take over!)

5. Avoid talking at all during the exercise. When you've finished, share your notes with your partner. Let him or her tell you whether you were on target or not.

GUIDED INTUITION

Another way—one that may be easier for you—to begin learning to receive telepathic messages is by asking your partner to focus on sending you a color. Your partner should let a specific color fill his or her mind without attaching it to a specific object. For instance, if your partner chooses orange, he or she should just focus on orange, not an orange piece of fruit.

When you feel comfortable with your success at the object-sensing exercise, try receiving an impression of a visual image. This exercise is similar to the popular psi experiments, referred to as ganzfeld tests, that we mentioned in Chapter 2. See how you do.

Intuition Exercise: Receiving an Image

Get your paper and pencil ready. Your partner will need a bell or other noise-making device. You and your partner should be in separate rooms but close enough to both hear the bell. Settle into comfortable positions in a quiet state.

1. Your partner should privately pick about five different pictures from post-cards, magazines, or books. You should not look at any of them ahead of time.

2. Your partner should focus on one picture at a time, trying to think of nothing but that image. He or she should do this for about one minute and then ring the bell.

3. When you hear the bell, record your impressions of the image, whether you prefer to write or draw what you perceived. Feel free to simply list or draw details if a specific image does not come to you.

4. Your partner should allow you about 20 seconds to record your impressions. Or, you can have your own bell to ring to let him or her know when you've finished.

5. Repeat this process for all five images. Avoid speaking to your partner during this time.

6. When you've finished, look at your notes together with your partner. Let him or her tell you when you were on target or not.

Pertaining to these exercises, theories differ on whether you should stop and discuss each image just after sensing it or go through all five before comparing notes. Basically, it depends on what you want to achieve. If you want to assess where you are right now without interrupting your concentration, go through all five images at once. If you want to develop your skills of telepathic discernment, stop to analyze which images transferred best—and why and how.

If you feel that you're not as successful as you'd like, don't be too hard on yourself. Remember that you'll often feel like you're just making it up. Be as willing to be wrong as you are to be right—you'll learn from your mistakes. Another factor may be your partner. It takes two to tango—and to talk telepathically. If your partner isn't focused or is having an off day, you'll be sharing that experience, too. Keep in mind that, for both of you, this is a new skill—and as with any new skill, it takes practice.

Sending Messages

Interestingly, scientists seem to know more about who makes a good receiver than who makes a good sender. Perhaps they tend to focus on *how* people receive information because that's how they have proof that psi exists. For example, a sender who has fantastic skills can't get his or her message across—and therefore can't be evaluated—if his or her receiver isn't effective. But that doesn't mean that sending isn't important. And you might have a special strength in that area.

To practice sending telepathic messages, prepare yourself in the same way that you would for receiving messages. Work with someone with whom you're emotionally close, and put your mind in a relaxed or meditative state. Check out these exercises and see how you do.

Prepare to Send

Sending messages is all about focus. The more you can focus your mind on the message you want to send, the clearer that message will be. And how do you learn to focus? Meditate!

Try to meditate daily, if only for a short session every day. If you have a regular mediation practice, that's great. Keep it up. If you don't, why not start now? Pick a guided mediation from this book, turn off your phone, take a quick bathroom break, focus, and relax. Alternatively, you can just sit in a quiet and comfortable place and concentrate on your breath as it enters and leaves your body.

If meditation is a stumbling block for you—and it can be for many of us as we rush about our daily lives—make a commitment this month to learn more and practice sitting in meditation for just a little while a few times a week. The more you do it, the better you will get—and the better you get, the easier it will be. If you're so inclined, check out *The Complete Idiot's Guide to Meditation* (Alpha Books, 2002) by Joan Budilovsky and Eve Adamson or *The Complete Idiot's Guide to Mindfulness* (Alpha Books, 2008) by Anne Ihnen and Carolyn Flynn. Both books will help you with techniques that will focus and relax your mind.

Intuition Exercise: Telepathic Telephoning

As a simple and fun experiment, try sending a telepathic message to a friend to call you. Pick someone who calls often enough that he or she wouldn't have to go out of his or her way to phone you, but not someone who calls you every single day. Sit calmly in a quiet place, close your eyes, and focus on the friend of your choice.

MIXED MESSAGES

Don't rely on telepathy to meet new people! If you're shy, you may be tempted to send a telepathic message to an attractive stranger—but, as you know, telepathy works best with people you already know well. The best way to start getting to know someone new is to strike up a conversation—out loud!

Say your friend's name in your mind and picture him or her clearly. You can even use words to tell him or her to call you. Then, envision your friend thinking of you, going to the phone, and dialing your number. Envision this very slowly and distinctly, taking the time your friend would actually need to do this in real life and including every detail of the scene—even if you've never been there before. For example, imagine where your friend's phone sits, how he or she would pick it up, and how your friend's fingers look as they push the phone's buttons. Then, hear yourself picking up the phone and saying, "Hello." The entire process should take 5 to 10 minutes.

When you're done, write down the time that you started and ended the exercise. Then, stop thinking about it. Your friend might not call immediately, but when he or she does, ask what your friend was doing when you sent the message. Perhaps your friend was busy but was thinking of you and waiting to be free to call. If you don't hear from your friend that day, call the next day to see whether the thought to call you did indeed cross your friend's mind when you sent the message.

If you don't succeed the first time or two, don't worry. Try a few more times, perhaps without calling your friend to ask why you didn't get a call back. Then, try the experiment with someone else.

Intuition Exercise: Sending an Image

Here's another exercise designed to help you practice being the sender. Because effective sending can be more difficult to measure, we recommend checking your results for this exercise after each attempt.

This exercise requires a little planning ahead. Select five or six pictures with specific images, which may come from magazines, books, or postcards. Don't let your partner see any of them. You may want to choose pictures that have an emotional content, as these are easier to send and receive.

Plan for your partner and yourself to sit calmly in a quiet place at the same time, whether you're in the same house or in completely different towns. During this quiet time, you look at one image while your partner simply sits and waits.

While concentrating on this image, describe it with words in your mind and also look at every line, shape, and color. Then, think about all the associations it brings up for you, whether good or bad. (Emotions are important for making an image have more impact on the receiver.) Continue thinking about the image for about 10 minutes.

Meanwhile, your friend should write down every impression he or she receives—visual, verbal, or emotional.

Try this exercise at various prearranged times for each of the five pictures. Discuss your results after each one, however. Discussing the results shortly after the experience will help you understand what impressions you sent that did or didn't work, which will help you improve your skills.

Lynn had her sending abilities tested while promoting the first edition of this book. She had gotten a call from Fox Cable News and thought it was just the little local affiliate station, but when Lynn arrived at the studio, it turned out that the show she was to be on was one that gets aired across the world! Was this broadcast going to turn Lynn into a celebrity, or would she just blow it completely?

During the interview, as if to add to Lynn's anxiety, the interviewer put her on the spot by suggesting they try a telepathy exercise on the air. She said, "You think of an object, and I'll try to pick up on it." The only thing that seemed to come to Lynn's panicked mind was the word "star." So she focused on that. Her emotional energy must have been strong enough to send that word out into the ethers, because much to Lynn's amazement her interviewer blurted out, "I'm getting a star!" When Lynn viewed the tape several weeks later, she saw that the look of relief on her face was priceless.

The Least You Need to Know

- You can develop your skills of mind-to-mind communication.
- Practicing open communication with people you are close to helps you sort out what's telepathy and what's not.
- It's easier to share telepathic messages with close friends than with people you don't know well.
- Having a clear focus, which you can develop through meditation, will help you become more telepathic.

Trusting Your Own Psychic Intuition

In This Chapter

- Using intuition on a personal level
- Evaluating your life with intuition
- Creating positive change with intuition
- Checking in for reassurance

We've talked about ways you can get in touch with your intuitive side and interpret messages. We've discussed how information may come to you and how you can transmit it. But we haven't said much about what you can actually do with this knowledge. How do you make intuition and its messages useful in your everyday life?

To put your intuitive messages to use, you'll need to assess what your intuition is telling you, evaluate what you're ready to do, and then take charge and actively direct your life in the direction you want to go—with your intuition as a guide. You can direct your thoughts and energy to move in a direction that's in tune with what your intuition wants for you: improving your life and furthering your spiritual growth. We'll show you how in this chapter.

Intuitive Intelligence

Most people consider the sixth sense to be an extra sense in addition to the five known physical ones. But the term also includes an interesting pun. The word "sense" suggests a type of intelligence. And that's another way of describing what intuition is. Here's a chart you can use to distinguish between the thinking that comes from the logical/rational side of your mind and that which comes from your intuitive side.

Logical/Rational Mind	Intuitive Mind
fragments	whole
limits	expansive
slow	in a flash
either/or	many options
judgmental	nonjudgmental
needs proof	trusting
critical	loving
controls	has faith
attached to outcome	detached
exclusive	inclusive
prompt	flowing
linear	flexible
expectant	still, quiet
complex	simple
driven	calming
"I should"	"I could"
doubtful	hopeful
categorizes	sees overview
self-righteous	forgiving
hesitates	courageous
sameness	diversity
sees limits	sees potential
values structure	open to possibilities

Both types of intelligence have their own type of good sense. After you learn to bring them both into balance, you'll have a good chance at becoming something that people don't talk about very often: wise.

Information: Past, Present, or Future

When receiving intuitive information, try to do so with an open mind. Gaining fresh insight into past events or emotions can teach you how to change the way you are today, but you needn't consider it to be a reprimand or source of guilt. Similarly, information about future possibilities can reveal options and opportunities—not unchangeable inevitabilities. But taking a hard look at the negative side of what is likely to happen if you pursue a certain path might help you redirect your focus and take more positive action.

When Lynn receives intuitive information, she perceives information about the past to her left, the present straight in front of her, and the future to her right. (Just to confuse you, Lynn has a friend who gets her information in just the opposite configuration!)

GUIDED INTUITION

Remember that receiving information is a highly personal experience. Although Lynn and her friend perceive past, present, and future information based on certain locations (that is, coming from the left, right, or straight ahead), other people do not work this way at all, and can receive information in any number of ways. Strive to find the way that works best for you, without comparing yourself to anyone else.

Often, clients ask Lynn about a hoped-for relationship. If she is immediately drawn to her left (the past), Lynn assumes that something has been unresolved in a past relationship and asks her intuition for information on that. Lynn might ask her client for the first name of a person in a previous significant relationship and then give the client information that could help resolve the conflict.

When asked about a potential future event, Lynn often sees probabilities rather than certainties. Let's explain. Lynn often sees alternate paths or choices that someone may make. They actually look like strands of light going off into the future. Many times one of these paths lights up in her mind's eye. Lynn interprets this to mean that this particular path is the most likely one for the client to take. Then Lynn describes what she sees as the outcome of this path. Lynn also describes the other choices.

Here's an example. Lynn had a client she'll call Ruth. Ruth sat down on Lynn's couch and asked quite bluntly, "Am I going to get a divorce?" She told Lynn her husband's name was Bob. When Lynn tuned into Ruth and her husband, Lynn felt instantly that things were quite rocky between them. They had a lot of miscommunication and hurt feelings. Lynn saw the paths of light into the future and unfortunately the one that indicated divorce lit up, which told Lynn that their marriage was indeed in trouble.

Lynn felt a wave of sadness and regret wash over her as she related this to Ruth. Lynn could see in her mind's eye that other paths of light, indicating other possibilities, were not completely dim. Lynn asked her intuition if anything could be done to save their marriage.

Lynn immediately received information about Bob, showing that he was filled with regret. She perceived him as a rather stubborn fellow who, Lynn suspected, might have had an affair. Lynn felt that Bob didn't want a divorce and was, in fact, quite distraught over this prospect. However, he had no idea what to do to communicate to Ruth that he loved her. The way he saw it, Ruth was angry with him all the time and he just wanted to avoid her at this moment.

MIXED MESSAGES

When consulting about relationships, you might feel pressured to respond with an outcome your client considers positive, but stay open to the true messages you receive. Moving on may be the best option for the individual, even if he or she doesn't yet realize it.

Lynn asked for guidance about what Ruth could do and how she could better communicate with Bob. As she was relating all of this information to Ruth, Lynn could see that the strong light on the path to divorce was becoming dimmer and the light on the path to reconciliation was becoming brighter. Lynn ended the session by giving Ruth a referral to a marriage counselor and reinforcing the issue of choice and free will. Later, Ruth reported that she and Bob had stayed together and were making progress with a therapist.

When Lynn consults with a client about a relationship, she doesn't always focus on whether the relationship will work out (that is, have a "happily ever after" ending) or not. Lynn asks her intuition about what her client needs to learn in the relationship. For Lynn to say "Yes" or "No" takes away from all the learning that's part of a relationship. That learning might include ways to make a relationship work—or lessons about moving on.

Using Your Sixth Sense

To fully use your sixth sense, you need to become more self-aware. You can do so by paying close attention to your inner dialogue—the voice inside your head that murmurs messages about your life and your self-image. So often when Lynn consults with clients she picks up on how much they put themselves down or engage in *negative self-talk*. This type of thinking drowns out what your intuition might be trying to whisper in your ear. It also defeats your hopeful efforts at trying to create positive change.

> **DEFINITION**
>
> **Negative self-talk** is the inner voice in your mind that creates a running flow of negative thoughts about yourself and your actions.

It's Not About Predicting the Future

Often, what we tell ourselves—about life in general or about our abilities and talents—becomes a self-fulfilling prophecy. Lynn can make all sorts of wonderful predictions about your future, but if you go away from a session with Lynn thinking "I could never do that" or "I'm not that smart (or lucky or educated or ambitious)," then there's no real possibility of change. Henry Ford once said, "Whatever you think you can, you can. Whatever you think you can't, you can't."

> **ARE YOU AWARE?**
>
> Scientists have conducted research indicating that people who believe psi exists are more likely to experience it. On the other hand, skeptics that question the existence of psi have the greatest difficulty experiencing it. ESP tests clearly show believers scoring much higher than skeptics.

Your subconscious mind considers whatever you choose to tell yourself to be the truth. If you tell yourself you're always unlucky, your mind believes it and creates proof of that belief in your reality. What are some positive beliefs you hold that help you succeed? What are some negative beliefs you hold that hinder your success? Are you willing to change them?

Lynn is often aware of the power her consultations have on the eventual outcome. Although Lynn encourages people not to take what she says as gospel truth, many do. They think they have a future that is etched in stone and that Lynn has the ability to read it. Nothing could be further from the truth. We shape our future by the thoughts we hold, the dreams we dream, the beliefs we carry with us, and also by our willingness to make choices, act, and take risks.

Lynn has many clients she would define as successful in life. In many respects, they are the easiest clients to work with because they don't let a lot stand in their way. When they decide they want to create something, all of their positive beliefs engage to help them create their desired outcome. Here's a sampling of common beliefs Lynn sees that these successful people hold:

- "I can make things happen in life."
- "I love my work because I do what I enjoy."
- "My work and my life are the same."
- "People like me and trust me."
- "I trust my hunches and gut feelings."
- "I'm lucky. Situations unfold for me at the right time."
- "I believe there's enough for everyone."
- "I'm willing to take risks when I feel guided to do so."
- "I'm good at what I do."
- "There is a purpose and meaning to my life."
- "I enjoy being of service in my field."

When you hold such positive beliefs about life, then you're more likely to take the steps necessary to make your dreams come true. As part of those positive beliefs, your intuition is guiding you every step of the way. It gives you input, saying "Yes. This is a good decision" or "No. Stay clear of that direction. Go the other way." When you learn to pay attention to your inner sense, it leads you to greater joy and peace.

However—and this is a big however!—trusting your intuition does not mean nothing bad will ever happen to you. It means that you can make wiser choices, experience greater calm, and understand a greater purpose—even during difficult times in your life.

Finding Your Inner Confidence

Lynn tries to give her clients hope for the future and the tools they need to accomplish their dreams. One of the most important tools is recognizing and accepting the power of your own words and convictions. Are you truly in touch with your core beliefs? You better be, because they really help shape the way you experience life. Creating change in your life might require you to modify or even eliminate some of your core beliefs. But first you need to know what they are. Get out your notebook and a pen and take a moment to complete the sentences that follow.

Intuition Exercise: Your Values and Beliefs

I believe that in order to have a happy life I have to _____.

People who are successful are _____.

People with money are _____.

I believe that in order to get ahead in life you must _____.

People who are poor are _____.

To be spiritual you should _____.

People who are psychic are _____.

My worst fear is _____.

My greatest hope is _____.

My biggest obstacle is _____.

My greatest strength is _____.

> **GUIDED INTUITION**
>
> Be honest about your true beliefs. No one is judging you, and you certainly don't need to judge yourself. However, if admitting a certain belief or two bothers you, make a mental note and come back to that one later. Your intuition may be telling you that you need to work on this issue.

One of the first principles in creating a life you love is to act "as if." If you start behaving as if you have the qualities you need to have a successful life, your unconscious mind won't know the difference and will start to feel successful and will draw new and positive experiences to you. Your intuition will provide you with information about going in the new direction that you have chosen.

Take some time out to answer the following questions. You don't need to write anything this time, just allow yourself to picture and imagine how you'd feel.

What would your life look like if you acted as if you were:

- Highly intuitive

- Confident and successful

- Extroverted

- Well-liked

- Destined to succeed

- Full of energy

- Filled with creative ideas

- Courageous

Hold onto these images and feelings; they represent an exciting step toward creating inner confidence. The more familiar you become with these positive sensations, the more they will come to you naturally. This is an early step toward replacing old negative thoughts with new healthy ones. Paying attention to your beliefs and to the way your inner dialogue supports them is another step along the way to creating the life you want.

So now that you know what your current beliefs are, are you ready to decide how you'd like to change the ones that need changing?

Intuition Exercise: Your Treasure Map

We've talked a lot in this chapter about using your beliefs to create what you want in your life. What do you want—*really* want—for yourself and your future? If you're like most people, that isn't an easy question to answer.

In this exercise, you're going to create your own treasure map—one that can lead you to the greatest treasure you've ever dreamed of: your innermost dreams and desires. We're asking you to work with symbols. Symbolic images are one of the primary ways that your intuition speaks to you.

This treasure map, or dream collage, is a visual representation of your hopes and dreams. In addition, it's fun to do, and it might just remind you of being in kindergarten. So let your inner child out to play and enjoy! You will need:

- A large piece of poster board or foam core
- A pair of scissors
- Liquid glue or a glue stick
- A bunch of old magazines
- A few new magazines

Go through your magazines and cut out words and pictures that inspire you. Pay attention to what excites you. If you've always wanted to travel, for instance, cut out a picture representing your dream destination and paste it on your board. Same goes for a picture that represents an exciting career, or a beautiful body, or a great relationship. Cut out and paste any photograph, drawing, or other visual representation of your goal or goals.

When you're done cutting and pasting, put your collage in a place where you'll see it frequently. Creating and displaying your treasure map brings your secret dreams and desires, aims and ambitions, out into the open. As your eye catches it from time to time, you'll be reminded of that side of yourself that isn't always doing the expected, rational thing. With time, the strongest parts of that "secret" side will start to jump out at you. They'll remind you not only that they're there, but also that they're ready for you to start making them real in your everyday life. And you can turn to your intuition for help on how to create that reality.

Using Intuition to Change Your Life

Many people come to Lynn with a vision of what they want to create in their lives—and, more often than not, they simply want Lynn to affirm that they'll get it. The pressure to say, "Yes, you will get that new home, new relationship, new career, new car ...," is enormous. Who wants to go to a psychic and hear that the relationship you just started is not going to work out or that you may lose your job instead of being promoted?

Lynn's always found it difficult to tell her clients that things are not going to work out exactly as they planned. She used to feel that she could devastate them, or at the very least crush their dreams. How is it possible to be honest about what Lynn sometimes sees psychically, and yet avoid forecasting failure?

Lynn's prayed a lot about this. She wants to guide her clients toward success—not just predict success or failure. Over time, Lynn's begun to see a connection between someone's internal condition—what he or she is thinking or feeling—and what ultimately happens in reality. And you must keep this in mind as you explore your own intuition or, especially, if you visit a psychic for guidance. You are the architect of your world. You create your life experiences through your beliefs, the images you hold, the guidance you follow (or ignore), and the actions you take. It is within your power to create a life you love.

People often come to Lynn expecting to hear phenomenal predictions or witness miraculous events. Lynn can tell them only what she sees and provide them with what she understands to be the tools to create the reality they desire. The rest is up to them. One of Lynn's favorite quotes is from Lewis Carroll's *Alice in Wonderland:* "There's no use trying," Alice said. "One can't believe impossible things." "I daresay you haven't had much practice," said the Queen. "When I was your age, I always did it for half an hour a day. Why sometimes I've believed as many as six impossible things before breakfast."

What the Queen was on to is a philosophy called *metaphysics*. It's derived from the Greek words *meta*, meaning "going beyond," and *physikos*, meaning "the physical plane." It suggests that a connection exists between what goes on in your mind, beliefs, and consciousness and what you create in your life.

DEFINITION

Metaphysics is a branch of philosophy that looks at the nature of reality, existence, and the structure of the universe.

Using Your Mind to Create Success

"There is nothing either good or bad, but thinking makes it so," says Hamlet. We believe that this principle can apply to how you approach your life. If you believe your life's miserable and will always stay that way, then it will. If you want it to improve and you plan positive changes, then your new future has already begun.

GUIDED INTUITION

Stating clear intentions is a powerful way to achieve goals. Affirmations are especially helpful in changing thought patterns and redirecting your life. For more on affirmations, check out Lynn's website, where you will find some downloadable teleseminars: http://lynnrobinson.com/category/products/teleclasses.

But despite the best intentions, you'll still need to do more than wish and dream. I consider the following four steps essential to achieving your goals and creating a life you love.

- Know what you want. Have a clear vision of what you want to create. Don't spend a lot of time figuring out how to achieve your goal. Just do what the Queen suggests to Alice: Believe impossible things!

  The universe has amazing tools at its disposal to help you create what you want. When you're honest and clear about what you want, your higher self takes the long view of the connections and situations that must occur before you attain what you ask for. It begins drawing together the people, opportunities, and events that you need to create what you want.

  Your higher self finds opportunities for you and provides the necessary impulses for appropriate action so that you're attracted to those opportunities—and they're attracted to you! Your feelings, hunches, and flashes of insight signal what actions to take. Your willingness to be spontaneous, follow your inner urges, listen to strong feelings, and act upon them can lead you to your goals.

- Believe in yourself. One of the biggest reasons people become unable to create the lives they want is lack of self-esteem and self-love. Do whatever it takes to start believing in yourself—see a therapist, work with your minister or rabbi, write in your journal. If you believe you're worthy of your goals and are capable of achieving them, you're well on your way!

- Know the "science" of creating/manifesting. Thoughts, beliefs, and emotions help create your reality more than you might imagine. Researchers at the University of California discovered that individuals who believe strongly that they can change or control their destiny are more likely to persevere in a difficult task.

Lynn had a teacher, Tom, who taught her a valuable lesson. Whenever she spoke to him about any type of limitation, such as, "It's so difficult to start a business in this economy," he would counter with, "If you say so." It annoyed Lynn terribly at the time. But now, whenever she hears herself saying something in her mind like "I can't ..." or "It's hard to ..." she also hears Tom reminding her, "If you say so." Lynn usually stops doing this negative thinking right away. Richard Bach addresses this issue in his book Jonathan Livingston Seagull: "If you argue in favor of your limitations, you get to keep them."

- Start a plan of action. Lynn calls this "putting energy out there." What one step can you take? Start. Do it. Then take another. Follow your inner guidance. What is it telling you to do? Is there anything that feels appealing or fun? Do that. Someone once said, "If you always do what you've always done, you will always get what you've always gotten."

Planning Your Ideal Life

As we've discussed, the first step in creating a life you love is to be clear about what it is that you want. Lynn uses the questions in the following exercise to identify her true thoughts and feelings, which she can later refine and expand if need be. You try it!

> **ARE YOU AWARE?**
>
> Psi research shows that the best research subjects are those who concentrate well. Various studies along this line of testing indicate that mental focus is a key factor in psi subjects successfully achieving the goals of the experiment. When using intuition to improve your life remember the importance of focusing on your goals.

Intuition Exercise: Your Ideal Life

Write a paragraph describing your ideal life in each of the first three areas. Choose two more that are important to you from the list in "other areas" and write about them also. Be as descriptive and specific as possible. The questions listed after each area are just to get you started. Follow your heart to write about what's important to you.

Work

(What would you do, even if you weren't getting paid for it? What kind of situation would you work in: alone, self-employed, or a large corporation?)

Money

(How much monthly or yearly income would you like? How much money would you like to have in investments and in savings?)

Relationship

(If you are in a relationship, how would you like it to be different? If you are not in a relationship, describe what you would like to create.)

Choose Two Other Areas to Write About

(Physical health and appearance; creativity; home and possessions; "free time," hobbies; spirituality; family; education; community or volunteer work; travel; friends; associates)

After you have your wish list, underline some of the most important words in each paragraph. This will get you started at creating your own written goal, or list of goals.

Your Goal

Write down your goal(s) in two or three sentences.

Intuition Exercise: Verbalize and Realize

Remember the suggestions we made in the positive self-talk section of Chapter 7? Those tips can help you to turn your goals into positive statements. Your intuitive mind can then interpret those as what your future is intended to be.

GUIDED INTUITION

Remember that intuition comes in many different forms, so stay alert to new ways that it appears to you. Once you've gotten used to receiving messages in a certain way, don't always expect them to come to you in exactly that same way, or you might close off valuable opportunities for learning. Your intuitive messages can come to you from a source as "solid" as another person (maybe even a stranger) who suggests a good idea, or from a source as ethereal as a dream. Because it's operating 24 hours a day, your intuition has a lot of leeway in its role as your internal guidance system.

Following are some sample affirmations to help inspire you. This list of statements offers examples of affirmations that can help you reach your specific goals. You can create your own affirmations, or use these singly, mixed and matched, or as springboards to create your own personalized affirmations. In other words, use them in any way that works for you.

- My intuition continues to direct me in manifesting miracles in my life.
- Infinite riches are now flowing freely into my life, and I deserve them.
- I find it easy to take appropriate risks and actions.
- I love and trust myself. I make appropriate decisions for my career success.
- I trust my intuition and have the courage to act on its wisdom.
- I feel confident in all that I undertake, and I succeed.
- I use my abundance wisely in ways that are of service to my community and to the resources of the earth.

Write down your affirmations now. Put them on the back of an envelope if that is what is nearby, or put them in a notebook or calendar. Or, if need be, write them in the margins of this book! The point is: record your affirmations by writing them down.

Intuition Exercise: Visualize and Realize

What will it look like to achieve your goal? Picture yourself living in the situation you want to create. Many people imagine their visualizations as a series of snapshots or slides illustrating the outcome they want to achieve. What three images come to your mind as a result of realizing your goal?

Write down your visualizations now.

When you have a clear sense of your goal, go back and observe what actions appear to you as the steps you need to take to reach that goal.

Write down three things that you feel guided to do as steps toward achieving your goal.

Following Through

Now that your plan is in place, don't look back. Don't second-guess yourself or give way to doubt. Don't worry if your plan of action seems irrational or silly. Unless your ideas are actually harmful, trust your hunches. Your intuition is guiding you along new pathways toward your goals. Trust that your intuition got you this far and that it won't leave you now. This is the time that it can really get into high gear and show you all it's got to give. But in case you have a tendency to second-guess yourself, here are a few guidelines to keep you on track:

- Pay attention to your thoughts. Listen to what you tell yourself about your life situation. Pay particular attention to your beliefs about your ability to achieve what you want. Erase negative self-talk.

- Practice your affirmations and visualizations. Practice these at least twice a day. Often, the morning and evening are the best times for most people to focus their thoughts.

- Pay attention to what excites you. Continue to think about what you would like to create in your life. Focus on what brings you joy in your life today and what might bring you joy in the future.

- Take action. Take action on at least three things that can move you closer to your goals/visions/dreams. If you're after a new career, for example, call a job counselor, interview someone who works in your desired industry, sign up for a related class, or do some research on the web or at the library. Small steps count! By taking them, you're building a bridge to the life you want!

 GUIDED INTUITION

To keep your affirmations in the front of your mind, tape up affirmation "memos" around your home or office. They'll give you quick reminders, even when you're too busy to take time out to initiate the process of creating positive thoughts.

Owning What You Know

One important way to build confidence in your ability to pursue your dreams and goals is to give yourself a pat on the back for opening up to your intuition. Following are some suggestions for staying in touch with the psychic side that brought you this far on your journey:

- Begin each day by asking for guidance. You might do so when you first wake up in the morning, when you're having your morning coffee, or even during your shower. If you need information about something specific, ask your intuition about your problem. Otherwise, ask for general guidance and wisdom.

- Take time out every day for a 10- to 15-minute meditation break. Experiment with doing it at different times during the day, then decide which one works best for you.

- Remember that your guidance might come in a variety of forms. It might appear as an internal nudge to read a certain book or to call a specific friend. You might experience your intuition through a spontaneous feeling of joy when you do something that you love, which is your intuition's way of saying, "Do more of that!" You might get a gut feeling or another body sensation that indicates you're on the right or wrong track regarding a decision. Learn to pay attention to all the ways your guidance speaks to you.

- Follow your impulses. Be spontaneous. When you overanalyze something you might be arguing yourself out of your intuition's input.

- Ask your intuition for help. Get in the practice of speaking to it like a trusted friend. You'll be rewarded with an ever-increasing channel of communication in return.

All of these suggestions are intended to get you using your intuition as often as possible. Try to avoid asking for intuitive guidance and then just ignoring the messages you have received. Everyone likes it when his or her advice is listened to and acted upon. Your intuition is no exception! Remember to check in on a regular basis, just to make certain that you're still on track. You'll feel all the better for it.

GUIDED INTUITION

It's easier to maintain (or start) a good habit, such as meditating, if you repeat the ritual at around the same time every day. This advice applies to touching base with your intuition, too. The more regularly you check in, the more reliable your intuition will be.

Well, we hope we've guided you toward getting up a good head of steam when it comes to realizing your psychic side. And now that you've done that, you're ready to "break on through to the other side." Next, we're going to show you a different realm, one that transcends your own mind, your own life, and your own body. We're going to talk about leaping the barriers of space and time.

The Least You Need to Know

- Intuitive intelligence offers its own brand of knowledge and wisdom, which can create a perfect complement to your rational mind.
- Intuitive intelligence teaches valuable lessons, whether based on past errors or future possibilities.
- Glimpses of the future are not set in stone; they offer a chance to compare and consider options.
- Two factors are essential to creating change: choosing a goal and taking action.

Leaping the Barriers of Space and Time

Travel—right from the comfort of your own home! Forget about fancy time machines; you can do it yourself by taking an incredible journey with your own mind.

This part talks about some pretty far-out stuff—exploring previous lifetimes, spirit messages, and getting to know your second self. It might sound strange at first, but when you think about it, these are just further steps along an ever-evolving path of awareness and spiritual potential.

Precognition, ESP, and Regression

In This Chapter

- Perceiving beyond the senses
- Knowing the future
- Sensing energy
- Taking it in or tossing it out

By now, you know that you can use your intuition in the here and now to help improve your relationships, professional opportunities, and physical and mental health. You can tap into it as a way of understanding your emotions and use it to help you overcome obstacles.

But that may not be all. You might also be able to use this power—the all-knowing, omnipresent force within you—for insight into, and influence over, events outside yourself. We call this power extrasensory perception, and that's what we'll talk about in this chapter.

The "Extra" in Extrasensory Perception

As defined in Chapter 1, ESP stands for extrasensory perception. The "extra" refers to the ability to receive or send information without using your normal five senses of sight, sound, taste, touch, and smell. It involves knowledge that comes via a nonrational pathway.

Many experts divide ESP into three main categories:

- Telepathy (communicating mind-to-mind)

- Clairvoyance (seeing events or objects by using an inner sense of sight rather than an external one)

- Precognition (knowing about events before they occur)

Other experts who really like to go into detail add two more categories under the blanket term ESP. They are more pertinent to perception of the past than seeing into the future, but they're interesting to think about:

- Retrocognition (knowing about past events without using the five senses)

- Psychometry (learning the history of a particular object without using the five senses)

All these categories share a common characteristic: perception that extends beyond the use of the five senses. Intuitive insight about the future can come to you in a variety of ways, including the following:

- A vision of the future

- Words of warning or prediction

- A sense of knowing in the mind

- A feeling of warning

We're sure it's no surprise to you that these pathways loosely correspond to those generally used to gain intuitive insight in any area. After all, in some peoples' view, sensing the future is the quintessential type of intuition.

For some people, their impressions of the future are so strong that they know they've experienced something more than a hunch. This happens when someone has that most definite form of proof: a vision of an event. Whether in a dream or in the mind's eye, sight creates a definitive image—the impression of which remains long after the image itself has passed. People who experience future insight through sounds or words are less likely to be as confident of their knowledge.

With clairsentience, certain insights tend to catch your attention because they arrive out of the blue, yet give a strong and clear sense of instantaneous knowing. Although this information can pertain to the past or present, insights about the future will usually strike you as the strongest. The reason why clairsentience about future events seems more typical is because you revisited these feelings in your mind. That is, when the foreknown event actually occurs, you remind yourself of your previous thoughts or feelings about the future. In this way, future insights are reinforced in your mind and therefore seem most common later.

Another familiar form of future insight involves fearful warnings or feelings about future events. Most people have had this experience, and it's not usually a fun one. We'll talk more about this later in the chapter. For now, let's introduce you to the technical name for foresight, or knowing beforehand.

Knowing Beforehand: Precognition

Some people use the term ESP to refer specifically to *precognition*. What distinguishes it from other types of ESP, however, is its relationship to time.

DEFINITION

Precognition can be defined as foreknowledge or awareness of a future event before it occurs.

While telepathy and clairvoyance have to do with perceptions occurring across distance, precognition focuses on perceptions that occur across time—specifically, perceptions of future events. Precognition, or foretelling the future, is what many people automatically think of when the ideas of ESP or psychic ability come up. But, as you know from reading this book, there's more to psychic awareness than that.

Precognition doesn't work as simply as just rubbing a crystal ball and then seeing someone's life pass before your eyes. For many people, precognition is completely unexpected and certainly wasn't asked for. People often don't know that they've experienced precognition until after their insights regarding a future event have come to pass.

Precognition can also be hard to pin down because it's experienced in a variety of ways. Among the most common are through the emotions, brief inner glimpses through the mind's eye, or through dreams. However, one aspect of precognition seems to stand out as its trademark: the sense of certainty.

GUIDED INTUITION

As a general rule of thumb for identifying true precognition, remember: the less likely it is that you could know the information ahead of time, the more likely it is to be precognition.

Sensing Emotions

Many people receive a strong sense or feeling that something's coming but have little information about what it might be. They might recognize a precognitive experience only after the actual event occurs. A precognitive sense or feeling of a future event is called *presentiment*.

Like telepathy and clairvoyance, precognition tends to involve people on an emotional level—particularly those who have close emotional ties. Also, like telepathy and clairvoyance, precognition seems most likely to occur when concerned with potentially dramatic or catastrophic moments, which naturally include extreme emotional states. Interestingly, this special ability to sense others' feelings, especially intense ones such as those associated with a crisis, also shows empathic intuitive abilities.

Whether in regard to others or yourself, a precognitive sense of an unfortunate event is called a *premonition*. These forewarnings are an especially common type of intuitive ability for people to experience. A popular theory is that premonitions are an age-old evolutionary device developed for self-preservation. If premonitions do indeed meet a basic evolutionary need of every individual, does it follow that intuition is an innate ability among everyone and has evolved as a positive characteristic for survival and growth? That's a question we're still pondering.

> **DEFINITION**
>
> **Presentiment** is a sense or feeling about a future event. **Premonition** is a foreboding of an unfortunate future event.

The warnings that come through premonitions usually occur as intense feelings, rather than visions or the calmer feelings that accompany other types of precognitive experience. Oddly enough, premonitions usually allow enough time to change the behavior or plans that could cause the trouble.

Information About Events

If you've experienced precognition of an event, try to follow up after the event has occurred. This will help you get a sense of whether your precognition was presentiment or foresight into an actual occurrence.

A very specific aspect of precognition that refers to the foreshadowing of future events is *second sight*. This term suggests that you see actual future events in a vision or visions. People who have this ability are called seers.

> **DEFINITION**
>
> **Second sight** is the ability to see future events. It is a general term that can refer to wisdom, prophesy, or divination through the use of a device such as a crystal ball or by means of palm reading.

Another way you might receive visual information about future events is through precognitive dreams. Of course, not all dreams foretell future events—but those that do are usually clear and easily recalled. Have you ever had an experience that seems familiar, but you don't know why? This might actually be a dim recollection of a precognitive dream.

Ways You Can Experience ESP

You're all familiar with dreams, but how do you know when you're seeing into the future within these reveries? For that matter, you can ask the same question for visual images, sensed phrases, or strong feelings. How do you know whether they actually reveal present or future events or whether they are merely unexplainable episodes? Well, the obvious answer is to wait and see. But along the way, you can learn a lot by paying close attention. (Keeping good notes in your psychic journal helps, too.)

Psi researchers recommend the following tips for tracking your precognitive abilities:

- Always follow up by finding out what actually happens. That way, you can track how well your feelings or visions describe the future.

- Stick with events that take place in the near, rather than distant, future. In other words, try describing events that take place tomorrow or next week, rather than those five years down the line. We'll give you some tips on how to do just that in the exercises that follow later in the chapter.

Next, we provide you with a few simple exercises to help you get in touch with your precognitive ability. Try to keep the previous two tips in mind as you explore. Because people typically have less anxiety about the past, that's where we'll start—and from there, we will move boldly forward into the future.

Intuition Exercise: Encountering the Past

Begin this exercise by getting into a relaxed, meditative state. For the first part of the exercise, count down from 10 to 1. As you do so, imagine yourself moving downward into your consciousness, as if you were walking down stairs or descending on an escalator or elevator. When you get to the bottom on the count of one, ask your guide to show you information about a newsworthy, well-known past event. Observe and remember your own feelings and sensations regarding this news.

Feel free to ask your guide questions about these events and interact with him or her in any way that feels comfortable.

When you're ready, return to the staircase and walk back up the stairs. As you do, feel yourself returning to "normal consciousness"—refreshed and energized.

Intuition Exercise: Encountering the Future

For the second part of the exercise, again settle into a meditative state, and count down from 10 to 1. As you do so, picture yourself flowing gently downward into your consciousness on a feather, cloud, or magic carpet. When you arrive on the ground on the count of one, ask your guide to show you information about an upcoming event that will be noteworthy and possibly newsworthy. You might feel that you receive this information telepathically, through feelings, through images and pictures, or even through sound. Observe and remember your own feelings and sensations regarding this news. Feel free to interact with your guide, asking questions or making comments.

When you feel ready, count from 1 to 10. As you do so, feel yourself coming back into "normal consciousness" and open your eyes.

Pay careful attention to the difference between your feelings and perceptions of information about the past and what you learn about the future. An important aspect of this exercise is recording everything you experience as soon as you are done—and don't forget to date it. Over time, you may see your new "news" about the future come true, and you'll be glad you wrote your personal "headlines" down.

GUIDED INTUITION

A website specifically designed for testing precognition and psi ability is www. gotpsi.org. At the site, you will have an opportunity to try five different tests, including two different card-based tests, a location test, and a remote-viewing test. Like all good precognition experiments, this site gives you prompt feedback.

Intuition Exercise: Creating a Screen

This exercise is designed to both test and improve your precognitive abilities. Imagine in your mind's eye a screen, such as a blank television screen or a calm pool of water, on which you can see tomorrow's events. Position your screen in an environment you feel comfortable with and enjoy. Then, sit back, relax, and watch your screen. Try to picture tomorrow's headlines, lottery numbers, or the winners of a local sports competition. (We don't advise betting money on them—just check it out for fun!)

It will probably be easiest for you to access information from the near future in an area in which you have a specific interest. If you normally read the newspaper, envision yourself getting up and following your regular morning preparations before sitting down with the newspaper. Then, open your imaginary newspaper. Use the following tables to record your insights, or copy the information into your psychic journal. You might receive words, a fleeting impression, or a symbolic picture for an answer. Copy the following chart and keep them in your journal.

What unusual subjects or issues will be in the local news …

Today?	Tomorrow?	This Week?	This Month?

Choose an issue from the national news. What will be the likely outcome of this issue …

Today?	Tomorrow?	This Week?	This Month?

Choose a stock to track. What will that stock close at …

Today?	Tomorrow?	This Week?	This Month?

Choose another topic of your own to track precognitively.

Today?	Tomorrow?	This Week?	This Month?

Pay attention to whether events about which you have psychic knowledge that occur tomorrow feel differently from those that occur a few months from now. Notice whether the knowledge that you gather through precognition feels differently from what you learn through retrocognition. Sense and assimilate the atmosphere, sounds, and physical sensations of various shifts in time.

Hooking into your precognitive abilities will further increase your openness to all psychic information. The sense of connection—to other minds, to other times, and possibly even to a "higher" mind—can be a great source of comfort and joy and at the same time can aid you in developing greater psychic awareness.

Receiving Guidance from Past Lives

According to many intuitives, including Edgar Cayce, access to past-life information is possible because it all still exists and is stored in the *Akashic Record*. This omniscient record is like an ultimate, conscious computer data bank. It contains information about every aspect of every person's life, including body, mind, and soul.

Another theory goes that specific information, whether from the Akashic Record or not, might be forwarded to you by beings who assist you in your current incarnation. Some people call them guardian angels and believe that they may even be tied to relationships from past lives.

DEFINITION

According to Edgar Cayce and others, the **Akashic Record** is a sort of universal memory bank or an invisible record of everything that has occurred in the universe, including details of every soul and every life ever lived.

Dreaming a Wake-Up Call

All through her childhood, Lynn had recurring dreams of a large mansion that had a nightmarish quality. Often, part of the house was burned—and she found herself wandering through it looking for something she couldn't find. In one dream about this place, she was standing outside watching the mansion burn to the ground. People from the village were also watching, but she stood apart from them, distraught and sobbing.

When Lynn was about 20 years old (in this life), she met a man about her age. At dinner one night, he casually mentioned that he had taken a class in reincarnation and experienced a past-life regression. Lynn was fascinated and asked him what he remembered. His first words were, "I remembered this big house ...." Much to Lynn's embarrassment, she burst into tears. She grabbed a piece of paper and drew the floor plan of the house from her childhood dreams. It was the same house he saw in his regression.

What they were able to piece together from his past-life memory and Lynn's dreams were that they had been married in that life and had two young children. He discovered that she had been unfaithful and came to realize that he was not the children's father.

He had set the house on fire to punish her—without realizing that the children were inside until it was too late. He remembers that he killed himself shortly after this. Lynn remembers being ostracized by the townspeople. She finally left that area and lived a few more years, wandering from town to town before experiencing an early death.

After bringing this to light, Lynn saw the young man again only a few more times (in this life, anyway), and she never had the "mansion dream" again. But what she learned was that in that past life, she seemed to be someone who judged others—a wealthy woman who lived apart from the common folk. She thought that her way was the best way and that God was on her side and had rewarded her with a life of privilege. After the fire, she learned that all she'd really had was material possessions, that she had no true friends, no real meaning in her life, and nothing of substance on an inner or spiritual level.

Lynn believes that what that life gave her was an understanding of people from all walks of life and an ability to see things from all sides. It also made her look at the issues of forgiveness and judgment. She finds all these lessons to have been extremely helpful in the work she does now.

Recognizing Karmic Life Lessons

To make yourself more aware of past lives and open to recalling them, try to take mental notes of your unique reactions to what's around you. Also, try to avoid judging yourself and what you see according to long-established belief systems (especially those that don't include reincarnation).

Intuition Exercise: Regression

This exercise is designed to help you address an issue in your life—a fear of speaking your mind, a concern with commitment or decision-making, or an inability to let go of an old relationship—that has been left unresolved. Usually, the first thing that pops into your mind is the best issue for you to pursue. Write your issue in your journal.

This exercise uses a regression technique. You might want to record it or have someone read it to you.

1. Begin by closing your eyes. Uncross your arms and legs. Relax. Take a deep breath and let it out slowly. Continue taking several more slow, deep breaths and concentrate on your breathing. Then, breathe normally.

2. Visualize a circle of white light forming in front of you. Now, bring this stream of light through the top of your head down through your body from head to toe. Take the time to fill any spot in your body that feels dark or heavy. Saturate each area with the white light. Imagine this light flowing through you and then surrounding and protecting you.

3. Relish this feeling of being relaxed and safe. Allow a peaceful state of mind to flow through you.

4. Now, imagine that you are being taken to a place where you will be shown your past life that most influences the issue you are concerned about.

5. You are being taken to a temple. This beautiful building has a colossal double doorway placed squarely beneath huge arches and twin spires. A massive set of stone steps leads up to the entrance. Concentrate on bringing in every minute detail of its elaborate masonry. Now, see yourself alone, poised at the foot of the steps, looking up expectantly at the doorway. Start climbing the steps; notice the rough-hewn granite as your shoes touch one step after another.

6. When you reach the top, stand beneath the immensity of the wooden doors. Breathe deeply, pause, and then stretch out a hand to feel the texture of the wood.

7. Open the doors and find yourself in a vast, open room filled with light. The air smells of sweet incense, and you feel enveloped by the stillness and magnificence of the scene.

8. As you take in your surroundings, you notice that you are not alone. A very kind old man dressed in a long robe approaches you and lovingly takes your arm, then points at a door across the room. He walks with you, and you precede him through the doorway and down a stone stairway. The steps are narrow and well worn, and they lead down to the cellars. Move down these steps; feel yourself descending deeper and deeper into the very foundations of the temple.

9. At the foot of the steps, the old man explains that he is the guardian of the Hall of Records and has been expecting you. He asks that you take a few moments to explain to him why you are here. You explain your quest for self-exploration and ask that you be shown a past life that will assist you in your self-understanding. The old man, bowing his head, listens attentively to your explanation and grants your request.

10. Now, the old guardian beckons you to follow him. You seem to float behind the flapping tails of his robe as he sets off through the seemingly endless corridors, past shelf after shelf piled high with books. At last, he halts before a door. He stands there for a few moments before pointing to another door he would like you to enter.

11. You are about to enter a past life when you walk into this room. You are completely safe as you observe your former self. Your guardian beckons you to open the door and walk in. As you do, you feel yourself changing as you step into a different time and place.

12. Take a few moments and observe who you are. Absorb what you see and feel—calmly, passively, and without emotion. In a few moments, you will ask yourself some questions about what you are seeing; you will later remember everything you see and experience, but for now, simply observe your surroundings.

- What are you wearing?

- What fabric is your clothing made of?

- Are you wearing anything on your head?

- Are you male or female?

- What is the shade of your skin?

- What is the color of your hair?

- Are you inside or outside a structure?

- What does it look like?
- Is it night or day? Cold or warm?
- Are you alone or with someone?
- What are you doing?
- What language are you speaking?
- What country are you in?

13. As the scene in front of you continues to unfold, ask yourself the following questions:

- What did I learn in this lifetime?
- What did I not learn?
- What things was I good at in this lifetime?
- Do I recognize anyone?
- Who is my mother ... father ... spouse? Who are my significant friends? Do I have children? Who are they?
- What do I want to bring back from the past to enhance my present lifetime?

14. Now, as this past-life personality, complete these two sentences:

- "I will never ...."
- "I will always ...."

15. Allow yourself a few more moments to finish your viewing of this lifetime. Complete anything that is left incomplete.

16. Now, you are ready go out the door you came through. Your guardian is waiting for you outside the door. He motions for you to follow him once more through the labyrinthine library to the stairway leading back to the light-filled temple. You walk behind the old man, climbing up the cellar stairs with him. He walks you across the grand hall that is filled with light to the door where you first entered the temple.

17. Now, you step outside the beautiful, glowing temple and slowly descend the stone steps. As you move one foot before the other, you find that normal consciousness is slowly returning. By the time you reach the foot of the staircase, you are once more fully aware of your surroundings.

18. Take a moment to write in your psychic journal. Write down any details of what you remember. Do you feel that you received an answer to your initial concern? If so, what do you feel you learned?

Did you learn anything new about yourself? Perhaps you gained a sense of where you'd like to start making some changes. Perhaps you learned something about the history of your own emotional reactions. If nothing else, maybe you can become more conscious of who you are, as influenced by—and separate from—where you are right now. That's another way to expand your consciousness!

Opening to your abilities in the area of retrocognition will further expand your mind and increase your sensitivity to all psychic information. Your connection to other times, to other minds, and possibly even to a "higher" mind can aid you in developing greater psychic awareness and a larger consciousness.

What to Do with Information When You Get It

Seeing the future or the historic past can, understandably, set off all kinds of emotional alarms. When you get past thinking that you're crazy, you immediately start to ask two questions: "Why is this happening?" and "Why is this happening to me?"

In the face of a premonition, you might initially feel fear. However, if self-doubt or confusion prevents you from taking action, you may begin to feel guilty. If a crisis does occur, you could be left wondering whether you should have done something to stop the event. And yet, the action to take isn't always clear or possible to control.

MIXED MESSAGES

Let go of the guilt. Many people who foresee unfortunate future events start to think that their thoughts actually cause unfortunate incidents to occur. Just because you can pick up on an energy does not mean you are responsible for creating it. Remember this if you start to feel bad about your intuitive knowledge.

Consider taking action if the path to do so appears clear. Please be sensitive about how you share your intuitive information with others. Announcing, "I'm psychic and here's what I get about you!" may be more than a little off-putting. Instead, you might try phrases like, "My sense is …" Or, "I have an idea I'd like to share with you …."

If the solution does not appear clear, you don't have to consider it your responsibility to take action. Consider that the information is intended as a lesson to help you, not a responsibility to fulfill. Many people who report experiencing precognition also report one of the greatest lessons that can come from it: spiritual transformation. Realizing that a source of knowledge exists—one that exceeds any power they previously believed possible—can dramatically change the life of the person who experiences it.

Often, people who experience revelations of intuitive insight begin to follow a spiritual path with a newfound belief and openness. By getting in touch with an infinite, eternal power, they begin to explore the grander scheme of what life is all about. That path leads many to explore the extension of intuitive knowledge beyond present lifetimes to past and possibly future ones. Want to travel the path of a karma chameleon? Read on to the next chapter.

The Least You Need to Know

- You can receive information about the future in many ways and on various levels.
- Precognition involves a strong sense of "just knowing" that your intuitive insight pertains to the future.
- You can develop your ability for precognitive intuition.
- Your intuition can help you understand and learn from your previous lives.
- Accept information that comes to you as a gift, not as a burden.

Messages from Beyond

In This Chapter

- Contacting the great beyond
- Channeler, medium, or charlatan?
- Messages and meanings
- The role of spirit guides

Just because you can't see something right in front of you doesn't mean it doesn't exist, right? That has been the theme of this entire book, hasn't it? And the theme continues in this chapter, where we discuss the possibility that the souls of people living and dead exist among and around us, available for consultation and information—available even to you if you know how to ask.

So you can contact your Aunt Sadie, your first-grade teacher, a dearly departed friend, or even your childhood dog. You can ask beings who have passed over for advice or reassurance, or you can get in touch just to say hello. The choice is up to you. Who and what do you want to know from the other side?

Communicating with the Other Side

According to those who are in the know, humans can communicate with ethereal beings on a variety of levels. A person who communicates with spirits is called a *channeler*, a spirit messenger, or a psychic medium. Today, many people in this field prefer the term "psychic medium" or "spirit messenger" to channeler because they think that channeler sounds old-fashioned. Other practitioners of this art, however, continue to call themselves channelers. Some people use all these terms interchangeably.

Others, though, make a distinction between mediums, who are seen to communicate with the spirits of the deceased, and channelers, who are said to communicate with our higher selves and with angels and to carry messages for soul development and spiritual growth.

DEFINITION

Channeling is the process of communicating with spirits. A person who communicates in this way is called a **channeler,** a medium, or a spirit messenger.

Before we delve into mediumship, though, are you ready for a joke? Detectives were searching for one particular psychic medium who had escaped from the local jail. In the newspaper, they asked readers to be on the lookout for a blond man of about 5'4" who was last seen wearing a black sport coat. The article's headline read: "Small Medium at Large!" Okay, now back to work …

When we discuss mediumship (the art practiced by psychic mediums) in this chapter, we're really talking about contact with spirits—in other words, contact between spirits (either those of people once living or spirits who never had bodies) and living human beings. Many people use their special skills in this area to contact loved ones who have passed on. Using techniques of mediumship, you can contact your own deceased relatives, others' relatives, and spirit guides as well.

You may have heard of a number of famous mediums or spirit messengers, such as John Edward, James Van Praagh, Sylvia Browne, John Holland, Gordon Smith, George Anderson, Michael Wheeler, or Doreen Virtue. (You may also know the show *Medium*, which aired from 2005 until 2011, and is based on the experiences of medium and profiler Allison DuBois.) These professionals are able to help lay people make contact with the spirits of the dead. For example, on his television show *John Edward Cross Country*, John Edward delivers messages from those who have passed on to audience members eager for information. In recent years, mediums and their messages have been steadily gaining in popularity. But the public's interest in the spirit world and its messages is in no way a new phenomenon.

Famous Mediums in History

The Fox sisters, three young women from Rochester, New York, first brought public attention to the phenomenon of table rapping—the announcement of a spirit's arrival during a *séance*—in 1848. The enthusiasm for other-worldly phenomena carried over to levitation of tables and other objects and led to the growth of the immensely popular Spiritualist movement in the later decades of the century.

DEFINITION

A **séance** is a meeting, session, or sitting in which a channeler attempts to communicate with the spirits of the dead.

By the middle of the nineteenth century, Spiritualism had two million followers! Devotees of Spiritualism believe in life after death and feel that the dead are able and willing to communicate with the living. The movement became so widespread that 15 years after the first spirit visit to the Foxes, a bill was proposed in the U.S. Congress to organize a committee to investigate the Spiritualism phenomenon.

Among the most famous mediums of the period was D. D. Home, whose reputation for his remarkable abilities and pristine integrity earned him a place in the history books. Reports of his demonstrations during séances include levitating his own body, having an invisible spirit play the accordion, and even having spirit hands appear in the air and pour water into a glass—without spilling a drop.

Another famous medium during this time was Nettie Colburn, the trance channeler whose spirit guides advised President Lincoln. Between 1861 and 1863, Mrs. Lincoln called her to The White House to use her skills to present information and advice to President Lincoln on a wide variety of subjects, which he was known to have followed on many occasions. Her guides counseled Lincoln not to put off enacting *The Emancipation Proclamation*. She also gave him advice on ways to raise morale among the Yankee troops, and her advice worked.

Lenore Piper, born in 1859 in New Hampshire, was a medium in Boston for most of her life. Known to be a consistently effective full-trance medium, she was investigated by the Harvard-educated philosopher and psychologist William James. He was later quoted on his experience with Mrs. Piper: "Science, so far as science denies such exceptional occurrences, lies prostrate in the dust for me."

Mrs. Piper channeled a physician named Dr. Phinuit, who apparently knew all about William James. During the hour-long session, the spirit relayed through Mrs. Piper the details of a recent letter James received from one of his New York aunts, the whereabouts of a missing waist coat, and a rug. Even the hard-line scholar James was forced to admit, "Insignificant as these things sound when read, the accumulation of a large number of them has an irresistible effect."

Mrs. Piper eventually began working as the house medium for the Society for Psychical Research, where a private detective (hired by the society) made certain that she received no information about the people she read for through any other source than intuition. No evidence was ever found to indicate that her exceptional information came from any source other than her spirit guides.

Of course, certain old-time mediums were probably faced with the temptation to make their sittings as exciting and dramatic as possible. In a sense, they were performers. Interestingly, certain mediums considered to be truly psychic, such as Eusapia Palladino, were also occasionally caught in the act of embellishing their demonstrations. Of course, this cast doubt on all the good work they—and their more highly principled counterparts—had accomplished.

How Mediumship Works

Before you can act as a medium, you must actively seek out guidance from a spirit. Indeed, a basic understanding within the psychic world is that each being, including you, has free will and that no spirit can force another, or be forced itself, to do something against its will. A spirit cannot communicate through a medium (or a channeler) unless the medium agrees to it; the spirit must have an actual invitation from the medium before it can establish contact and start to send its messages. Although many people believe that to communicate with a spirit, the spirit must be of someone they know or someone once alive, that doesn't appear to be the case.

MIXED MESSAGES

The important thing to remember when exploring mediumship is that, in the spiritual realm, your free will reigns. You can always exert control by asking a spirit, or spirits, to leave. Similarly, if a spirit suggests that you do something that seems wrong to you, don't do it—and seek help from a professional in the field to help you understand what type of experience you are having.

As John Holland, author of the excellent book *Born Knowing: A Medium's Journey—Accepting and Embracing My Spiritual Gifts* (Hay House, 2003), describes it, a medium naturally has a special kind of energy vibration. The spirit world, which is all around us all the time, vibrates at a higher rate than our physical world does. The only thing that separates us from the spirit world is this difference in vibrational frequency. A medium either has a higher vibration to begin with or is able to raise his or her level of vibration toward the spirit world. At the same time, the spirit who desires contact will lower its vibration to help reach the medium.

Different mediums, of course, have different methods of raising their vibration. Although some mediums fall into a deep trance and wake up knowing nothing of what has occurred (as so often depicted in Hollywood), that's not the only process available. Some mediums are fully conscious of their physical surroundings while channeling a spirit and can even pause to attend to some interruption before continuing. Other mediums work in intermediary states of altered consciousness that they have found to be most effective.

Altered States

There are three main types of channeling states that fall along a wide spectrum. All these states involve an altered state of consciousness to some degree:

- Full-conscious channeling
- Light-trance channeling
- Full-trance channeling

A medium who is a full-conscious channeler has raised his or her vibrational level—and, at the same time, can move around, stop, and then restart the process. Trance channeling involves someone who seems to enter another realm. A light trance is less intense, and information may be exchanged telepathically between the spirit's and medium's minds. A heavy trance involves the medium's complete loss of consciousness, perhaps occurring when a spirit enters the person's body.

ARE YOU AWARE?

Jon Klimo, professor of clinical psychology at Argosy University in San Francisco, California, and author (with Pamela Heath) of *Handbook to the Afterlife* (North Atlantic Books, 2011), describes a form of entity-less channeling that he calls "open channeling." He also points out that many important figures from the past, including Moses, Solomon, Muhammad, and Merlin, all practiced channeling.

Although the historic stereotype portrays the medium or channeler in a full trance, a new school of medium is inclined to be more conscious while channeling. No one way is best for everyone. Each person's comfort level and increased spiritual insight are what matter most.

Is Anybody Home?

To begin with, the medium offers an invitation—either through feelings or thoughts to the spirit world. Some mediums might have certain phrases or rituals that they repeat in their minds as a way to prepare themselves. In most cases, they simply express their intention to connect. Remember, a lot of contact with spirits is tele-pathic. Any words formed would more likely occur in silence and be transmitted telepathically.

After a medium opens himself or herself to receiving a message by raising the vibration, he or she then begins the process of connecting. At this point, the medium enters an altered state of consciousness. If the medium's style is to enter a less-changed state, he or she then opens the energy field that surrounds him or her to create a form of merging or opens the mind to telepathic communication while remaining aware of what occurs.

After establishing a connection, with his or her own spirit guides or with other spirits who want to communicate, a message starts coming through. At first, the connection might be a bit rough. But as the medium and spirit begin to merge more completely, the information becomes clearer. If the medium feels that the connection isn't right, he or she can ask for further clarification, visualize a better connection, or ask the spirit to stop "transmitting."

Certain mediums feel that the message is not strictly dictated by the spirit; rather, it is a melding together of the medium and the spirit. One analogy that clarifies this relationship is to think of a medium's work as similar to a translator's work. Although the speaker offers information in a single language and format, each translator may translate the message somewhat differently.

What to Expect from a Psychic Medium

As we mentioned, you can think of a medium as a connection between the material and spirit worlds—a translator of the spirit language into the human lexicon. The original message may come in a clear, sequential order or in abstract images. To effectively sort out this much information, a medium needs to be flexible, intelligent, educated, curious, open-minded, imaginative, and even empathic. He or she needs to step outside himself or herself and be willing and able to step out of his or her personal viewpoint to see things from various perspectives—and sometimes from various perspectives at once. This is important because the spirit world involves view-ing information from different dimensions—beyond the third (physical) and even the fourth (time).

A medium may offer information that seems baffling (or at best, irrelevant). But with time, the meaning of this information often comes to light as making profoundly simple sense. For example, you may not understand now why you receive a certain message when something disappointing happens to you, and yet someday a better opportunity comes your way and the special message you received helps you put it all in perspective. This goes back to the idea that everything is somehow connected; a perfect pattern underlies apparent chaos. In many ways, channeled information isn't all that much different from information received in a regular psychic reading; it's just one more way that your intuition may provide you with information. If this topic interests you, do a little homework before you sign on for a session with a medium. Carole Lynne's book *How to Get a Good Reading from a Psychic Medium* (Red Wheel/ Weiser, 2003) provides a wealth of information to prepare you and help you get what you want from a reading.

GUIDED INTUITION

When you have a session with certain mediums, you might notice a change in their voice when contact has been established with a spirit. The channeled voice often sounds quite different and distinct from the medium's own and might have an accent that does not belong to the medium naturally. But this altered voice is not a prerequisite for proving a spirit is present.

If you are looking for a well-trained medium, you may want to check out the National Spiritualist Association of Churches (NSAC). Yep, the Spiritualist movement is alive and well! NSAC is the oldest—they have been around since 1893!—and largest organization devoted to "the Science, Philosophy, and Religion of Modern Spiritualism" in the United States. Spiritualist churches all over the country hold regular services with prayers and the singing of hymns. They also devote part of services to mediumship, where trained practitioners will pass on healing messages from the other side to individuals in attendance. To find out whether there is a Spiritualist church near you or to get a more in-depth look at NSAC and Spiritualism, visit NSAC's website: www. nsac.org.

Who Do You Want to Talk To (and Why)?

Spiritual beings who can be channeled exist on many levels. Some people refer to these levels as dimensions. The idea is that humans live in the third dimension, which is physical reality, and attempt to progress up through higher dimensions.

Indeed, some people believe that spiritual beings can exist in more than one level—sort of keeping tabs on where they're at in each particular level simultaneously.

There is a wide range of beliefs about who spirit guides are and where they come from. According to whom you listen to, these may include human beings, aliens, enlightened masters, angels, gods and goddesses, universal powers that be, your higher self, or the universal mind. With all these options, you start to get the idea that someone out there probably has a little free time to spend with you. And they do it not for their own entertainment but to provide you with the information you need to continue along your path of spiritual awareness and development.

Channeling Loved Ones

When the idea of contact with spirits comes up, most people think of encountering loved ones who have died. According to a 2009 study by the Pew Forum on Religion and Public Life, almost 3 in 10 Americans responded that they had been in touch with someone who had died. Some people sense this as a feeling of a presence nearby, whereas others might hear or see the loved one.

Many people feel solace and comfort when sensing that their loved one has passed to another realm but is still around them—just on another plane. Others experience frequent visitations with their loved ones, involving a series of conversations or communications that help the still-living individual build a new life and release remaining negative feelings, such as guilt, regarding the loved one.

ARE YOU AWARE?

Many people get messages from loved ones in their dreams. Some people have even reported dreams that include an acquaintance delivering a message, often about the acquaintance's death. When the dreamer awakes, he or she receives news that the acquaintance has just passed away—under circumstances that make sense in the context of the message.

These experiences most often occur spontaneously, without the help of a medium. In a sense, the individual is independently experiencing his or her own type of channeling with a loved one. But what if your loved one does not contact you? Many people often become quite distraught that the spirits of their loved ones have not been in touch. But the fact is that they have. We have become so conditioned by sensationalist television programs and movies that we tend to believe that any information from a spirit will be a grand and dramatic happening. In real life, though, this is rarely the case. Often, the spirits of your loved ones will come to you as a feeling, a flash of memory, or a passing thought. Remember, according to the basic precepts of mediumship, the spirit world is all around us—so your loved ones who have passed on are also all around you. If you are not seeing, feeling, or sensing their messages, slow down, make sure to breathe, continue to practice meditation, and keep working to hone your psychic awareness.

Channeling Spirit Guides

Many professional mediums ask their spirit guides to access information for their clients. For example, during a session the medium might ask his or her own spirit guide for helpful information for the client. The medium may also ask his or her own guide to collect a message from the client's loved one. Alternatively, the medium's guide may communicate with the client's guide.

Guides, as we discussed in Chapter 5, exist to love, support, and encourage you. They also deliver good advice. Here's a story we like: a particular minister, who is known as a teacher in intuitive circles, was faced with the decision to retire early from her lifetime work at a prestigious institution. She secluded herself in a country house and spent several days meditating on the question. She eventually emerged with the advice her guides had given her and a determined conviction to follow it.

When she announced that she was going to resign early, despite being one year away from getting full retirement benefits, everyone told her she was crazy. But halfway through the year, her department disbanded. She had been spared all the anxiety, disappointment, and bitterness experienced by many of her colleagues who had remained—and she gives her guides the credit for that. (She still has a healthy pension to help her financially.)

This woman contacts her spirit guides as friends and advisors, seeking their advice on any matter that concerns her. Her experience is rather like using intuition as a guide. Clearly, she has learned to trust their guidance, maintaining a very personal relationship with them, and she rarely channels for other people. When she does receive input regarding other people, she might try to help them with subtle suggestions without telling them her source.

In contrast, some mediums receive requests from their spirit guides to share their messages with the world. In 1963, Jane Roberts became the first channeler to do this in published form. With her channeled guide "Seth," she produced the best-seller *Seth Speaks*, as well as several other books, before she died in 1984. The public was ready to receive Seth's message of a multidimensional reality and each person's potential power to shape it. Sanaya Roman and Duane Packer work in a similar tradition to Roberts. They were asked by their guides, Daben and Orin, to teach people how to channel in workshops and to write about the subject as well. For more extensive information about their work, visit their website at www.OrinDaben.com. Esther Hicks and her group of teachers in the spirit world who go by the name Abraham have also produced enlightening work in this mode. You can access some of their wisdom at www.Abraham-Hicks.com.

You as a Psychic Medium

Channeling is a skill you can learn, just as you're learning to develop other aspects of your psychic abilities. As you learn, though, it's important to remember that everyone has a different experience of what it's like to channel. Your style will depend not only on who your spirit guide (or guides) turns out to be but also on your particular energy level, clarity, and focus. You might experience a feeling of expansive energy flowing through you or a tingling or buzzing feeling throughout your body as you channel. Others who channel report a sense of floating upward or of seeing lights and colors.

The message you receive might come in any number of different forms. Spirit guides use images, feelings, words, and concepts to give you information. The information that they bring you might be from them or from other spirits, such as deceased loved ones. Many individuals who have experienced channeling report that the information is simply transmitted telepathically and you "just know" the answer. When you channel, you are the person who translates the information sent to you from your guide. You might feel as if you've received a big block of information and you must search to understand what it means and how it feels. Often, you'll feel the words form in your mind just at the moment you speak them. Or, you might find that you're simply present as a vessel for healing energy—and words or ideas never come into play at all.

GUIDED INTUITION

For a beginner's guide on how to channel, check out Sanaya Roman and Duane Packer's book *Opening to Channel: How to Connect with Your Guide* (HJ Kramer, 1993). For some terrific guided-meditation how-to tapes on channeling, see Appendix B.

Intuition Exercise: Channel It!

This exercise will help you develop your channeling powers. Because it's a meditative exercise, you might want to have a friend present to take you through the process by asking questions to focus your energy. Or, record yourself reading the following text so you can listen and focus without the distraction of a book in front of you. Soothing music may also help you deepen your meditative state. If you have never contacted your guides before, you may want to start with the exercise "Meet Your Guide" that we presented in Chapter 5.

You might experience your guide as light or energy, male or female, someone you have known, or someone you have never met. Your guide will help you with this exercise. He or she will adjust your energy and align his or her energy with yours. Your guide might change over time as you evolve and have different needs and questions. If you feel uncomfortable at any time in this exercise, just open your eyes and return to normal consciousness.

1. Sit comfortably in an upright position, either on the floor or in a chair. Make sure you're in a position that you can hold comfortably for 15 to 20 minutes.

2. Close your eyes and relax your body. Take several slow, deep breaths. As you slowly inhale and exhale, imagine your emotions, thoughts, and physical body becoming calm. Feel yourself slowing down and relaxing. Take a few minutes to relax deeply.

3. Feel and imagine light and love coming to you from a much higher dimension. Imagine it flowing to you, surrounding you and filling you. Feel yourself lifting to a spiritual, beautiful place that is filled with brilliant white light. Imagine that you are traveling in a bubble of light into the sky, floating through the stars. As you move higher and higher, you are filled with a feeling of perfect love and safety. Carry this feeling with you as you move higher and higher.

4. Adjust your posture to a position that allows you to feel open. You may want to move your arms, head, and shoulders so you can feel as expansive as possible. Slow down your breathing, and imagine yourself opening up even further to all the love and hope that exists in the universe. Feel yourself floating higher and higher.

5. You may feel yourself growing warmer and feeling a buzzing or tingling sensation. Just notice whatever you experience. Take another deep breath and exhale. Imagine that your emotions are calm and balanced. Make the energy around you feel as beautiful as possible. Imagine that rays of love and joy are pouring down upon you. They open you up and make you appear radiant and filled with love.

6. Go as high as you can imagine, moving into finer and finer energy. At last you enter a high dimension that is bathed in flowing light. A doorway opens before you, and many guides and masters are there to greet you. They usher you forward into the light. They tell you they are taking you to meet your guide—the one who is right for you to work with. This guide has been especially chosen for you, and he or she is closely aligned with you.

7. Your guide is coming to meet you. A path is being made clear as he or she gets closer. Your heart opens, and you feel yourself being surrounded by an incredible feeling of peace and love. Your imagination is telling you all about what is happening around you. The other guides and masters slip away and leave you alone. At first you are simply adjusting to your guide's energy. Feel all the sensations, impressions, and images that flow through your mind.

8. Your guide is speaking to you telepathically. You find yourself hearing words and feeling sensations. Concepts may come flooding into your mind. This is your guide communicating to you. You can carry on a mental conversation with your guide. Ask him or her questions, then listen and feel for the response. The information might come to you in any of the ways that you may receive psychic information, including through images or sensations.

9. Ask your guide whether he or she will continue to work with you to help you be more open to receive information and to be able to channel. Ask whether you need to do anything to prepare to channel.

10. Ask your guide a question and see whether you feel comfortable speaking the answers aloud. You might be more comfortable writing the answers or might choose to simply continue as you've been doing in speaking telepathically to your guide. Whatever is easiest is fine.

11. Complete anything you need to say or do with your guide. Thank your guide, and ask whether you need to hear anything right now. Now, take a deep breath and come back to normal consciousness. Open your eyes.

12. You might find it helpful to move around, walk, and stretch. If you still feel a bit spacey, go out for a walk for a few minutes and focus on your feet as they touch the ground.

Learning anything new takes practice to get it right. If you are doing this for the first time, don't be discouraged if you don't connect with a guide right away. If you simply succeed in feeling expansive or experience a feeling of openness and compassion, that's a great start. Remember that your guide will be using your own thoughts to transmit images, feelings, and concepts. We'll say again here what we say for each exercise: you will feel like you're making it up! Because your guide will be using your voice, your imagination, and your ability to translate the information, you might feel as if it is all coming from you. With practice, you will have a clearer sense of your guide and feel his or her presence and energy.

As you continue to practice, you will begin to feel the guide as an energy presence that is different from yours. When a guide works with you for the first time, it is generally a very subtle experience. Nevertheless, you'll probably feel energized, focused, and filled with well-being during and after the experience.

ARE YOU AWARE?

If you ever want to take a vacation with your guide, Cassadaga Spiritualist Camp is just the place. Located in central Florida, it focuses on helping mediums use psychic techniques to get in closer contact with the spirit world. Established in 1894, the camp currently hosts about 100 full-time residents and about 50,000 visitors every year—just counting the humans! For more information, check out the camp's website at www.cassadaga.com.

Messages from the Spirit World

Many channelers report that their guide is like a best friend. When you feel comfortable receiving messages, your guide will inform you about what needs to be done. Your guide will help you and leave you with positive feelings and hope for the future and your continued spiritual growth. If you can offer advice or help to others without revealing your guide as the source, you are wise to choose that route. Stick with offering information in subtle ways, and then trust the recipient's own intuition to help him or her apply your input in the best way possible.

True and trustworthy spirits are not busybodies. They have a purpose for contacting you and accepting your invitation to communicate. They might have a complex message or a simple reassurance to offer. Their lesson might be to open your mind to undreamed-of possibilities or to explore unknown ideas and feelings. The sense that you gain from this experience is likely to change your life forever—not necessarily leaving your established path but becoming profoundly aware of it.

We will discuss yet another level of awareness in the next chapter. On this level, your spirit takes its own journey, rather than receiving spiritual visitors "at home." So grab your hat and get ready to explore the realm of out-of-body experiences.

The Least You Need to Know

- Communication with spirits is called channeling and is practiced by mediums, spirit messengers, and channelers.
- Mediums can work in various ways but usually experience some sort of altered state.
- You can practice channeling privately for personal growth or with two or more people present to gain access to otherwise unknown information.
- Channeled messages should give you hope and help you in your spiritual growth.

Out of Your Body

In This Chapter

- Your second self
- Bargain travel
- Near-death know-how
- Out-of-body experiences

"There are more things in heaven and Earth, Horatio, than are dreamt of in your philosophy," says Hamlet. This statement certainly applies to your inner world as well, which—according to many philosophers and yogis—exists on many levels.

Many Westerners grew up with the idea that the individual exists on just two levels: body and soul. Other cultures and belief systems, from the Egyptians to the Theosophists, express the idea that each individual exists on several different levels—five, seven, ten, or more. As we'll show you in this chapter, traveling through those levels will allow you to explore yet another aspect of your psychic abilities.

The Astral Body: Your Second Self

You know that you are more than just the sum of your body plus your mind. You also know that human beings live on many different levels of consciousness and existence. Various esoteric traditions talk about the many "bodies" that each person has. Some people think of these different aspects as "subtle bodies," or selves that exist on a parallel plane. In this view, these different aspects are all part of a larger consciousness. This theory emphasizes the idea that the body itself does not contain these aspects.

Rather, this larger consciousness contains the body, as well as the other levels of existence, as just part of its manifestation. You can learn to create a closer connection to any of these aspects within yourself.

A commonly recognized "extra" self is the *astral body*, also called an energy body. The astral body exists on the astral plane and is made from the vibrations of the physical body. The astral body may also be called a double, because it is an exact duplicate of the physical body. The Theosophists refer to it as the "etheric double."

According to shamans (healers who act as intermediaries between the physical world and the realm of spirit) and Theosophists, the astral body resembles the physical body but is made of a very fine and flexible material. Driven by emotions, passions, and desires, the astral body is thought to be a bridge between the physical brain and a higher level of mind. It also offers a special ability: the most extensive travels you can dream of.

If you have read any mystical writings, you may have heard of another level of the energy body—the shining body, which is made of light. This light represents the divine and its higher dimensions of consciousness. As your shining body, you might take the form of a single, condensed point of light. Sometimes, this body is described as a flame rather than a point of light.

DEFINITION

The **astral body,** also called an energy body, is made up of a subtle field of light that encases the body. And of course, "astral" literally means of or from the stars. It is thought that when you're sleeping, the astral body can separate from the physical body, which results in flying dreams.

From Unconscious to Conscious Projection

The astral body is capable of a very special type of travel. While leaving the physical body at rest, it can get up, walk around, and look back at its physical body, explore its immediate surroundings, and then journey to new places. What makes this experience really amazing is that you are fully conscious and in control throughout the experience.

This process of consciously leaving the body and traveling free of physical constraints is often referred to as *astral projection* or *astral travel*. Although many people use the terms interchangeably, experts distinguish astral projection as an awareness of separating the conscious mind from the physical body. With astral travel, an individual uses this conscious awareness to experience a sense of flying to new, nonphysical realms as well as to physical ones.

DEFINITION

Some people make a distinction between astral projection and astral travel, but others consider these two terms to mean essentially the same thing. For those who do see a difference, **astral projection** refers to the conscious separation between your consciousness and physical body, whereas **astral travel** goes further and allows you to actually travel to a different location while being conscious that you are not in your body.

How the conscious mind disconnects from its everyday consciousness and separates from the body remains a mystery. It is difficult to prove what really happens during astral travel—and one way or the other, it doesn't really matter. Because astral travel is no easy task to master, whatever works for an individual who can make it happen is just fine, regardless of the process or what you call it. Indeed, experts say that naming or analyzing the process may only interfere with the process itself.

Dream Journeys: Astral Travel

What is the process involved in astral travel? Experts agree that having a relaxed focus, such as with meditation and other forms of altered consciousness, helps you reach this state. A regular meditation practice and the physical and mental discipline it brings will lend you the strong focus necessary for astral travel. As usual with altered states, the idea is to sidestep normal conscious awareness.

If the idea of astral travel and leaving your body scares you, don't worry. If you are uncomfortable with this concept, you don't have to think about it. You do not have to engage in astral projection to be psychic. Many talented (and successful!) psychics do not practice astral travel at all. And if you try to go on a journey on the astral plane and fail, don't feel that you are a failure as a psychic being. This technique takes practice, and even then it is not something that everyone will master (and neither will every psychic want to). If you are interested in trying astral travel, though—and why not give it a shot?—we have some tips.

MIXED MESSAGES

When you begin to experiment with astral projection, you might experience some anxiety. When your body is completely relaxed but your mind is aware, you might feel unable to move—much the way that you do as you begin to fall asleep. Although this is a perfectly normal physiological response, some people are frightened by this sense of paralysis and wake themselves up. Don't worry; this feeling that you can't move actually provides the perfect opportunity for astral travel.

When preparing for astral travel, several steps can help you induce the experience, including the following:

1. Pick a quiet space and lock the doors. Choose a place that you consider a sanctuary, where you will not be interrupted by the phone ringing or by other people entering.

2. Choose where, or whom, you intend to visit. (Thinking of where you want to go, rather than focusing on simply leaving your body, seems to work best.)

3. Using the power of your imagination, create a shield of light around you to protect yourself psychically. In addition, envision yourself filled with light. Any time you prepare for astral travel, invoke whatever divine force or powers of good you believe in to protect you.

4. Find a comfortable position, either lying down or sitting upright in a comfortable chair.

5. Use progressive physical relaxation techniques, such as breathing, counting, meditation, or visualization, to relax your body but allow mental alertness.

6. Review your emotions and release any negative feelings of fear, anxiety, or guilt.

7. Listen to a repetitive sound, such as drumming, a certain line from a song, or your own heavy breathing. Choose a sound that has positive or neutral connotations. (For example, if you are not drawn to the Christian tradition, you might want to avoid listening to a tape of Benedictine monks chanting.)

8. Concentrate on a spot three feet away; you can gradually increase the distance. Visualize a gateway, such as a doorway or window that you have seen in a previous dream. If you're trying to visit a specific, real-life destination, visualize its doors or a similar image. Guided imagery can help you here. (During your first few astral traveling experiences, you might find that you don't get beyond the astral projection phase, which means that you might just feel or see yourself floating above your body.)

ARE YOU AWARE?

The Monroe Institute (www.monroeinstitute.org), a not-for-profit educational and research organization in Virginia, teaches people to explore astral projection and life beyond the physical body. Robert Monroe, the institute's founder, believed people are highly suggestible to sound and that certain sound patterns could alter brain waves and help people achieve a higher consciousness. Although Monroe died in 1995, his institute remains famous for training people to have out-of-body experiences. For more about astral projection, look for Robert Bruce's *Astral Dynamics: The Complete Book of Out-of-Body Experiences* (Hampton Roads, 2009).

After you've taken these steps, you might become aware that your mind is awake while your body is asleep. Try to calm your mind in response to this realization. You may then hear a sound of roaring, sense a flashing light, and/or feel an electrical vibration on your skin. Any or all these can build until suddenly you hear utter silence and see complete blackness.

This is the final step before beginning your journey. Now, you're ready to soar.

GUIDED INTUITION

If you are unable to move freely while attempting astral projection, use your imagination. Imagine where you'd like to go and think of how you'd like to get there, but don't stick to simple walking or ascending directly upward. Fly with flair!

A Flying Dream ... or More?

In the next phase of astral travel, your mind switches from its normal reliance on verbal thoughts to a nonverbal awareness. You witness all that happens but experience no separation between thought and action. Here's what you may experience:

1. Soon, you realize that you're moving. You can move in an astounding variety of directions—not just up or down, but spinning, soaring, or flying—and not just in one direction but many at once.

2. You might grow outward in all directions at once and then move inward again. You can experiment with this sense of expanding and contracting. You might feel this movement localizing around specific parts of your body and can change this by changing your focus.

3. Instead of seeing only in front of you like normal, your point of view changes. You can also see in all directions at once; imagine yourself as being simply an eye or a sphere.

4. Once you get used to moving, you can choose to visit whatever or whomever you wish. Do remember your etiquette, however. While you are meant to feel at home in this realm and are free to go anywhere, remember that you are a newcomer. A little humility is always wise in new territory. Treat any being you meet with respect.

5. When you have completed your journey, just think yourself back to your physical body. Move your body until you feel comfortable back in your room and are fully conscious. Take a moment to acknowledge whatever source gave you the protection that you requested.

ARE YOU AWARE?

Theosophists theorize that an infinitely long and strong silver cord connects the astral body to the physical one. You might not sense it during your astral travels, but many people from various cultures have. Their descriptions include "a coil of light," "a kind of elastic string," "a lighted cord," "a thin ray of light," "a thin, luminous ribbon," "a beam of light," "a smoky string," and "a slender, slightly luminous cord."

Meeting other beings is a characteristic that makes astral travel unique. Although it might happen in lucid dreams (see Chapter 9), reports of this are rare. Otherwise, lucid dreams share many traits with astral travel. Indeed, some expert astral travelers enter or exit their astral travel through a lucid dream state. Not surprisingly, many people who are experienced with creating lucid dreams are also adept at astral travel.

The line between astral travel and lucid dreaming can become confused at times. In both, subjects are aware of being in an altered state and having an ability to control it. They are fully conscious, and the world within their experience also maintains a certain consistency that adds to its feeling of reality. However, in both states, their world appears somewhat different from the real world and has many properties of an imaginary or dream world.

The main difference between lucid dreams and astral travel is that with lucid dreaming, the subject fully realizes that he or she is dreaming—whereas in astral travel, he or she feels that he or she has actually left the body. With a lucid dream, the subject begins the experience when he or she is clearly asleep, whereas astral travel can actually begin from a very relaxed, awakened state.

As we say with all the other experiences we have discussed in this book, write down what you experience. You can keep any astral travel information in your psychic journal or in a separate astral travel journal if you prefer.

Fear of Flying?

Many people who are interested in astral travel also have certain fears about the practice. Here's one of the most common questions that people ask: "Is it possible that after an astral travel experience I won't be able to get back into my physical body?" We can answer with assurance a resounding "no." There is no danger that your consciousness won't be able to find your body again or get back in. Think of it this way: in many ways, you engage in astral travel every night when you dream. When you use astral travel, though, you are conscious that you have entered and are moving within a different dimension. The difficulty that you will most likely have with astral travel is not that you won't be able to get back, but the opposite—it's quite difficult to stay on the astral plane. Most people get pulled back to normal consciousness much too quickly. Don't worry about losing either your body or your mind!

Another question that people often have also has to do with their fears. Many people find that they get scared as soon they start to travel, and their fear snaps them right back into their bodies. These people want to know what will help them deal with their fear and learn to stay on the astral plane. All we can say about this is practice, practice, practice! The more you practice, the more relaxed you will be and the more ready your mind will be to let go and allow you to fly. We'll also point out that the more regularly you meditate, the better able you will be to calm your mind and the more open you will be to experience life on this other plane.

Individuals who have had success with astral travel sometimes worry about how they feel after they've come back to normal consciousness. If you feel spaced out after an out-of-body experience, try grounding yourself by drinking a glass of cool water. A cool shower will also help, as will taking a walk while concentrating on the feeling of the ground beneath your feet. Feel free to use any other grounding techniques—such as guided meditation, counting your breaths, or hugging a tree—that works for you.

Doubling Your Double

A special type of mental projection that lends proof to the idea of body doubles is *bilocation*. This occurs when a person who is currently living and breathing appears in two places at once and is equally "solid" in both places. The person appears to be doing normal activities and might even speak to you. Historically, these travels were reported to occur when a person was not able to leave home but somehow "traveled" to a faraway locale to deliver an important message. Instances of bilocation tend to occur with people who are mentally active and so full of ideas that their minds are "divided." The idea is that someone might be thinking of one thing and doing another, causing his or her physical body to be in one place and the double to appear in another.

> **DEFINITION**
>
> **Bilocation** is the state when a living person is able to be in two places at the same time.

Activating Your Second Self

Experts at astral travel tell fascinating stories of their experiences. Some prearrange to meet fellow travelers and compare notes the next day. Others travel to secret realms where they visit inner sanctuaries to study deep, spiritual insights. They can meet with teachers who help them learn or spend hours researching ancient texts in unknown languages. And when they wake up, their clocks show that only a few minutes have passed.

In all likelihood, you won't be able to accomplish these feats on your first attempt. But here's an exercise to get you started on the astral traveler's path.

Intuition Exercise: Activate Your Second Self

1. While relaxing in a protected space, visualize your second self. Imagine it positioned just in front of or above you (depending on whether you are sitting or lying down), in the exact position of your physical body.

2. Carefully observe how your double looks, and see yourself from a different perspective. Check out the back of your head and body—parts of yourself that you don't normally see.

3. Allow your consciousness to move to your double. Begin to look through its eyes.

4. Look at your surroundings from this new perspective. Then, move around the room, looking at everything through these new eyes.

5. What would you like to do next? You can stay close to home and look at your other rooms. Or, you might try reaching through your walls and moving around your neighborhood. Or, you might venture even farther—perhaps farther than you can now imagine.

Remember that you are always in control—and relax. Many people who are experiencing their first astral "flight" react with fear, which immediately brings them back to consciousness and ends the experience. If you become afraid, remind yourself that you *want* to have this experience and that you can end it whenever you choose.

You might also want to visit a place or person who is normally far away through a process called *targeting*. This can be done by focusing on the image of the location or the person's face, then seeing it at the end of a tunnel. You then move yourself through the tunnel until you arrive.

DEFINITION

Targeting is a technique for shifting consciousness during astral travel by focusing on a person or place in ordinary reality in order to visit.

Near-Death Experiences

Another type of experience that involves the sense of separating from the body (and often traveling through a tunnel) is a *near-death experience (NDE)*. NDEs stand out from astral travel in one big way: they do not require conscious control.

DEFINITION

A **near-death experience (NDE)** occurs when a person who is considered dead experiences a vivid awareness of separating from his or her body before being revived and returned back to life.

In 1975, Dr. Raymond Moody, Jr. originated the term "near-death experiences" to describe clinical death and a return to life. There are a number of popular books on this topic, including *Evidence of the Afterlife: The Science of Near-Death Experiences* (HarperOne, 2011) by Jeffrey Long and Paul Perry and *Into the Light: Real-Life Stories about Angelic Visits, Visions of the Afterlife, and Other Pre-Death Experiences* (New Page Books, 2007) by John Lerma.

What You See and Feel

Because of medical advances, more people are now able to have a close encounter with death and then live to tell the tale. These people share similar experiences, and their similarity is what makes them remarkable. Here's a list of traits shared in many NDEs:

1. A person feels that he or she is dying and hears himself or herself being pronounced dead by a doctor.

2. The person hears a loud noise—usually a loud ringing or buzzing.

3. The person also feels himself or herself moving through a long, dark tunnel.

4. Suddenly, the person discovers he or she is outside the physical body. However, he or she remains in the immediate physical environment.

5. The person sees his or her own body from a distance, watching the resuscitation attempt from this strange point of view. Emotional upheaval or detachment also accompanies this.

6. Eventually, the person collects himself or herself and adjusts to this unusual condition.

7. The person discovers he or she has a new body that has unique powers separate from the physical body he or she just left.

8. Soon, spirits of former loved ones appear.

9. A warm and loving spirit appears as a being of light who asks questions. These are nonverbal and intended to help the person examine his or her life. Panoramic playbacks of major life events appear.

10. Gradually, the person approaches a border that seems to represent a barrier between life and death. For unknown reasons, he or she must turn back to an earthly life. His or her time to die has not arrived.

11. The person resists returning after glimpsing an afterlife of immense joy, love, and peace. But he or she returns to the physical body.

After having such an experience, many people have difficulty talking about it. For one thing, it's hard to describe with mere words. Also, many people they talk to cannot understand or believe the experience. The person is changed forever.

ARE YOU AWARE?

The Gallup Organization and near-death research studies estimate that 13 million adults have had NDEs in the United States alone. Worldwide, that number is much larger. NDEs are experienced by people of all nationalities, races, backgrounds, and ages. On the average, these people are no more or less religious than any cross section of the population, coming from agnostic and atheistic backgrounds as well as religious ones.

How NDEs Can Change You

Actor Kirk Douglas reportedly had a near-death experience when a helicopter he was flying in collided with another aircraft. Douglas, who suffered severe back and head injuries, was left fighting for his life and actually died for a few moments before being resuscitated. He states, "There was never a moment I was as close to God as I was then. I will never take life, things, or people for granted again. I'm more appreciative of being able to open my eyes in the morning and see those I love close by."

Those who have had an NDE show a dramatic change in their attitudes toward life and death. You can see a fictional but well-drawn example of this type of change in the Clint Eastwood movie *Hereafter* (2010). The film not only details the impact an NDE has on a French journalist who survives the 2004 Indian Ocean tsunami, but also follows the story of a reluctant professional psychic (played by Matt Damon). Surveys show that people who have had near-death experiences no longer express a fear of death. They also have a stronger belief in the possibility of an afterlife—or gain one if they previously did not believe in an afterlife. We cannot declare that NDEs prove that life exists after death, but they do suggest that consciousness continues on some level after physical death.

When asked about what the near-death experience taught them, survivors all share similar answers. They emphasize the importance of learning to nurture a true and profound love for others. And another lesson is to focus on seeking new knowledge, rather than limiting one's views. Survivors' values also might change. For instance, the drive to get ahead financially or professionally might seem insignificant in the face of their revelation about the meaning of life. As we have seen, all these lessons are important in the intuitive areas we have explored. Indeed, some who have NDEs report an increase in their intuitive and psychic abilities.

Have You Ever Had an Out-of-Body Experience?

Both astral travel and NDEs are called *out-of-body experiences (OBEs)*. They share the sense that the duplicate body or second self has left the physical body behind and taken off in flight. Some subjects report seeing objects positioned in places that they could not have seen from the viewpoint of their physical bodies.

OBEs are actually more common than you'd think. Various surveys of how many people have had OBEs show different results, but their estimates range between 1 person in 10 and 1 in 20. Although OBEs can happen to anyone—including you!—most occur when people are resting, sleeping, or dreaming. However, researchers report that an out-of-body experience can happen just about anywhere; they've received reports of it occurring during high-speed motorcycle and airplane rides.

DEFINITION

Out-of-body-experiences (OBEs) are unusual and brief occasions when a person's consciousness seems to depart from the body, allowing him or her to observe the world from a point of view that transcends the physical body and bypasses the physical senses.

Are you wondering whether you've ever had an OBE? Or do you think you were just dreaming? Here are a few questions to help you distinguish between an OBE and a dream:

- Have you ever had the sense of being outside your physical body?
- Have you had the sense of being outside your physical body and observing it?
- Did you have a tremendous sense of energy?
- Did you feel vibrations?
- Did you hear strange or loud noises?

- Did a sensation of bodily paralysis accompany the experience?

- Was the experience very vivid, resembling an everyday waking experience more than a dream?

If you answered "yes" to most of these questions, you probably have undergone an OBE. If you're still not sure, be aware that out-of-body experiences usually have an awesome impact on people who experience them. If you haven't experienced one, don't be afraid to keep trying. As we've said before, practice makes perfect.

Out-of-body experiences can be both awesome and intriguing, but don't get too carried away with the idea. The important thing to realize is that the point of an OBE, like any psychic experience, is to learn why you're having it and how you can grow from it. If you really want to have this type of experience, your dedication and perseverance will lead you there. But if you start to feel frustrated by your failed attempts, consider that this might not be the path for you. Explore other areas that have a greater pull on your imagination and energy.

If you're beginning to think that astral travel is too far out for you, get ready to come back down to Earth. In the next few chapters, we're going to explore psychic phenomena that are more physical than the mental trips we've been taking. We're about to switch gears to psychic stuff that you can see, touch, and "talk to."

The Least You Need to Know

- A duplicate self can separate from your physical body and travel without the restraint of physical laws.

- With the strong focus gained from a regular meditation practice, you may be capable of learning to travel on the astral plane.

- Astral travel involves an extremely clear and controlled level of conscious awareness.

- In near-death experiences, a person separates from his or her physical body and sees from new perspectives.

Listening to Your Intuition

This part focuses on some information that may surprise you and some with which you will want to become super familiar. We start by looking at psychokinesis—the way the mind can move physical matter. We'll also touch on ghosts and other paranormal phenomena. We'll move on and talk about certain types of psychic "paraphernalia," devices that can help you access your intuitive know-how. Then, we'll provide you with essential hints and tips for doing your own readings—and finally, we'll leave you with some wise words about the future.

Psychic Feats, the Paranormal, and Psi

In This Chapter

- Moving matter with the mind
- Concentrated can-do
- Far-out psi: the paranormal
- Uninvited guests and what to do about them

So far, you've learned about fantastic astral flights and infinite expansions of consciousness, space, and time—events and experiences that seem to occur in other dimensions and in higher spiritual realms.

In this chapter, we'll look at how psychic energy can impact physical reality by talking about ways in which the mind can move objects, overcome physical obstacles, and affect matter. We'll also investigate paranormal phenomena while keeping an eye on psi.

Psychokinesis

As you've discovered, with forms of psychic activity such as telepathy, clairvoyance, or precognition, the mind receives incoming information about people, objects, or events. In the cases of mind over matter, the mind projects an influence outward toward other objects or people.

Psychokinesis (PK) is the general term for using the mind to control matter without any technological help. PK can include quiet activities such as prayer and healing or fantastic feats such as table tipping, fire walking (ouch!), or that all-time classic—spoon bending. Remember Neo learning from a child how to bend a spoon in *The Matrix* while he waited for an audience with the Oracle?

DEFINITION

Psychokinesis (PK) can be defined as the creation of motion in inanimate objects (which are often far away) through the use of psychic powers. In other words, your mind and soul, working on an unseen plane, have the ability to interact with matter and affect it.

Will Wishing Make It So?

Clearly, creating PK effects is more complex than simply wishing hard, clapping your hands, or clicking your heels together. And yet, there's a certain side of it that requires not trying. The idea of letting go of your focus often comes up when discussing what makes PK work.

As in other areas where psychic skill comes into play, experts recommend achieving a state of relaxed concentration. In this state, which often occurs during meditation or hypnosis, the rational mind takes a backseat—allowing a deeper level of consciousness to direct the types of thought, or energy, that pass through your mind. This process is quite different from wishing, which is based on a rational effort to direct very focused thoughts.

Physics, Magic, or Intuition?

Theories on how PK works are about as numerous as types of PK feats, ranging from complex explanations of physicists to skeptics who cry fraud. In fact, we can't possibly list all the theories that physicists have put forth, and the scientists themselves don't even agree upon any one of them. But some scientists are beginning to see similarities between the seemingly bizarre events associated with psi and the workings of subatomic particles (bits of matter that are even smaller than atoms). Both appear to act randomly, without specific patterns.

Other researchers look at neutrinos as possible prototypes for how psi works. These particles move at the speed of light and may even pass through physical matter because they consist of pure energy. Some recent scientists extend this concept to theorize the possible existence of psi particles, giving them names such as mindons, psychons, and psitrons. Pretty original names, huh?

Other scientists present ideas that do not try to specify physical mechanisms, such as neutrinos or psi particles, that make PK work. Some suggest that PK results from nonphysical energy—a psychic energy rather than a physical one. It might originate from a person's mind or already exist in the universe, while being susceptible to the mind's mental manipulations or directions. Another theory is that some form of biological gas emanates from the body and forces an object to move. But various experiments have done a pretty good job of ruling out this possibility.

ARE YOU AWARE?

Some time ago, a group of eight skeptical people in Toronto decided to use their imaginations to create a "spirit," complete with his own personality and detailed life story. Then, they tried to conjure him up. And indeed they did! Philip appeared and communicated with them via table rapping, which they monitored closely to make certain there was no fraud. So what made a completely nonexistent character appear? The theory is that Philip was a product of the group's unconscious mind, creating a type of group psychokinesis.

We tend to lean toward another theory, which seems to have a strong following in the scientific community as well. It is derived from David Bohm's theory that combines relativity and quantum theories, which we describe in Chapter 2. For an excellent overview of how these various theories come together, check out Chapter 5 of Belleruth Naparstek's book *Your Sixth Sense* (Harper San Francisco, 1997).

When You Concentrate

We've talked about how the body is made up of energy vibrations. This idea is not so hard to accept when you realize that the body is composed of gazillions of atoms. Atoms contain more than 99 percent space, with their remaining miniscule particle of matter contributing less than 1 percent. That's a lot of empty space—and yet what holds it all together and fills in the empty gaps is energy.

Each being and every thing has its own sort of "energy print" (like a fingerprint), which we call its vibration. These vibrations have rhythmic up-and-down patterns that move almost constantly. The catch here is the word "almost." When a vibration reaches the top or bottom of its pattern, it has a moment of potential rest. (This principle was referred to as a pendulum effect by physicist Itzhak Bentov.) At this precise moment of rest, called the "stillpoint," your vibration meets up with and matches that of the ultimate stillpoint.

This ultimate stillpoint is the original and ideal state of all vibrations. The idea behind this is that every dimension, entity, and object is interconnected at some level of existence—within a dimensional realm that is much different from the physical world that we perceive. Rather than existing as hierarchical levels, they are multidimensional—where each ones fits inside another and they all interconnect. At the heart of it all, and running through everything, is the vibration that we're calling the stillpoint. Ironically, it seems to vibrate at such a high speed that it has no movement at all—which suggests that it includes the entire spectrum of vibrational speed and movement. By having access to all vibrations, this state contains an intimate knowledge of them all.

In a sense, all beings "blink" in and out of this vibrational state quite often. (It's estimated at around seven times a second for humans.) It happens so quickly that you aren't even aware of it on a conscious level. But the same part of your mind that sidesteps the conscious mind and taps into your intuitive side is aware of this stillpoint vibration. Indeed, that's how our intuition accesses information that we do not otherwise realize we have access to. But how does PK fit into this scenario? What makes it work?

When you are more aware of and attuned to your ability to tap into this stillpoint vibration, you attract more energy to yourself. In a sense, when opening to new levels of vibration, your own levels tend to expand. This explains why simply opening up to intuition causes you to receive more insight and information. But with PK, after realizing the energy is there, you must learn to direct it toward material objects.

ARE YOU AWARE?

Some researchers believe that psychokinesis and levitation were used in ancient times to erect large temples of worship and other structures. Some of the most famous edifices in the world are thought to have been erected using these psi techniques. Among them are the Egyptian pyramids, Machu Picchu in Peru, Stonehenge in England, and the famous lines and desert drawings on the Nazca Plains.

Before directing this energy outward, however, the key to controlling it comes from within. To become more closely aligned with it, you can practice making your vibrational level more closely match it. How do you do that? Surprise! You meditate—or practice similar methods of altering consciousness—because these states create vibrational levels closer to the stillpoint. The more time you spend increasing these levels within yourself, the more closely connected you'll be to this tremendous vibrational force that permeates everything.

What do you call this force? Well, if you're an Eastern yogi or mystic, you would call this energy prana or chi or ki. If you're a Western mystic, you could call it God. If you're a scientist, you might call it electromagnetic energy. If you're a psi scientist, you call it psi. Regardless of what you call this energy, it shows one interesting trait: it responds to what comes from within you and not to external forces.

The Paranormal and You

"Paranormal" is a catch-all word for any experience that people can't explain with science. In a way, then, psi could be a subset of the larger term "paranormal." But psi scientists strongly resist this usage because they don't want their discipline grouped together with unusual—and perhaps spurious—phenomena such as Bigfoot sightings or alien abductions.

Researchers have found one underlying theme that seems to surface fairly often: paranormal sensitivity and psychic insight might be linked in some way. This connection raises the question, "Does psychic sensitivity open one up to paranormal experiences, or does an experience with the paranormal increase one's psychic ability?" Although there's no definitive answer to this question so far, the two types of awareness often seem to go hand in hand. Have you had an experience that seemed to be paranormal? If so, you are not alone.

Ghostbusters

Is there any truth to the seemingly silly stories of ghosts and goblins haunting nearby locales? Indeed, these tales extend far back in time, beyond mere children's tales to some of the most basic beliefs in many cultures. *Ghosts* certainly are not a new phenomenon. Experts in the field have tried to categorize the various experiences people have reported in an attempt to understand what really is out there. The most commonly described categories include *apparitions*, *hauntings*, and poltergeists (which we'll discuss in the next section).

DEFINITION

Webster's defines a **ghost** as the soul of a disembodied spirit, imagined to be wandering among the living. Actually, the word is used to describe various phenomena, some of which do not involve a soul or a spirit at all. An **apparition** is probably closest to what people usually call a "ghost"—a spirit with an image that can be seen and can interact with its observer. A **haunting** is a repeated perception of an image, whether it's a sight, sound, or sense of movement. Experts suggest that it doesn't involve a spirit but an "energy imprint."

What most people think of as a ghost is called an apparition by those in the know. This spirit form may appear physically. It looks more like an image projected on a movie screen than a substantial body. (Remember: spirits are a form of energy.) In addition to showing itself physically, an apparition usually communicates in some way with its observer. It might acknowledge your presence by looking at you or even speaking to you.

Typically, an apparition remains attached to the physical realm because of the psychological problems its human antecedent had. A person who died through trauma or who had a strong attachment to a certain place is more likely to come back as a ghost or apparition. He or she might need encouragement or help to move on to another realm. Experts in the field of paranormal studies consider apparitions to be harmless. As the famous ghostbuster Loyd Auerbach says, "The ghost can't hurt you. However, the ghost experience itself can hurt you psychologically, depending on the way you react to it." (If you have a ghost living in your home, you might need expert help to remove it.)

True apparitions are considered very rare. Slightly more common are "hauntings" (which is a noun). These repeated perceptions are thought not to involve spirits but to be imprints of past events. The idea is that the vibrational frequency of a certain event was so intense that it left a strong imprint behind at the location where the original event occurred. This imprinted image appears like a film clip; it repeats the same brief image each time it appears.

A classic example of a haunting involves the frequent sightings of Anne Boleyn in the Tower of London. Over the centuries, people at the tower have reported seeing her ghost near her place of execution. The theory is that the intense emotions surrounding the event left their mark on time.

The most common category of ghost that people perceive actually comes from within their own homes and minds. And yet, they're not imagining it!

Poltergeists: Uninvited House Guests

Poltergeist (1982), the famous horror movie, actually depicts the power of PK quite well. What happens is that objects move, shake, or levitate in response to intense mental energy coming from someone living in the house. This energy is not created consciously, which is why people suspect a ghost.

DEFINITION

A **poltergeist,** which means "noisy ghost" in German, isn't a ghost at all. It's a form of PK (psychokinesis) that is usually generated unconsciously.

Although the movie *Poltergeist* associated this phenomenon with ghosts, this isn't accurate. Also, the phenomenon is often pinned on young children, but the little guys really don't deserve the bad rap. Usually, the source of this energy is adolescents, who are known for their intense emotions, or from adults, who are known for unconsciously burying some pretty heavy feelings of stress. Often, repressed feelings of anger are involved. The good news is that after the source is identified, the odd events quickly stop. By acknowledging that you have intense feelings, you can begin to deal with them. This opening up quickly clears the air.

Housecleaning: A Little Psychic Feng Shui

In recent years, an ancient Chinese art has traveled westward to help us do a little spiritual housecleaning. *Feng shui* (pronounced "fung shway") promotes the idea that the physical environment expresses—and affects—the people who live in it. It encourages people to become aware of their physical surroundings and to embrace them as part of themselves.

DEFINITION

Feng shui is an ancient Chinese philosophy of, and method for, creating harmonious environments.

Feng shui combines a common-sense approach to arranging your home with transcendental techniques for balancing unseen life energies. If you want to balance your surroundings, first imagine the ideal environment, filled with a nurturing sense of love and light. Then, compare your ideal with your reality.

To create your newly realized ideal, examine your internal world as well as your outer one. You will probably find that they reflect each other—and in a big way! To help you focus on these issues, we've prepared an exercise for you. Why not read it and then commit to doing it sometime this week?

Intuition Exercise: Energy Clearing

Start by answering the questions that follow in your psychic journal. After you have contemplated your answers, make sure to move on to the next phase—action!

Phase 1

1. Is your home filled with clutter and possessions you aren't even sure why you own? If so, list some of those objects.

2. Could it be that you are holding on to the past? Although it may feel comforting, is it possible that hanging on is preventing you from moving ahead? Take a few minutes to write about your feelings regarding this issue.

Phase 2

When you let go of physical objects, you become part of the universal flow of giving and receiving. You can begin to clear the energy in your home by cleaning out your closets and clearing out your unused stuff. Don't be afraid to let go of old material attachments and the old stuck energy attached to them.

Make a commitment now to get rid of the old stuff in your home that is cluttering up your life and bogging down your energy. Write down the date that you plan to complete this task.

Phase 3

Now that you have gotten rid of your old things, it's time to clear out the old energy that's hanging around. To do this, you will need any of the following items that appeal to you:

- Incense

- A sage smudge stick

- Candles

You also might want to get some bells, chimes, or any other small instrument that appeals to you. Light your incense, sage, and/or candles. Sing and dance through your home while accompanying yourself. Feel the vibrations of your song. Imagine that you are driving any negative or stale energy out with the force of your love and light. Chant a mantra or affirmation while you dance, if this feels helpful, and visualize your home full of vibrant, nurturing energy.

GUIDED INTUITION

Practicing feng shui in its tangible terms involves many complex principles. For example, colors in your home should be balanced between all the primary colors. Often, these are associated with the colors of the seven chakras: red, orange, yellow, green, blue, indigo, and purple. Because each color has its own vibrational frequency, creating this color harmony is one way of balancing energies in your home.

Feng shui acknowledges the important role that intuition plays in properly understanding and using this ancient philosophy. Your intuition can help you gain a sense of aspects in your environment that need to be reassessed and improved. These lessons also offer insight into past habits, thinking, and feeling that may create unnecessary burdens for you today.

Taking Possession

Whereas feng shui focuses on how the "spirit" of material objects can interact with—and even dominate—their surroundings, this section talks more about a much different type of dominating spirit. Many people believe that certain not-so-nice spirits exist that can take over a human's body. Others suggest that just part of another spirit might become fragmented and attach itself to a human. Usually, that human is someone who is depressed or feeling hopeless. Still others suggest that a person may lose a fragment of himself or herself, perhaps by remaining overly attached to someone who is no longer part of his or her life.

The traditional view of spirit possession is that an evil, inhuman spirit attempts to take over a person's soul in order to bring the soul over to the side of evil. Possessed people may start to act in a bizarre fashion and report hearing voices, imagining seeing awful beings in mirrors, seeing strange lights or movements, and noticing a haunting phenomenon in the home. Evidently, when caused by a malicious spirit, these occurrences quickly escalate in frequency and severity.

MIXED MESSAGES

Don't face your fears alone. If you feel that you or your home may be visited by an unwelcome guest, don't hesitate to contact a qualified expert in this area. Do an internet search for "Paranormal Association." There are chapters in many states. A visit to one of their websites may give you some tips on how to release your "guest." The site may also have a list of experts in your area.

In such extreme cases, experts use *exorcism* to ask unwanted spirits to leave a person. Exorcism exists in the Christian, Islamic, Jewish, and Hindu traditions. There are even some Buddhist sects that hold exorcisms. Although this procedure has historically been practiced by religious authorities, such as the Catholic priest in the movie *The Exorcist* (1973), a new breed of helper has come on the scene in recent years. These are specially trained therapists who use hypnosis and past-life regression to ascertain and aid a client in clearing negative energy.

DEFINITION

An **exorcism** is the act of expelling an unwanted spirit through religious or solemn ceremonies.

Some of these specialists have found that a person who has chronic depression or lingering feelings of guilt or despair might be helped by this treatment. According to these specialists, although the despairing person may not be overtaken by negative spiritual energy, the person experiences enough of it that it has seriously dampened his or her spirits.

If you find yourself falling into the habit of fearing something you can't understand, affirmations offer a simple way of facing your fears. If you ever start to feel frightened when thinking about possible unfriendly visitors, try repeating this affirmation, which comes from the Unity Church, a religious movement within the wider New Thought movement. (If the concept of or word "God" doesn't feel comfortable to you, feel free to choose the word "universe," "spirit," or whatever feels right.)

> The Light of God surrounds me,
>
> The Love of God enfolds me,
>
> The Power of God protects me,
>
> The Presence of God watches over me.
>
> Wherever I am, God is.

As we've said before, it's up to you to choose what you believe and how you think. The ability and responsibility to decide for yourself is what makes you *you*.

MIXED MESSAGES

Resist the temptation to blame bad spirits for your problems! For example, if you've been working all day on your computer and it suddenly starts acting up, take a break! It's not a malicious spirit, but it may be a hint from your intuition that you're overdoing it.

Keep an Open Mind

If you find yourself thinking that paranormal experiences sound too foreign to possibly be true, just think of your own experiences. Since you've begun to practice some intuition exercises, have you begun to notice some odd occurrences, unusual impressions, or astounding insights? Do you find yourself accepting possibilities and believing ideas that you would have shrugged off a few months ago?

The impressions and experiences you've had may seem simple. People start calling you more often when you're thinking about them, you suddenly know a bit of information that can help you out in a pinch, or perhaps you feel filled with a sense of peace or energy when you're meditating. Any or all of these show that you are more in touch with a greater awareness—your inner knowing. And how could you prove any of it to anyone? Your only proof, unless you've already had some documented PK experiences, is that you yourself have felt it.

We'll talk more about how psychic energy interacts with objects and events in the "real" world in the next chapter.

The Least You Need to Know

- Your mind can exert control over matter without the help of any physical force.
- You become more closely aligned with the vibrating energy all around when you meditate. And doing so will help you open to your intuition.
- Ghosts may exist in various forms, and most are harmless.
- When considering possible realities, remain open-minded and respectful—without obsessing!

Psychic Tools
of the Trade

In This Chapter

- Psychic paraphernalia
- News from natural forces
- Information or imagination?
- Always having free will

We've been looking at how the mind moves matter and at what might be moving the mind. It's fascinating stuff, but how can you use this intuitive insight and psychokinetic potential in your own life? Of course, you start by learning to trust your own intuition. But if you'd like a little backup, or even just a fun way of conducting your own homegrown experiments, you can try playing with a little psychic paraphernalia. A gadget or two might help you express your openness to receiving information and provide the tools for translating it.

Various devices can provide options for ways to tap into your intuitive insights. Many of these are especially useful when you are seeking specific information, such as "yes" or "no" answers to questions. In contrast, devices aren't all that helpful if you're seeking inspiration on an art project or insight into a complex mathematical formula. As you develop your intuitive abilities, you'll learn which methods work best for obtaining certain types of information; no one method is right or wrong. The important point is just to enjoy the experience, which is a more productive attitude for learning something as well! But just in case you're looking for an extra helping hand, we'll show you some options in this chapter.

Spell It Out: Ouija Boards

Among the classics of spiritualist paraphernalia is the *Ouija board* (pronounced "WE-ja"). Depending on who you talk to, the source of the name could be either ancient Egyptian for "good luck" or a combination of the French and German words for "yes." Various people also claim to have invented the board, which has been around for about a century.

DEFINITION

The **Ouija board** contains a planchette, a platelike device designed to glide easily, and a larger base with letters, numbers, and words printed on it. People lightly place their fingertips on the planchette as it moves across the base to spell out answers to specific questions.

The Ouija board consists of a smooth surface (usually a rectangular board) on which the letters of the alphabet, the numbers one through nine, and the words "yes" and "no" are drawn. Participants place a planchette, a smaller platelike device equipped with a pointer, atop the board. During a séance, two or more people place their fingers loosely on the planchette, then ask a carefully worded question. Apparently directed by a spirit guide, the planchette's pointer glides around the board, pointing letter by letter to spell out an answer. Although the messages might appear a bit non-sensical at first, they eventually seem to flow more smoothly.

People who experience the phenomenon are amazed at how accurate answers can be but usually emphasize the importance of wording the questions clearly. (Remember the oracle who promised the king that a great army would win the battle? The king mistakenly assumed the oracle meant his army. Needless to say, he was extremely disappointed when he suffered a devastating loss.) Foolish, impossible, or unclear questions lead to garbled answers.

If you decide to use a Ouija board as a way to communicate with a spirit guide, make sure to think through your questions carefully before you begin. Also ponder who you want to seek information from. If you seek valuable news from a specific entity, you'll need to make this clear. Like other psychic exercises we've described, we recommend asking good and loving guides for their protection, both before and after the session.

Some Ouija supporters suggest that the Ouija board enables otherworldly spirits to communicate freely without having to work through the mind of a medium. Others would argue that the Ouija's spelled-out messages come from a part of the mind that sidesteps rational thought. Where the message itself originates, whether from a spirit world or one's deeply embedded personal intelligence, remains a fascinating mystery.

MIXED MESSAGES

Be careful who you connect with! Ouija boards have a history of being used for fun; they also seem to attract "fun-loving" (mischievous) spirits. Some experts claim that these tricksters are lower-level spirits who might not have your best interest at heart. For this reason, some people discourage using the Ouija board at all.

Going to the Earth's Source

While many people believe that their source of spiritual or psychic information comes from the heavens, others believe that it comes from nature and the earth underfoot. Do you remember when we talked about the Gaia theory in Chapter 2? This is the idea that the earth is a living entity in and of itself, and each individual is just a smaller part of that greater level of consciousness.

In that vein, some people suggest that other aspects of the earth—streams, rivers, grass, trees, rocks, and mountains—also have individual identities that fit into the grander scheme of the earth's purpose. In addition to providing tremendous natural resources, these entities provide great amounts of psychic power. Some followers of this theory claim that certain notable sites mark areas in which the earth's forces contain exceptional power, including Stonehenge, the Egyptian pyramids, and Buddhist monasteries.

But how do you discover these forces, know where they are, or tap into them? One way is by using the ancient intuitive art form of divining with sticks (or, as they're called in their new-and-improved version, divining rods).

Dowsing

Ancient cave drawings going back 6,000 years show people holding forked sticks. The practice appeared in prehistoric pictures in places as diverse as Egypt, China, and Peru. *Dowsing* for water would, understandably, be an essential use of divination for the early nomadic tribes who often traveled through dry territory.

DEFINITION

Dowsing is traditionally considered a method of detecting underground sources of water and other material by using divining rods. Although most divining rods are fabricated forked sticks, a tree branch with this Y-shape also works well.

Dowsing works according to the same principle surrounding psychometry. Like tuning in to the vibrations linked to a certain object, dowsing tunes into the vibrational information regarding a specific place. A dowser performs the procedure by clearly formulating in his or her mind what he or she is seeking, then holding divining rods and walking through the chosen area. When the dowser crosses a spot that contains the sought-after substance, the rods move. By walking back and forth near this spot, the dowser can ascertain the line that the water, or whatever material, follows.

Perhaps dowsing has survived from ancient times to the present because it has so many uses. Among its uses are dowsing for oil, minerals, lost objects, archeological sites, and even spiritual landmarks that might have been buried over time. Dowsing can also be done from afar by using a map and a pendulum—and in search of something far different from a bit of water!

Pendulums

Dowsing for information can be done with a *pendulum*. In addition to pointing out the location of physical materials on a map, pendulums can locate information within the human body (especially when it comes to pinpointing a site of disease), answer "yes" or "no" to specific questions, and even make stock market predictions. Anyone can learn to use a pendulum; the hardest part is asking an appropriate question and phrasing it properly.

DEFINITION

A **pendulum** is an object suspended from a fixed point that moves in response to a natural force.

Working with pendulums is a good way for newcomers to psychic ability to gain a sense of confidence.

Intuition Exercise: Let the Pendulum Swing

With very little practice, you can make a pendulum work and see for yourself that you can get immediate feedback. You can even create your own pendulum.

1. Make a pendulum by attaching a weight or solid object to a string or light-weight chain that's about 6 to 12 inches long.

2. Hold it several inches above a flat, clear surface or clean sheet of paper.

3. Ask it a very basic question that you already know the answer to, such as, "Is my name (fill in the blank)?" Note which direction it moves toward—that is your "yes" answer for the rest of this question session. Then, ask a question that will clearly elicit a "no" response to ascertain which direction will mean "no" for the rest of the session. (This process should be repeated each time you begin a new pendulum dowsing session, as the direction for a specific answer may change with time.)

4. Prepare some questions that require "yes" or "no" answers. Try to focus on an issue or event that will not require a long wait before the future confirms the answer you receive. So avoid long-term questions such as, "Will my daughter grow up to be a doctor?" You'll also want to avoid formulating an ambiguous, frivolous, or insincere question.

5. Hold up the pendulum again and command it to be still. It should come to a complete rest.

6. Ask the questions you prepared. If you sense that a certain question is not getting a clear response from the pendulum, repeat the question or try to reword it.

The same basic approach can be applied to map dowsing if you'd like to ascertain the location of a person, object, or source of information. To do this, ask the whereabouts of something important to you as you hold the pendulum over each section of a map. Gradually, you will zero in on the location of the information in question.

Look Into My Crystal Ball: Scrying

Scrying is an old-fashioned practice of divination that involves staring into a reflective object, such as a magic mirror, crystal ball, or a still pool or bowl of water (as Nostradamus did). The act of keeping your eyes open while staring into a shining, reflective surface works like a form of meditation or self-hypnosis—the prime state for opening your awareness to psychic insight.

DEFINITION

Scrying is the practice of divination that induces clairvoyance as you stare into a reflective surface and enter into a trancelike state.

Although the famous mystic, seer, and author Nostradamus (1503–1566) used a bowl of still water as his reflective surface of choice, modern scryers most commonly use crystal balls, which are usually 3 to 6 inches in diameter. The ideal crystal ball is made of quartz, not glass, because quartz crystal is said to increase psychic energy. It should be placed (or held) against a dark background, such as a black velvet cloth. To prepare for scrying, darken the room, leaving only a candle burning.

When staring into the reflective surface of your choice, avoid using a hard, focused stare. Keep your eyes relaxed, don't strain, and gaze beyond the surface to the inside center of the ball. After much practice, a deep darkness may appear within the ball. After more practice, cloud forms appear, which eventually may be accompanied by colors or light. And after even more practice, images may begin to appear. As you become experienced, you can see an answer—including information from the present or future—in picture form when you gaze into the surface and ask a specific question.

Traditionally, images moving to the right are considered symbolic, and those to the left are considered actual occurrences. Another theory suggests that images that appear farther away occur farther away in time, but those that appear closer take place closer to the present time.

You will need to learn what each location means for you personally. One thing to keep in mind: scrying takes many hours of practice before you can achieve results. It is not for the impatient and therefore has few practitioners. In general, scrying works best for people who have a visual bent. It provides an image, then allows you to translate it in a way that makes sense to you. For example, Nostradamus tended toward flowery descriptions. When he saw visions of machines that didn't even exist yet, he had to create his own verbal imagery to describe them. For those of you who are visual but prefer an additional verbal and metaphorical approach to divination, there is the tarot.

GUIDED INTUITION

Limit your scrying session to 20 or 30 minutes to avoid causing your eyes to tear or burn. When learning to scry, you might notice that the area near your third eye begins to burn. This is actually a good sign—as long as you don't let it distract you.

Archetypes and Metaphors: Using the Tarot

The *tarot* is surrounded by mystery; even its true origins are unknown. The earliest decks appeared in Italy in the late 1400s when they became part of a popular Renaissance parlor game. However, some historians believe that the images on the cards came from ancient Egypt and India and that sages secretly preserved their sacred symbolism by placing them on playing cards.

DEFINITION

The **tarot** refers to a special deck of 78 cards that are used to predict the future.

Typically, psychics read the tarot to foretell the future. A seeker usually has a specific question or issue in mind when asking for a reading. The psychic prepares to read the cards with meditation or a similar relaxation technique. The psychic has the seeker shuffle and cut the cards. At this point, the psychic draws cards from the top of the deck and lays them out in a specific order and position, which are associated with certain aspects of the seeker's life, such as inner feelings, the past, the near future, and the environment.

Of the 78 cards, 22 are called Major Arcana and are symbolized by characters that suggest certain traits. For example, the Magician suggests self-control and taking charge. The Lovers suggest love, sex, and emotional success. The Sun suggests happiness, rebirth, and freedom. Where these cards are placed and how they relate to the others' placement are part of the interpretation. The remaining 56 cards in the tarot deck are divided into four suits—Wands, Cups, Swords, and Pentacles—each with their own associations.

Along with its unknown origins, the way tarot works remains a mystery. Although skeptics argue that cards are chosen randomly, tarot readers raise the question of what "random" really means. They suggest that the seeker's intuition leads him or her to shuffle the cards in a certain way, which affects which card appears in what place during the reading. In addition, the seeker's intuitive guidance influences how the cards are read, just as the psychic's intuition provides an appropriate interpretation of the cards.

GUIDED INTUITION

If you're just beginning to work with the tarot, you might want to start out using only the Major Arcana. These 22 cards have strong images and thus provoke many fruitful associations. After you gain confidence with these powerful cards, you can develop your skill with the more subtle Minor Arcana. If you'd like a good guidebook for learning more about the tarot, check out *The Complete Idiot's Guide to Tarot Spreads Illustrated* (Alpha Books, 2006).

Each individual has a personal interpretation of what each card means, which usually comes from his or her intuitive sense. Because the cards are based on visual images, you can derive this personal interpretation without consulting books. Once you have a strong sense of what a card means for you, you can compare your impression to classic interpretations described in books. Interestingly, the two meanings—private and universal—tend to come together, linking your personal sense to symbols of a universal scale. This supports Jung's idea that all people share experiences that are represented by archetypal images.

Exploring the I Ching

The *I Ching* is a book that explains an ancient divination method practiced in China for centuries. First written down in about 500 B.C.E., the I Ching is also known as the "Book of Changes." It is designed to show how any and every event is susceptible to change. People who are well acquainted with the book claim that it seems to possess its own form of intuition. It adapts and expands its meanings in ways that reach its reader, regardless of the reader's level.

DEFINITION

The **I Ching** is an ancient Chinese book of divination that guides its user in casting coins and then understanding eight basic symbols, their pairings, and their interpretations.

When consulting the I Ching, a "reader" throws three coins and, based on the heads/tails positioning of six different throws, looks up their interpretation in the book. Using this interpretation, you can divine how a specific issue or event is likely to be affected by various actions. While showing the effects of these actions, the book also offers guidance as to what would be the wisest path to pursue. The I Ching is based on the principle that two basic forms of energy run through everything: yin (negative and receptive) and yang (positive and assertive). Each energy is represented by a line: yin is broken, and yang is solid (or strong). These lines are combined into sets of three to create eight basic symbols. These eight symbols, arranged according to a random coin toss, are used to create a series of 64 hexagrams. This pattern of hexagrams is used to do a reading. To understand how all the symbols combine to create the meaning of each hexagram and influence the interpretation of the whole, the reader consults the I Ching.

Sound confusing? Well, like most methods of divination, I Ching gives you a certain amount to work with, then leaves the rest up to you. Mainly, the application of the message's meaning is left to you—which is where your intuition comes in. After obtaining a reading, you may instantly recognize what you can learn from it. That's the familiar form of clairsentience: knowing without knowing how you know. On the other hand, you may perceive the message as a riddle. You will need to take time to ponder it and question yourself. In this way, you can learn to look at the situation from many perspectives, and thus to come to better understand your own motivations.

ARE YOU AWARE?

If you really like numbers and want to learn an entirely different, mathematical approach to divination, check out numerology. This intuitive art is based on the idea that each number has its own vibration and significance. For example, the number three is associated with self-expression, creativity, inspiration, and joy, whereas the number seven is thought to represent philosophy, mystical tendencies, and intuition. Numerologists believe that numbers in your life can reveal a great deal about your destiny, life purpose, personality, and fortunes.

Charting the Stars: Astrology

Astrology is another ancient form of divination. When using astrology, you study the stars and planets, and observe the patterns of their movements in relation to your life and actions. The idea is that movement in the heavens is reflected in similar actions in your life. As astrologers say, "As above, so below."

DEFINITION

Astrology is the study of how the heavenly bodies influence human affairs.

To give an accurate reading, an astrologer usually needs to know the exact time of your birth. If your parents don't remember the exact time of your birth, check your birth certificate; they often list time of birth. If you don't have your birth certificate, check with the office of records in the town where you were born. Where you were born also has an impact on how an astrologer casts your chart. But don't worry; a good astrologer has ways to work around the lack of this information if you don't have an accurate record.

With the exact time and location of your birth, you can have a map made to show how you relate to and interact with the cosmos: your astrological birth chart. The 360 degrees on the chart are divided into 12 sections, or houses, that describe various facets of a person's life, such as his or her philosophy, family, intimate relationships, career, hopes, and friends.

By examining your relationship to these various personal areas, you can better understand yourself and the actions you have taken. You can use your birth chart to see where your strengths lie, and to assess where these traits can probably lead you. But it's important to realize that your fate is not sealed in an astrological chart. By becoming aware of likelihoods, you can gain the opportunity to change them. Astrology is a complicated science, which goes far beyond the scope of this book. An excellent reference to get you started on learning about astrology is *The Complete Idiot's Guide Astrology Dictionary* (Alpha Books, 2010). You can create a birth chart using an astrology software program or by going to a website that allows you to create charts online from birth data.

Using awareness to create an opportunity to change is the principle underlying all forms of divination. By gaining a larger view of who you are and by getting insight into deeper meanings in life, you give yourself the chance to change old patterns and unconscious habits. You help yourself put your inborn gift of free choice to good use.

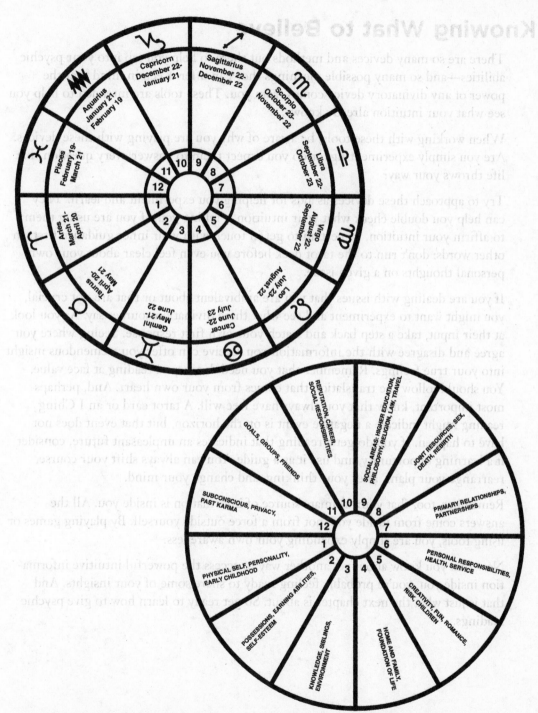

Look for your Sun sign on the Zodiac Wheel. The astrological houses reveal the energies of specific areas of life. You'll want to take note of where the planets appear in the houses of your astrological birth chart.

Knowing What to Believe

There are so many devices and methods out there to help you tap into your psychic abilities—and so many possible meanings they can offer. Keep in mind that the power of any divinatory device comes from you. These tools are intended to help you see what your intuition already knows.

When working with these tools, be aware of why you are playing with these devices. Are you simply experimenting, or do you expect them to answer every question that life throws your way?

Try to approach these devices as aids for helping you experiment and learn. They can help you double check what your intuition is telling you. If you are using them to affirm your intuition, be certain to get in touch with your inner guidance first. In other words: don't run to the tarot deck before you even feel clear about your own personal thoughts on a given issue.

If you are dealing with issues that you are ambivalent about or that are not crucial, you might want to experiment and see what these divination sources say. As you look at their input, take a step back and watch your own first response. Seeing where you agree and disagree with the information you receive can offer you tremendous insight into your true feelings. Remember that you needn't accept a reading at face value. You should follow the translation that comes from your own heart. And, perhaps most important, know that you always have free will. A tarot card or an I Ching reading might indicate a negative event is on the horizon, but that event does not have to happen. If you do get a reading that indicates an unpleasant future, consider it a learning opportunity, and use it as a guide. You can always shift your course, rearrange your plans, alter your thinking, and change your mind.

Remember, too, that your ultimate source of information is inside you. All the answers come from inside you, not from a force outside yourself. By playing games or using tools, you are simply expanding your own awareness.

Now that you know about yet another way to access the powerful intuitive information inside you, you're probably feeling ready to share some of your insights. And that is just what the next chapter is about. So get ready to learn how to give psychic readings.

The Least You Need to Know

- Divination devices can offer insight into the patterns of your inner and outer worlds.
- You can find a specific method of divination that works best for you.
- Have fun! Your sense of play and experimentation are important facets of your intuition and its further development.
- What you discover about the future isn't etched in stone; it's a guidepost for where you can create change.

Giving a Psychic Reading

In This Chapter

- Reading yourself
- Reading someone else
- Possible pitfalls
- Intuitive interpreting

A reading is the forum in which most people want to put their intuitive abilities to use. It sets aside a specific time and place to truly focus on what you want to learn about the bigger issues in life. It's also what takes this amazing knowledge base you've tapped into out of some faraway realm and puts it right in front of you, with a specific sense of what it means in your life—and what your life means. A reading helps both the reader and the sitter (the person who's receiving the reading) feel connected with the universe.

Giving a Reading: You Can Do It!

Why book an appointment with a psychic when you're wired for psychic insight yourself? We've told you from the start that you have this ability—now here's your chance to test your wings.

A reading will probably draw on all the various skills you've developed. You won't know ahead of time how information will come to you, so be prepared to take it as it comes—in whatever form it arrives. Because you'll be focusing all your abilities on one person, the information is likely to come in a way that's best suited for his or her—or your own—understanding. That principle applies whether or not the sitter is a complete stranger, a close friend, or even yourself. In fact, when you first start to give readings, you might want to start where you know you'll get the most feedback: with yourself.

Reading Yourself

In Chapter 12, we talked about the Akashic Record—the extrasensory information that exists in another dimension, kind of like the ultimate, cosmic library. The records contain information about your lives—past, and present (and perhaps, future). It also contains this information about everyone else, so it's basically a history of the world.

What's important for you is that the Akashic Record contains information about your soul's growth and your present life's goals and purposes. The following meditation is a way to access the information about why you chose this lifetime and the people in it. Knowing this can help you understand what your life lessons might be and how you can better serve the world.

Intuition Exercise: Journey to the Akashic Record

As with many of the meditations in this book, you might want to record this yourself or have a friend read it to you. Quiet music in the background may help you focus your thoughts.

1. Get into a comfortable, relaxed position and close your eyes. Imagine that you are in your inner sanctuary. You and your sanctuary are surrounded and filled with a brilliant, white light. As you bathe in this light, imagine it becoming even more beautiful and radiant.

2. Imagine now that a bubble of light comes to you; you are able to step inside it. You feel safe, protected, and relaxed. The bubble of light carries you up and up, into a higher, finer dimension. Take a deep breath, exhale, and imagine you are moving into a higher, finer vibration.

3. The bubble sets down and releases you at a magnificent library. You stand in awe of its brilliance and light. You feel drawn to go in. As you enter the library, you see many rows of books lined up, from ceiling to floor. You understand that this is the Hall of Records. You are here to find the book that represents your soul's history.

4. A wise woman dressed in flowing white, a very high being, comes to greet you. She mentally asks you to sit for a moment and rest. She asks you to pause while she sends you light. You feel your heart, third eye, and crown chakras opening, and feel surrounded and filled by her love.

5. Mentally you tell this wise being that you would like to be shown your book from the Hall of Records. She has been awaiting your arrival and gestures to a table, which holds a thick book that shines with light. You look at it closely and find it has your name emblazoned on the front.

6. Your guide instructs you to think of a question that you would like the book to answer. Take a deep breath and exhale slowly. What would you like the book to reveal?

7. Open the book. It immediately falls open to the page that contains your answer. (pause)

   What does it say? (pause)

8. The next page contains information about the qualities, such as love, patience, and honesty, that you are to develop in this lifetime. Turn the page. You are able to read the answer. (pause)

   What does it say? (pause)

9. The next page contains information about your contribution to the world in this lifetime. Turn the page. You are able to read the answer. (pause)

   What does it say? (pause)

10. You can return to the Hall of Records at any time. Are there any last questions you would like to have answered? Turn the page. You are able to read the answer. (pause)

    What does it say? (pause)

11. When you are ready to leave, you walk outside the Hall. You see your light-filled bubble, like a chariot, is awaiting you. You step inside and are transported back to your inner sanctuary.

12. Rest here for a moment and reflect on all that you have seen, felt, and heard. If you have a guide who works with you in your sanctuary, ask him or her to be present to help you process the information or to sit quietly beside you and send you light.

13. When you feel ready, slowly open your eyes and come back to the room.

This journey to the Akashic Record is a very personal meditation. It enables you to directly access information from your own higher mind. You can go there whenever you want to understand how specific issues in your life fit into the grander scheme of things. But when it comes to someone else, you may not be able to read the book with that person's name on it. You'll want to develop a separate set of skills for accessing someone else's information.

Reading Someone Else

As mentioned several times already, when you receive intuitive information you might often feel that you are making it up. Lynn has heard many of her students tell her the following just before they have a brilliant, highly accurate psychic perception:

- "I don't know how to do this."
- "You can't just make it up and claim it's intuition."
- "This doesn't make sense."
- "This is really stupid, but ...."
- "How can anyone know this?"

You might feel or believe any or all of the above, but try to have fun with these exercises. Play at them. Loosen up and give it a try. It's really the only way to learn.

Here are some steps to help you get started doing a reading for someone else. Beforehand, make sure you both feel comfortable enough around each other. Ask the person ahead of time what he or she is interested in learning. You'll do best when you have the right frame of mind: focused relaxation.

GUIDED INTUITION

When doing a reading for someone else, keep in mind that information often comes in images—symbolic or literal. If you receive an impression of an odd image, don't try to assign it a meaning. Often, the person you're reading will be able to tell you what it means.

1. Quiet your mind. Take a few deep breaths. Let go of any worries. You might find it helpful to do one of the relaxation exercises we described earlier in the book. Some people do the exercise "Meet Your Guide" in Chapter 5 before giving a reading.

2. Focus your attention. Concentrate.

3. Ask your intuition a question about an issue or problem the person you are reading has presented. You might also simply ask your intuition, "Please give me information about this person that will assist him."

4. Allow information to come into your mind. Receive it. Don't push it. You might receive this information in words, images, symbols, dialogue, physical sensations, feelings, and/or ideas. However you receive it is right for you.

5. Verbalize all the information coming in to your mind. If you are not clear, you may ask your intuition for more information. Pay attention to all of your impressions. Your conscious mind may want to censor the information because it doesn't "make sense." State what is coming to you anyway. Remember that you are learning a new skill. You will get better at this with practice and become more sure of your information and your accuracy. Later we'll address the issue of what to do if you receive bad news or negative information.

6. If information comes in too quickly, ask for it to slow down. If it comes too slowly, ask it to speed up.

7. If you are not receiving information about a specific question, there might be a reason. The answer might interfere with the lesson the person is learning around this issue. Ask the question in a more general way, such as "What can I say about this issue that would be helpful?"

8. Don't edit the information. It may make sense to the person you're reading. Check it out with him or her when you have finished receiving your impressions.

Remember that helping someone gain insight is the main purpose of giving that person a reading. You don't need to know his or her life story or predict his or her future. The important thing is to share the impressions you receive and try to help the person understand them. Here are a few more miscellaneous tips to keep in mind when you're first getting started:

- If you are just beginning to use your intuition, you may not be 100 percent accurate. Be gentle with yourself. Remember, every skill takes practice.

- You might find it helpful to close your eyes or look down in order to concentrate better.

- You might find it helps you to hold an object or a photograph belonging to the person you are tuning into. (In Chapter 4 we discussed how you can receive intuitive information using the skill of psychometry.)

When Lynn first began developing her psychic abilities, she practiced with friends and family a lot. But she began to realize that it could be difficult to read for people you already know, because you have too much information to be objective. So she asked her friend Sarah to help. Sarah comes from a large family, and Lynn hadn't met any of her family members. Lynn asked for their names and the towns that they lived in. (The latter helps her focus.) Lynn then described what psychic impressions she received about Sarah's siblings and parents. Sarah was able to confirm when Lynn was accurate, or not, which helped Lynn hone her skills.

GUIDED INTUITION

If someone is abusing drugs or alcohol, that person might be difficult to read. Lynn also finds this to be true of someone who is testing her. In addition, extreme anxiety in your sitter can make receiving intuitive information about him or her a challenge.

Doing a Minireading

Lynn calls these unofficial readings "minireadings." As a way to practice, Lynn asks friends for the names and locations of their friends and relatives. For example, her friend Sarah could tell Lynn whether her information about Sarah's Uncle Herbert was correct, but neither Lynn nor Sarah told Uncle Herb Lynn had done the reading and neither did they tell him what Lynn picked up about him. You can use this technique to practice your skills, too.

Here's an exercise that you can do to practice your own minireadings. It's most useful when you can get psychic impressions about someone you don't know, so ask your friend to give you the name of someone he or she knows well, but whom you don't know at all. Clearly, the person you're reading doesn't need to be physically present for you to get information about him or her.

Try to have fun with this exercise for evoking your intuitive impressions. Lynn consistently finds that people who feel okay about sounding a little silly and "making things up" get better results. Perhaps it's an aspect of that relaxed focus that we keep mentioning.

Intuition Exercise: Evoke Intuitive Impressions

The following list contains the general areas that Lynn tries to tune in to and receive information about when she's giving a reading for a client. When you're doing a reading, as you look at each word on the list, quickly write down your very first impression as it pertains to the other person's life. You don't have to write your responses in the exact order of the list. Information about a certain area, such as childhood, might pop into your mind first; then something about the person's relationships might come next. Follow your inner prompting.

- Relationships
- Career/work
- Goals
- Talents
- Childhood
- Health/physical body
- Emotions
- Home
- Greatest strength
- Greatest obstacle
- Greatest potential
- Other spontaneous impressions

Now evaluate the information you received:

1. Check this information with your friend to see how you did with your psychic impressions. Were you completely right? Was anything completely wrong?

2. How did you receive the information? Did you get it in words, images, feelings, a body sensation—or did you "just know"?

3. When you were wrong about a piece of information, do you remember how you felt when you received it? Did it feel fuzzy? Were you feeling blocked? Was an image or word unclear in some way? You can become a better psychic by understanding when you're not receiving clear information as well as when you are. If you're unclear, you might try asking the question in a different way. Instead of asking your intuition, "What does their home look like?" You might ask, "Do they live in a large house or a small one?" By varying the question, you might receive the information differently.

4. When you were accurate about some information, do you remember how you felt when you received it? Did you feel tingly, or simply certain you were right? Was there anything different that you felt when you had a correct answer versus a mistaken one?

GUIDED INTUITION

Remember to keep track of all the readings you do in your psychic journal, even if they are minireadings or self-readings. If you start to do a lot of them over time, you might want to start a separate notebook that includes just the date of the reading, who it was with, and any impressions that really stand out.

Lynn does this exercise frequently in her class "Developing Your Intuition." She is constantly amazed at what beginners in the class come up with. One man's partner in the class was a lively, nicely dressed, older woman. He went through the exercise quickly, easily using his intuition to fill in the whole list—with one exception. The only category he couldn't figure out was "Career." He kept hearing the word "none," so he assumed she didn't work. When it came time for the partners to process the information, Lynn heard a loud guffaw from the older woman. Then she exclaimed, "How could you possibly have known that I am a nun!"

Another student in the class was working with a partner and got stuck on the category of "Home." She found she kept getting impressions about the woman's kitchen. The student was concerned because the room kept changing from yellow, to light green, and then to peach. The woman laughed and explained that she was planning to have her kitchen painted. That morning before the class she had been going over color swatches with her husband. They were trying to decide between yellow, green, and peach!

Creating the Right Environment

Feeling comfortable with others—and with yourself—is essential to building the confidence that is necessary to gain trust and offer insight. When someone arrives at Lynn's office, she tries to help that person feel as calm and relaxed as possible. This helps Lynn and her client work together as an intuitive team, which makes it easier for Lynn to tune in.

Another important part of getting a clear reading is to set aside as many of your own opinions, feelings, and judgments as possible. In this way, intuitive counselors are similar to psychotherapists. Lynn has found that much of the judgment she used to hold about others has diminished over the years as she have given more readings.

People usually act out, hurt others, and do irrational things because they've been so emotionally injured themselves. Not to condone that behavior, but if you are reading for people, you need to respect and honor their path. Ultimately they are the ones who are responsible for their direction in life and for the outcomes of the choices they make. You can only be there as a guide to help along the way.

When You're Stuck

Just as you strive to make a reading comfortable for others, you must do the same for yourself. Sometimes you might have such high expectations of yourself that you put far more pressure on yourself than anyone else could. Of course, this can't possibly help you achieve relaxed focus.

Your intuition rarely acts in a radical fashion, so it is extremely unlikely that it will just shut down. Take that to heart and help yourself to relax. When you feel that your access to intuitive information is blocked, try taking a few small steps:

- Quiet the chatter of your conscious mind through meditation.

- Schedule a retreat for yourself.

- Engage in meditative activities, such as art, knitting, making bread, daydreaming, or even walking.

- Create a healthy balance between work and recreation.

- Try new things; break patterns.

- Drink a glass of water.

- Take a nap.

- Make sure that you are eating healthful foods.

- Abstain from recreational drugs and overindulgence in alcohol.

- Do something to make yourself laugh.

- Try speaking your options out loud and seeing which one feels right in your gut.

- Go to your sanctuary and speak with your guide.

- Ask for a dream about your concerns.

- Pray to a higher power for guidance.

- Why not come up with a few of your own ideas?

The main thing is to relax. Stop pressuring yourself and start trusting your intuition. Trusting your intuition is what a reading is all about: a confident sharing of information that comes to you as a gift. Remember to celebrate that!

MIXED MESSAGES

Don't let yourself become overwhelmed by your psychic abilities. If you're ready for a break, stop making quite as much effort to open to your intuitive side. But if you do this, don't wait too long to get back on track; you can see that consistent awareness and regular practice help a lot in bringing you closer to your intuition.

Turning It Off

So we've told you how to get up a good head of steam to really get in touch with your psychic side. But what happens if your brain feels like it's in overdrive? How do you take a break?

To generalize a little, some psychics do seem to be "on" or "open" all the time. They constantly pick up information about people and situations around them. Lynn says she would find this exhausting. Once, after she had done a lot of readings in one day, she felt she couldn't shut herself off.

She went to a mall after seeing her clients and found herself getting swamped with psychic information about all the other shoppers. She walked through the mall while being bombarded with impressions. The guy in the gray suit was having an affair and felt guilty about it; the short man coming out of the drug store was worrying about his sick mother; the teenage girl sitting on the bench was obsessed with a boy who wasn't interested in her ... it went on and on. After only a few minutes of this, Lynn fled the mall, fearing she was wearing a sign that read "Beware: Psychic Snoop!" She went home, fell asleep, and felt fine the next day.

When speaking with other intuitive counselors about preparing for readings, they all said they did some meditation or ritual to open up to more psychic awareness, but that shutting down just seemed normal and didn't require a ritual of any sort. When the reading is over, they simply return to a normal state. One woman said that what shuts her down is a shift in awareness away from her client as she ends the reading. Another woman said that as soon as she hung up after a phone session or after the door shut behind a client leaving her office, she felt she returned to a normal state.

On the other hand, some intuitives do practice a routine of closing down after they do readings. Some find it helpful to be outdoors near nature or to go for a short walk. Others have a set of words they repeat. Still others do something creative with their hands, such as gardening or cooking. One woman holds a piece of green fluorite crystal at the end of her readings because she feels it helps keep her grounded. Turning off psychic input may take some effort, but it is totally something you can do.

GUIDED INTUITION

For people who like to draw on their visual resources, indigo is often recommended as the color of psychic protection. (If you recall, this is the color associated with the third-eye chakra.) After a reading, you can imagine yourself wrapped in an indigo cloak. Another spiritual color that evokes purity is, of course, white.

Setting Boundaries

Boundaries are imaginary lines you establish around yourself to protect yourself. Boundaries are the proverbial "line in the sand." They establish what you will tolerate in another's behavior, and thereby establish what people can and cannot do to you.

Knowing how to establish boundaries for yourself is a valuable tool, whether you are giving readings or not. When you establish clear boundaries for yourself, your anxiety lessens, people respect you, and you experience the world as a safe place. Generally you have more energy, as well as a sense of inner peace. Although most people have learned how to set boundaries of some sort between themselves and others, applying these principles to the psychic realm requires a different approach.

Psychic Protection

Lynn doesn't perceive herself as being at risk from bad energy when opening up psychically. But some people do, and many recommend establishing habits to ensure psychic protection. These may include doing a "psychic protection" exercise before opening up to do readings.

My favorite exercise for this comes from author and psychic Belleruth Naparstek: "I imagine being surrounded and protected by a magical cushion of protective, intelligent, vibrating energy, which draws to it all the love and sweetness that has ever been sent my way—every prayer, smile, good wish, and gesture of gratitude drawn there as if by a powerful magnet, to surround and protect me."

Lynn usually does a light meditation before she sees clients and asks her guides, angels, and God to help. She asks that she be a clear and open channel for the wisdom that her clients need to hear. Lynn finds that the best protection includes getting enough rest, paying attention to her intuition regarding her own life, eating a healthful balanced diet, setting appropriate boundaries in her work, and making sure she has enough time for play and fun.

Lynn usually finds her work energizing, and she enjoys it. She says: "It's a privilege to watch people grow and change, and I feel honored to be included in that process." She also has learned to be clear in her boundaries while doing readings. She knows she can do only four or five readings in a day or about twenty a week. If she does more than that, she gets exhausted. Further Lynn says: "I've learned how to say 'no' to requests that drain me."

Problem Clients

Of course, Lynn's life would be less interesting—and certainly less challenging—if she didn't have the occasional difficult client. For Lynn, a difficult client is someone who wants her to have all the answers. The difficult client hopes that Lynn will have a revelation that will dramatically change his or her life, yet this client does nothing to create any changes on his or her own.

Lynn says "I feel drained by people who don't take the initiative to help change themselves." If she reaches a point where she feels she can't help them when they call for an appointment, she makes an appropriate referral. She has a huge resource list of therapists, career counselors, mediums, holistic physicians, and personal coaches, to name a few.

Sharing Psychic Information

Receiving intuitive information is one thing; sharing it is quite another. Knowing how to share intuitive information is an art in and of itself. But don't let this intimidate you. For one thing, the "rules" are not etched in stone. Because each reading is different and presents its own unique type of information, no simple rules can apply to every reading. Your actions definitely depend on your own intuitive assessment of the situation. Following are a few guidelines to keep in mind.

Remember that receiving information doesn't always mean that you have to share it. You can't always judge correctly what it means, and the more serious the news is, the more cautious you should be in passing it along. Belleruth Naparstek states this succinctly: "It would be arrogant and intrusive to assume we'd all been deputized by God to interfere with other people's lives, sometimes even if they ask us to."

MIXED MESSAGES

Be careful how you handle the psychic information that comes to you. If information about someone comes to you outside of the context of a reading, then be even more careful about how you handle it. It might be news that's intended for your own growth—not for that of the innocent bystander the information concerns.

If the News Seems Bad

Lynn is often faced with the question of what to do when she receives difficult information, such as an impending death, illness, or accident. She is of two minds here, and her response depends on the situation and what she receives intuitively. Lynn's first impression is usually to say whatever it is that she's received. She tries to couch the information in a way that softens the blow. Sometimes she receives information as a warning, in which case Lynn informs someone in enough time for them to take effective action.

In very serious cases, Lynn gets quiet and asks her intuition for a way to talk to the person. If she shares bad news, she talks to her client about possible courses of action.

What's the Answer? Yes or No (or Maybe)

Lynn often has clients call and ask her to answer just one or two quick questions. She finds these "quick" questions difficult.

Lynn usually asks clients to make an appointment, so that she's in the proper frame of mind to give accurate input. In general, Lynn finds that these clients make the assumption that she's "on" all the time. There's also an assumption that Lynn's intuition has the right answer as opposed to their own remarkable built-in intuition. Here's an example, a client whose name we've changed to "Sally."

Sally called with a "quick" question: "Should I take this job that I've been offered?" To answer this question, Lynn would need to psychically climb into Sally's life. Here are the questions that Lynn would look at intuitively to answer the "quick" question:

What's going on with Sally? Is she in a life situation that supports a change? Does she feel confident? Would another job be better? Is there another job coming along soon? How does she feel about the job? Would she be happy in her new position?

What's the job about? Who's her boss? Will he or she be a good match for Sally? Will the company be successful? What are the political dynamics in the company? What would Sally's co-workers be like? Will they be a good team for Sally to work with? Is this generally a good career move for Sally? Is it a growing company? Would Sally's position change for the better or worse once she had the job? Will she still be there in a year?

Certainly you can get a general intuitive feeling about a "yes" or "no" decision. But, as you can see, a good many intricacies are involved in answering someone's "quick" question. Lynn would want to look at all of these issues so that she could answer with integrity.

You Can't Predict Free Will

In her practice, Lynn is often asked whether she is 100 percent accurate. She's the first to say, "No, I am not 100 percent accurate." She also doesn't believe that measuring percentages really means anything when it comes to readings. Lynn says: "It's extremely difficult—in fact, practically impossible—to assess a percentage of accuracy when it comes to intuition."

Even the most skilled psychic is wrong a fair percentage of the time. Remember all those scientific tests we have spoken about in past chapters? The highest scores on many of those tests are around 65 percent. And those scores are considered quite impressive.

Lynn is also a firm believer in free will. Without pushing, she often tries to steer clients away from what looks like a disastrous path. So then she has to ask: "Am I inaccurate because my client took my advice and the disaster didn't happen?" In that case, she'd be happy with a 0 percent accuracy rate!

You can't predict free will. The future is full of probabilities. If you go to a psychic who sees a future event for you, he or she is looking at one probable future for you. What happens to you is influenced by your thoughts, beliefs, and emotions. Whenever you change a belief, alter a thought, or release a strong emotion, you are changing your future.

As a psychic Lynn sees her role as helping you understand the path you're on and where it's heading at present. She tries to use her psychic abilities to help you see where you're blocked and help you get unstuck. She'll teach you to create a life you love rather than have you believe you're stuck with a life you don't want!

ARE YOU AWARE?

In their recent research with quarks, thought to be the smallest particles of matter, modern physicists have noted an interesting catch-22. Whenever trying to observe and measure these tiny tidbits, physicists find that the particles' expected "behavior" suddenly changes. The theory is that the act of observing them actually changes them. A similar principle may apply to psi. Taking it out of its everyday context of being useful on a spiritual level to scrutinize it in a laboratory test may change the nature of its response.

But some people believe that fate, or destiny, is inescapable. So many prophets, from ages past to just days ago, have foretold doom in the future. For those such as Nostradamus, who seem so right, is it now their fate to be proven wrong? You can take action to create the change you want. Find out how in the next chapter.

The Least You Need to Know

- You can do a reading for yourself or someone else.

- When doing a reading, your intuition helps guide how you share information as well as helping you receiving it.

- Your careful attention to your own condition will help to improve the accuracy of your reading for others.

- Because we all have free will, information offered in a reading is not inevitable; rather, it presents possibilities for change.

Put Your Psychic Intuition into Action

In This Chapter

- Your intuition and love
- Money and your inner mind
- Healthy and wise
- To work we go
- Grow and create

If you've been doing the exercises in this book as you read through the chapters, awesome! If not, why not try an exercise now? We're going to walk you through a number of things you can do that will improve both your psychic ability and your life. We'll start with relationships and then move on to your finances and your sense of abundance. We'll look at steps you can take to improve your health and sense of well-being. We're also going to talk about work and career goals, and finally we'll look at your creativity and ways you can continue to cultivate yourself and your inner resources.

All You Need Is Love

They say that love makes the world go 'round. And this very well may be true. Love and your love life can also be a source of stress and anxiety, however. Not to worry! We're here to help you out—and so is your intuition. We'll look at a potential love interest, an existing relationship, and a relationship that may be on the rocks. So let's start at the beginning.

Intuition Exercise: A Handsome Stranger?

"You will meet a tall, dark, handsome stranger." That's what the stereotypical movie psychic may say, but we're not going to. Instead, let's look at a real situation that you're quite likely to encounter.

You've met someone new and attractive. Your new love interest has just called for the first time and left a message asking you out for Saturday night. You're feeling attracted, curious, and a bit fluttery and nervous. You don't really know or trust this person. Should you say "yes" and go on Saturday? Or should you play it safe and stay home? Could your new date be your future mate? You don't want to get all moony and have expectations that are too high, and yet ... you need more information. You could call a psychic hotline or discuss this new person with a friend, but why not look at what you already know but may not be 100 percent aware of? Ask you intuition!

Your intuition has a wealth of information to share, even about someone you've only met once. If you listen to your intuition, you can learn who to avoid and how to take steps away from frustration and heartbreak and move toward love and the relationship of your dreams.

ARE YOU AWARE?

The English poet Lord Byron (1788–1824), in addition to being a leader of the Romantic movement, was known for his love affairs. In his epic poem *Don Juan*, Byron wrote, "There is no instinct like that of the heart." And what is instinct but another name for intuition? We think Byron would agree that when it comes to matters of the heart, your intuition knows best.

First, grab a pen and some paper, and let's get to work. Make a list of qualities that are important to you in a relationship. (If you need some ideas to get you started, many people include these words in their lists: trustworthiness, honesty, sense of humor, good communication, fun to be with, ability to work hard, kind, open, and/or warm.) Okay? Write your list.

Now, you're going to use your list and your intuition to learn more about your new date. For each word on your list, you're going to rate your potential date on a scale from one to ten. Ten means "absolutely, yes, my date has this quality," and one means, "No, my date does not have this quality." Look at your list. Imagine your date. Close your eyes and ask your intuition questions based on the words on your list. We started with "trustworthiness," so we'll ask, "Is my new date trustworthy?"

What number between one and ten pops into your head? Write it down. One by one, ask your intuition about all the qualities on your list.

How did your date do? If your date scored between seven and ten on most of your important qualities, your intuition says "Yes!" If your date racked up a lot of scores between four and six, your intuition is saying, "Take it slowly" and see whether this new person proves worthy. If you wrote down a lot of ones, twos, and threes, well ... maybe you really need to stay home on Saturday night and do laundry instead.

Intuition Exercise: Survive Your First Fight

But maybe you are already seeing someone. You've been dating a wonderful person for a few months, and you've been having fun—a great time, in fact. But then, you and your date have your first fight. And now, you're not sure. You may even be feeling downright miserable. You want to know, "Is this the beginning of the end?" Quick—call up your inner knowledge. Your intuition will come to your rescue!

Get out your pen and paper. You're going to write answers to the questions that follow. Pay attention to your feelings as you do so, and note any fleeting impressions, images that pop into your mind, and sensations in your body. As you write, don't worry about grammar, spelling, or punctuation. Write whatever is in your heart and mind.

- What's upsetting your date the most right now?

- How does your date perceive your relationship?

- What does your date need from you?

- What is the best next step for resolving your present conflict?

- What do you need and want?

- What is the best possible outcome?

If more questions occur to you as you write, answer them, too. Read over all that you have written. Do certain parts jump out at you and give you a sense of relief? Spend a few moments absorbing your intuitive wisdom. Then, consider what steps you can take to improve your present situation.

Intuition Exercise: Three Choices

Do you wake up in the morning feeling that your relationship is over? Maybe you'll end it now and get on with the rest of your life. But then, by afternoon, you might feel that you want to give your partner one more chance. Feeling ambivalent about the relationship you're in can be pretty awful. You may feel stuck and unsure, but your intuition can help you out of this mire.

When you think about all the options available to you, it can be pretty overwhelming. How can you possibly decide? The beauty of this exercise is that it limits your options to just three:

1. The person I'm currently seeing is "the one." I want to continue the relationship.

2. I'm going to give this relationship a few more months and see whether it will work out.

3. I want to end the relationship.

Settle down and take a few deep breaths. Imagine your partner. Now, imagine that you have made a decision about the relationship and that you have picked option number one: you're going to stay in the relationship. Feel your body's response to this decision. Do you feel light and relieved, or do you feel worse than when you started the exercise?

MIXED MESSAGES

Violence is never okay. It doesn't matter what dumb thing you said or did—your partner should *never* hit you or threaten you with violence. If this is happening to you, get help from a trusted friend, family member, clergy, teacher, or from law enforcement staff.

Clear your mind by taking a few more deep breaths (and maybe drink a glass of water). Then, imagine that you have chosen option number two: you're going to give the relationship more time. Note your physical response to this decision.

Shake off that vibe and try on the last option. Imagine that you've decided to end the relationship. Pay attention to what your body and intuition have to say.

Which scenario felt the best? Remember that your intuition does not lie, and it will not try to mislead you. Once you're clear about what you want and need, you'll be on the path toward real love.

Create Your Abundance

Some of people's biggest concerns center on finances and their sense of abundance. So if you're worried about money—and who isn't these days?—know that you are not alone! Your intuition can help you in this crucial area. And, we have some exercises for you that will help you access your inner wisdom.

Intuition Exercise: Financial Incubator

Maybe you're feeling financially stuck. Maybe you're scared or frustrated. Or, perhaps you're dealing with a mixture of these feelings. Probably these feelings are not helping you find a solution to your financial woes. In fact, they could be shutting down your intuition and making it harder for you to come up with any ideas. Check out this exercise, and free your mind!

This exercise has two parts. For the first part, grab your notebook and a pen. Think about your financial situation. Now, write five questions for your intuition. For example, you could ask your intuition questions such as these:

- How can I improve my financial situation?
- What's the best way for me to make more money?
- How can I save money?
- What life change can I make to allow me to have enough money?
- How can I have more abundance in my life?

After you've written your list of questions, circle the one that feels the most compelling. This will be the question that jumps out at you and gives you a feeling of excitement and possibility. (Remember when you were in school and the teacher asked a question, and you knew the answer—so you raised your hand? It may feel like that.) Now, you're ready to move on to the next part of this exercise.

GUIDED INTUITION

You're feeling the economic pinch, and that lack is pervading your life. It's important to acknowledge what you do have. Take a walk and breathe in the fresh air. Have you ever thought about how much air there is? Lots—plenty for everyone! Appreciate the wealth that is all around you, whether it's nature and trees, desert sands, or crowded city streets. When you feel gratitude, your intuition will be easier to access.

Ask your intuition to focus on your question. You probably don't have a ready solution to your problem, but allow yourself to imagine that there is a solution. Then, ask your intuition questions about your desired solution. You could ask:

- How will I know my problem has been solved?
- How will I feel when my problem is solved?
- How will my finances be different when this issue is worked out?
- What will success look like?

Use these questions—and any others that your intuition provides—to begin to focus and hone in on the outcome that you desire. The more clearly you can imagine your desired result, the more surely your intuition will lead you along the path to prosperity.

Intuition Exercise: Ask a Hero

We all admire someone. Maybe you adore your boss, your grandmother, your best friend, a sports super star, an actor, a musician, or Abraham Lincoln. Maybe *you* don't think of that person as a hero, but you could! One definition of a hero is a person "who is idealized for possessing superior qualities in any field." In the following exercise, you'll call on the power of your hero or of someone you admire.

Take a few breaths and imagine your hero or a person you admire. Pick the first person who pops into your head. Write that person's name down in your notebook. Now, close your eyes. Imagine as many physical details about this person as you can. Now imagine that you are this person—your hero. Ask yourself, "What would my hero do?" "How would he or she approach the financial issues I'm having?" Jot down all the ideas that come to you, even if they seem strange, funny, or impossible.

Intuition Exercise: Worrywart

Do you worry about money? Do you worry most of the time? Worry is a choice. It may not feel like that's true, but it is—and worry can shut down your intuition.

If you worry a lot, one of the best things you can learn to do is change the channel! If you catch yourself worrying, gently guide your mind away from distressing thoughts and think of something else. Some people find that replacing a worry thought with a positive affirmation is helpful. Know that worrying about your finances will not bring more money to you. If that were true, we'd all be rich!

This is an exercise that you'll want to do often. First, grab your pen and notebook. Start with a clean sheet of paper with no writing on the other side. Make a list of all the negative things that you tell yourself about your finances. Your list may look something like this:

- I will never have enough money.
- I am a financial failure.
- I'll never get a job that pays enough.
- I can't afford the things I need.
- Compared to me, everyone else is better off.

Now, rip the sheet out of your notebook. Start with your first negative sentence and turn it into a positive statement about your finances. "I will never have enough money" will become, "I have enough money" or "I am on the path toward having enough money." Write a positive statement for each of the negative sentences you've written. Now, tear up your list of negative sentences. Keep your positive sentences with you. Stick them in your pocket, wallet, or purse, and anytime you catch yourself worrying, repeat one of your positive sentences to yourself. Your intuition will thank you!

To Your Health

Your intuition can serve as a great bridge between your body and your mind. Listening to your intuition often means listening to your body and its needs for sleep, relaxation, healthful foods, water, and appropriate exercise. You can improve your health and sense of well-being by listening to your body's intuitive messages.

Intuition Exercise: Energy to Heal

Meditation in and of itself can be quite healing. If you're feeling stressed—and even if you're not—why not try this healing meditation and get in touch with your inner glow?

MIXED MESSAGES

Be smart about your health. Use your intuition and make sure to get regular medical and dental check ups. If you're having health problems, consult a doctor or other licensed medical practitioner.

You'll want to sit at your altar, if you have one, or in a special space that you use for meditation. If you've created such a meditation space, then you already know how restorative and meaningful a dedicated sacred space in your home can be. Creating an altar for your meditation space can further enhance that sacred feeling and you may find you will come to rely on the deep grounding and connectedness it inspires. Before you start your intuitive healing meditation, light a candle. Look at the flame and take a few deep, centering breaths.

Close your eyes. Breathe deeply and let your belly expand. Exhale slowly. Take in two more deep belly breaths.

Keep your eyes closed and focus your attention inside and up. Imagine your third-eye center. Ask your intuition and any divine spirits to sit with you and help you.

Feel yourself fill up with healing energy. Think of the situation or physical condition you would like to heal. Imagine the healing energy that is all around and inside you. See it moving and acting where it is needed most.

Stay in meditation as long as you like. When you feel ready, thank your intuition, your healing energy, and any beings who have helped you. Then, open your eyes and return to normal awareness.

Intuition Exercise: The Doctor Is In

Regular checkups with licensed medical and dental practitioners are important, but you know that, right? It's also important to check in with yourself every once and a while. How are you feeling today?

Maybe there's something bothering you and you'd like to feel better. Or, maybe you feel pretty good but would like to have more energy, sleep better, or enjoy exercise and your physical being more. Get in touch by taking the inner view of yourself.

Find a comfortable spot to sit or lie down. Close your eyes and take a few deep breaths. Feel all your muscles relax.

Gently focus your attention on your physical area of concern. Feel your attention hover gently above this part of your body. Imagine that your body can talk to you. Ask it, "What can I do to help you feel better?" Note any physical sensations you may have. You may also experience images, words, or emotions surfacing.

If you do get emotional, just breathe and let the feelings wash over you. Remember, it's okay to cry—and a good cry can relieve a lot of stress.

When you feel you have meditated long enough, open your eyes and return to normal consciousness. Get out your journal or notebook and write about your experience. Note any thoughts, physical sensations, images, words, or emotions that your meditation evoked—even ones that don't seem to make sense. You may find that in a day or two, the strange clues that have bubbled up will give you important information. And remember, if you need to see a doctor or dentist, please do so.

GUIDED INTUITION

Mona Lisa Schulz, MD, PhD, is a popular medical intuitive. She's also a neuropsy-chiatrist and a professor. If you want to know more about her work, check out her website: www.drmonalisa.com. She's also on Facebook: www.facebook.com/MonaLisaSchulz. On Twitter, she's DrMonaLisa2.

Intuition Exercise: Pain Free

With the stress that we all experience, many of us get headaches, pains in the neck and shoulders, or in the back. Do you hurt? Harness the power of your intuition to help you feel better and move toward being pain free.

You could reach for some aspirin, or you can try to get to the root of your problem. Harness your intuition and discover—and possibly eliminate—the source of your discomfort:

1. State your desired outcome. It can be general, such as, "I want to feel healthy and strong." Or, it can be more specific: "I want to be free from headaches."

2. Immerse yourself in information about your condition.

3. Use your logical mind to analyze the options available to you.

4. Allow your intuition to pick the best course of action. Do this by asking your intuition questions such as, "What should I do about my headaches?" "How can I avoid pain in my neck?" "What do I need to know about the discomfort in my back?" These questions will evoke intuitive information.

5. Take a break and go for a walk, or just relax for five minutes (if a walk is not an option for you).

6. After your break, quiet your mind with a breathing exercise or a simple meditation. Listen for your intuition. What is it telling you? Write down all the possible solutions your intuition comes up with.

7. Make a hypothetical choice. In other words, pick one of the solutions and try it on for size. Does it feel right to your gut? Do you feel energized by this decision? Can you see yourself successfully using this plan of action? If the answer is "yes," then you are on the right track. If the answer is "no," pick another solution and test it out. Keep testing your solutions until you find the one that fits best.

Jobs, Careers, and Directions

Work is pretty central to most of our lives. Some of us want careers, and some of us just want to put food on the table and seek our fulfillment in other areas. Using your intuition in the work realm can help you make good choices in advancing your career or settling into the job that best fits your lifestyle and values. You can also use your intuition to help you advance along your path and maybe even get that long-desired promotion.

Intuition Exercise: Why Am I Here?

You've probably heard people talk about their dream job. Do you have a dream? If so, that's great. But if you don't, how do you know what to do? How do you identify your purpose in life? Many people have a hard time figuring out what their goals are. So if this is your issue, know that you are not alone and that your intuition can help. Check out this exercise.

Your inner compass continuously gives you information about your life's purpose. Objects, activities, and events that make you happy are road marks on the path to your larger purpose. Paying attention to the smaller questions can lead you to a big answer.

This exercise has two parts. First, we're going to give you some questions for you and your intuition to answer. So get out your notebook and a pen.

- What are your hobbies?

- What do you love to do on weekends and vacations?

- What are you doing when time seems to fly by?

- If money were not an issue, what would you love to do for work?

- If your boss gave you a year off with full pay so you could contribute to your community, what would you do?

For the next week, spend five or ten minutes every day meditating on your answers. They may not feel as if they are leading you anywhere just yet, but stick with it. This month, make a commitment to yourself (and to your intuition) to do more of the things that you love. Doing what you love will help you open to your intuition and to the path that is right for you. After you've spent a week considering what you love, move on to the second part of this exercise. You'll want to record yourself reading the meditation that follows. Or, have someone read it to you. Have your notebook and a pen handy because you'll want to write after you're done meditating.

1. Close your eyes. Inhale deeply and exhale. Draw in another slow breath and exhale. Continue to breathe slowly. Observe your breath as it flows in and out of your body.

2. Keep breathing and imagine yourself bathed in soft white light. Spend some time feeling the light all around you.

3. Feel the light enter into your heart and fill you with love and compassion. Feel the light circulating throughout your entire body. Allow the light to ease any tension or worries. Know that this light surrounds you, and feel its uplifting presence.

4. When you're ready, ask your intuition these questions:

   - What is my life's purpose?

   - What can I do to become clearer about my purpose?

   - What is blocking me from my goals?

   - What am I here to learn?

   - What can I do to move closer to my purpose?

5. Ask any other questions that come to you.

6. Continue to meditate for a few more minutes or slowly open your eyes and return to the regular world.

7. In your notebook, write down any flashes of insight you experienced during your meditation. Remember to include physical sensations and images.

Your intuition may give you some answers while you are writing. Or, you may have answers come to you during the meditation itself. If neither of these things happens, don't worry. Some people find their answers later in the day, or you may dream them at night. Keep working with your intuition—and keep doing the things that you love—and your path and life's purpose will become clearer and clearer.

 GUIDED INTUITION

If you need help finding your purpose, you may want to consult Lynn's book *Compass of the Soul: 52 Ways Intuition Can Guide You to the Life of Your Dreams* (Andrews McMeel Publishing, 2003).

Intuition Exercise: Help Wanted

Say you have a job or the outline of a career, and you like what you're doing. But you're feeling just a little bit stuck. You'd like to move up and take on more, but it's just not happening. Let's put your intuition to work.

In this exercise, you write a letter to your intuition, higher power, or the god or goddess of your choice. Lynn herself has used a technique like this for years. She has a special box in her office where she places her letters asking for help. You'll want to find a box for your letters, too—or make one!—and keep your box in a special place.

When writing your letter, describe your situation the way you would to a trusted friend. Get out all your fears and anxieties related to your position.

It's nice to write your letter by hand. You can even use different colors of ink or draw pictures if that helps you express yourself.

Once you've described the situation, make some requests. For example, you could ask for more responsibility at work or for a specific job title that interests you. Or, ask for that beautiful corner office you've had your eye on. Make your requests as concrete and specific as you can.

Then write, "If what I've asked for above is truly in my highest interests, please work with me to manifest these things in my life. Thank you. I await your guidance." Sign and date your letter. Place it in your box, and wait for clarity and ideas about your next steps.

Cultivate Your Garden

You've probably already intuited that you can use your intuition to enhance your personal growth and creativity. Maybe you don't feel that you're growing and think you aren't especially creative? Well, we know that you are! You are growing and changing every day. And whether you're trying to make a business decision, worrying about what color to paint your bedroom, writing a play, or trying to get dressed in the morning, you are calling on your creativity and decision-making abilities all the time. So let's call on your intuition to help you be decisive and cook up some new ideas.

Intuition Exercise: The Yes Response

You need to make a decision between two things or courses of action—maybe two job offers or the opportunity to move to a new city. You need to make up your mind—now. Is the pressure stressing you out? We all are faced with so many choices and make so very many decisions in our daily lives. Sometimes just the idea that you need to decide can cause enough stress to make it impossible to decide. Take a few calming, centering breaths. Remember that your intuition is quick and ready insight, and you can harness it now. Try this:

- First, acknowledge your feelings of stress. Tell yourself that everything is going to be okay and that you will make the right choice.

- Breathe deeply and imagine that each breath fills your heart with more love.

- When you feel centered, get out a sheet of paper and a pen. Write a description of one of the choices you could make. Then, write a description of a different choice that is possible.

- Now, write a description of your *ideal* choice. So if you are choosing between two jobs, you'd describe what you want in a job—such as good pay, a flexible schedule, fun co-workers, a company that has a training program, and/or job security. If you're looking at a move, you'll want to write down features of your ideal town. You may consider public transit, good schools, parks, a feeling of community, and location of family members.

- Sit quietly and close your eyes if this helps you focus. Pay attention to your breath for a few moments. Then, bring your two choices to mind. Ask your intuition which is the right choice for you.

Pay attention to any words or phrases that run through your mind, and note any emotions or physical sensations that surface. Does one of your options feel as if it has more energy than the other? Which choice feels lighter? Which one seems heavier?

Is one of your choices saying "yes" to you? A "yes" will make you feel good. You may feel some excitement, a zip of enthusiasm, or a sense of peace. Take action on the option that says "yes," and your intuition will thank you.

Intuition Exercise: Creative Home

Maybe you're into crafts or your talents lean toward the fine arts. Perhaps you want to make more inspired choices with your clothes or in decorating your home. In short, you want to be more creative. Sure, you keep meaning to take a knitting class or finish that scrapbook project you started last year, but …. Lynn says, "Intuition is where your creativity lives." So why not give your creativity its own physical home?

One of the most straightforward paths to greater creativity is to give your creativity its own physical space. This could be your desk, a corner of your bedroom or office, or even an unused closet. (We know an artist who transformed a hall closet into her art room—cozy, cute, and inspiring!)

Look around your home, room, or office. Is there a space you can turn into your creative home? You don't have to start a construction project to do so—just find a corner that your creativity can call its own. You'll want make the area fun and inviting. A splash of your favorite color on the wall could be inspiring. Consider adding desk toys or a mobile. Your creativity will enjoy the sense of fun these objects can bring. You could also put up a bulletin board and post inspiring quotes and images.

Provide paper, colored pens, crayons, modeling clay, and craft supplies and add some music. Then, all you need is time! Spend some time in your creative home every day and see what happens.

The Least You Need to Know

- Your intuition is a great resource when dealing with matters of the heart.
- You can improve your financial situation with hard work, a little luck, and the power of your intuition.
- Your intuition, which is a strong link between your body and your mind, can help you feel better.
- Your intuition can help you find your goals and then pursue them.
- Decision-making and creativity are closely related and both have a large intuitive component.

Glossary

affirmations   Statements that create a reality or truth through frequent repetition and focus.

age regression   An application of hypnosis whereby the client regresses to a younger age (or a past life) with the guidance of a hypnotherapist trained in this technique. Usually this is done to explore unresolved emotional issues.

Akashic Record   A "cosmic memory bank" containing information about everything that has occurred in the universe, including details of every soul and every life ever lived.

apparition   A spirit with an image that can be seen and can interact with its observer; this is the closest thing to what people usually call a "ghost."

archetypes   Common themes that arise from the collective unconscious and repeatedly appear as symbols in myths, symbol systems, and dreams.

astral body   A "second self" or energy body that consists of a subtle field of light that encases the physical body. It is thought that the astral body can separate from the physical body during sleep, which results in flying dreams.

astral projection   An awareness that the conscious mind has separated from the physical body, usually during a sleeplike state. It enables one to float above oneself and view one's own physical body.

astral travel   A step beyond astral projection that enables a "dreamer" to travel to a different locale while being conscious that he or she is not in his or her physical body.

astrology   A form of divination that studies the positions of heavenly bodies to determine their influence on human affairs.

aura   The field of electromagnetic energies that permeate and surround every living being. The word comes from the Greek avra, which means "breeze."

automatic writing   A form of creative expression that involves writing words. It occurs during an altered state of consciousness, when the rational mind is shut off and the intuitive mind takes a more active role.

bilocation   A phenomenon that occurs when a living person is witnessed at a second location, while continuing to function normally in his or her physical body at his or her original location.

brain waves   Currents of electrical impulses that are constantly produced and given off by the brain.

chakras   Centers of energy that run throughout the body. The seven major chakras are situated between the base of the spinal column and the top of the head. In Western medicine, they are referred to as the nerve plexus.

channeler   A person who communicates with spirits. Also called a medium.

channeling   The process of communicating with spirits who do not currently inhabit bodies.

chanting   The repetitive singing of a short simple melody or even a few monotonous notes. This repetition of the same words or sounds aids in attaining a deeper spiritual state.

chi   According to ancient Chinese medicine, the universal energy that flows through the body's vital organs, bones, bloodstream, and other parts. The Japanese call it ki.

clairaudience   The ability to hear sounds that aren't accessible to the physical ear.

clairsentience   The ability to perceive information out of the range of ordinary perception. Translated as "clear thinking" or "clear knowing."

clairvoyance   The ability to perceive things that cannot be seen with the physical eye. French for "clear seeing," it also refers to keen perception and insight.

coincidence   A striking occurrence of two or more events at the same time that seems to happen by mere chance.

collective unconscious   A level of the mind believed by Carl Jung to be inherited and to contain a reservoir of ideas, symbols, and archetypes that form the world's myths and belief systems.

contemplation   Deep thought or reflection as a type of meditation or prayer.

creative visualization   A process in which you create an image of the outcome you desire. This image is often called to mind during meditation or deep relaxation.

discernment   In the telepathic sense, refers to the ability to discriminate between personal desires, such as wishful thinking, and intuitive information.

distant healing   The idea that healing can occur through directed thoughts, such as prayer, even when the patient is not present. Distant healing can be considered a form of telepathy.

divination   The practice of foretelling future events through supernatural means, prophecy, or intuition.

dowsing   A traditional method of detecting underground sources of water and other material by using divining rods.

essential oils   Oils obtained from plants that retain the aroma and other characteristic properties of the plant. Their scents are used as perfumes, flavorings, and medicines.

exorcism   The act of expelling an unwanted spirit through religious or solemn ceremonies.

extrasensory perception (ESP)   Perception of thoughts, situations, or issues without using one of the five "ordinary" senses.

feng shui   An ancient Chinese philosophy for creating harmonious environments.

field consciousness   The idea that awareness exists on a plane that is interconnected and shared by all minds. This suggests that mental awareness comes from a source beyond the physical cells contained inside each individual's brain.

focus   A central point of attention that aids in concentration.

Gaia theory   The idea that the earth is actually its own entity, an enormous biological system that embodies a single living organism.

ganzfeld German for "whole field," refers to opening the inner mind by shutting out external data, such as light and sound. When these distractions are eliminated, the mind is more susceptible to picking up psychic signals.

ghost A word used to describe various phenomena, the most common of which is the soul of a disembodied spirit, imagined to be wandering among the living. Actually, some phenomena that people call "ghosts" do not involve a soul or spirit at all.

guardian angels Loving spiritual beings who help guide you through life. In rein-carnation theory, they prepare and help you through your current incarnation.

guided imagery A technique in which you use your imagination and all of your senses to imagine a desired outcome. Seeing and feeling this outcome in your mind aids you in achieving it in real life.

haunting A repeated perception of an image, whether a sight, sound, or sense of movement, of a past event. Experts suggest that it doesn't involve a spirit but an "energy imprint."

hunch An unexplained sense of a future event or outcome.

hypnosis An altered mental state characterized by intense focus that results in heightened susceptibility to suggestion.

hypnotherapist A hypnotist trained to help people explore deeply buried sources of their problems in order to understand and change their life patterns.

hypnotist A trained expert who directs and leads a client through a hypnotic trance.

I Ching An ancient Chinese book of divination based on creating pairs of eight basic symbols and their interpretations.

inference The process of deriving logical conclusions from premises assumed to be true.

karma The collection of the consequences of all of your actions during the phases of your existence. Karma is sometimes thought of as a type of fate or destiny.

levitation A phenomenon whereby objects, people, and animals lift into the air without any physical means of support.

lucid dreaming   An awareness that occurs during dreaming wherein the dreamer consciously realizes he or she is dreaming and is able to continue. Novices may not be able to direct the dream, but they can eventually learn the skill of controlling the course of a dream.

mantra   A word or formula that is recited or sung repeatedly. The sound is intended to resonate in the body and evoke certain energies during meditation.

materialization   Making an object appear from seemingly nowhere.

medium   Someone who serves as an instrument through which a spirit personality can manifest itself. Also sometimes called a channeler.

metaphysics   A branch of philosophy that looks at the nature of reality, existence, and the structure of the universe.

near-death experience (NDE)   An occurrence wherein a person who is considered dead experiences a vivid awareness of separating from his or her body. He or she eventually revives, and reveals his or her experiences. The traits of near-death experiences appear similar for all those who report them.

negative self-talk   An inner voice that makes negative comments about you and your actions.

neocortex   The uppermost region of the brain, responsible for rational and higher thought.

nonlocal mind   In psi circles, refers to accessing a vast, eternal mind that transcends space and time. It suggests that individuals' minds are infinite and united in one whole.

nonlocal reality   The concept that events that are distant can, nevertheless, have a local effect.

nonlocality   The idea that a thing or a thought is not located in a specific region of space and time. This view suggests that the mind is not limited to given points in space or time, such as the body or the present moment.

Ouija board   A board with letters, numbers, and words printed on it that is paired with a planchette, a platelike device designed to glide easily along the board's surface. People place their fingertips on the planchette, and it moves across the board to spell out answers (supposedly from spirits) to specific questions.

out-of-body experience (OBE)   An unusual and brief occasion when a person's consciousness seems to depart from his or her body, allowing him or her to observe the world from a point of view that transcends the physical body and bypasses the physical senses.

paranormal   Beyond the range of scientifically known phenomena. This implies that although causes of paranormal phenomena are not currently known by scientists, they someday may be.

parapsychology   The branch of psychology that studies psychic experiences. This refers to the types of behavior that allow us to perceive information beyond the boundaries of space, time, and our ordinary senses.

past-life regression therapy   Therapy that, by means of regression, explores emotional and physical feelings in order to recognize and release past life problems that are deeply connected to present life issues.

pathological   A deviation from a healthy, normal mental state.

pendulum   An object suspended from a fixed point that moves in response to a natural force. In psychic terms, it responds to a mental inquiry.

phobia   A persistent, irrational fear.

poltergeist   A form of PK (psychokinesis) that is generated unconsciously by a person with intense, but unacknowledged, emotions. Although it means "noisy ghost" in German, it doesn't involve a ghost at all.

prana   According to the Indian yogic tradition, a form of energy that animates all physical matter, including the human body.

prayer   A solemn and humble intention to communicate, in word or thought, with a divine force.

precognition   Foreknowledge or awareness of a future event before it occurs.

premonition   A precognitive sense of danger or forewarning of an unfortunate future event.

presentiment   A sensing of a future feeling.

projection   A psychological term that refers to attributing your personal emotions or traits to someone else; this is usually done to avoid facing one's own feelings or traits.

prophecy   Foreknowledge that comes in the form of a vision or dream. Traditionally, its source is believed to be divine revelation.

prophetic dreams   Dreams that pertain to sensing or predicting the future.

psi   A letter of the Greek alphabet, and the first letter of the Greek word psyche, which literally means "breath" in Greek and refers to the human soul. In scientific study, it refers to the force that causes psychic phenomena.

psychic attack   An occasion when someone willfully and consciously directs negative energy toward another person. This energy usually does not come from someone who has developed psychic skills.

psychoanalysis   A systematic approach for investigating the unconscious as a means of mental and emotional healing.

psychokinesis (PK)   The ability to use the mind to move objects without touching them.

psychometry   The ability to touch an object and thereby tap into the past of it and its owner. This may occur when a person picks up the vibrations that accompany an object's past.

psychosomatic   A physical condition that is caused or influenced by the patient's emotional state.

random number generator (RNG)   A machine that creates random sequences of electronic bits that are equivalent to the "heads" and "tails" of a flipped coin. The pattern of heads or tails respond to thought patterns by becoming less random.

reflexology   A form of hands-on healing based on the principle that every part of the body directly communicates with a reference point on the foot, hand, and ear. Massaging these points helps the corresponding body part to heal by improving circulation, eliminating toxins, and reducing stress.

reiki   A method of hands-on healing, wherein a trained practitioner places his or her hands, using specific positions, on six points of the body. Doing this enables vital life energy to flow freely throughout the body.

reincarnation The belief that after death a person is reborn into another lifetime.

REM sleep Rapid eye movement is a phase of sleep when the eyelids appear to twitch constantly. It is closely linked to vivid dreams.

remote perception Similar to remote viewing, but refers to any type of sensory data (such as sound) perceived from a distance.

remote viewing Using the mind to see a person, place, or object that's located some distance away and beyond the physical range of sight. This ability also enables one to witness events at a remote site without using the known senses.

retrocognition A form of ESP wherein one has an intuitive knowledge of past events without having obtained information through the five physical senses.

schizophrenia A severe mental disorder marked by emotional withdrawal, intellectual deterioration, bizarre speech and behavior, hallucinations, and delusions.

scrying The practice of divination that induces clairvoyance when a reader stares into a reflective surface while deeply concentrating.

séance A meeting, session, or sitting in which a channeler attempts to communicate with the spirits of the dead.

second sight The ability to see future events. It can refer to a wide range of abilities, including being extremely wise, prophesying, or divining through the use of devices such as crystal balls.

shaman A healer who acts as intermediary between the physical world and the realm of spirit.

skeptic A person who questions the validity of something purporting to be factual and tends to maintain a doubting attitude.

spiritual regeneration A spiritual rebirth or religious conversion. It suggests that a person who experiences this is made over, usually in a new and improved condition.

spontaneous drawing A form of creative expression that produces visual images or pictures. It occurs during an altered state of consciousness, when the rational mind is shut off and the intuitive mind takes a more active role.

synchronicity A coincidence of events that seem to be meaningfully related.

targeting   A technique, used during astral travel, for shifting consciousness by focusing on a person or place in ordinary reality in order to visit that person or place.

tarot   A special deck of 78 cards that are used as an approach to predicting the future.

telepathy   The communication of thoughts and/or feelings between minds, without the use of the ordinary senses.

trance   An altered state of consciousness that involves complete mental absorption.

wishful thinking   An expression of personal inner desires that may distort the perception of reality to make the desires seem like external truth.

Resources for Tapping into Insight

Getting in touch with your intuition is just a first step along a lifelong path of discovery. We encourage you to continue seeking new growth within the wide world of intuitive insight. Listed here are a handful of resources to help you along. Let your intuition lead the way.

Organizations, Institutes, and Sites

American Society for Psychical Research
5 West 73rd Street
New York, NY 10023
212-799-5050
www.aspr.com

This membership organization publishes a journal and a newsletter. It also has an extensive library. The ASPR publishes a list of courses in parapsychology offered at colleges and universities around the world.

Association for Transpersonal Psychology
P.O. Box 50187
Palo Alto, CA 94303
650-424-8764
www.atpweb.org
Email: info@atpweb.org

This membership organization publishes *The Journal of Transpersonal Psychology*. It also publishes a list of transpersonal schools and programs and holds conferences.

Atlantic University
215 67th Street
Virginia Beach, VA 23451-8101
1-800-428-1512
www.atlanticuniv.edu
Email: registrar@atlanticuniv.edu

Atlantic University was founded by Edgar Cayce and offers a Master's degree program in transpersonal studies. Study can be undertaken via distance-learning courses or in residence.

Barbara Brennan School of Healing
500 N.E. Spanish River Boulevard, Suite 208
Boca Raton, FL 33431-4559
1-800-924-2564 or 561-620-8767
www.barbarabrennan.com
Email: bbsh.office@barbarabrennan.com

Barbara Brennan is a leading expert on working with auras in the area of energy healing. Her school offers training programs for developing these healing techniques.

Beliefnet.com
Beliefnet is a wonderful resource for finding articles, quizzes, a community of like-minded people, and information on spirituality and the world's religions.

The Boundary Institute
P.O. Box 10336
San José, CA 95157
408-996-0190
www.boundaryinstitute.org
Email: info@boundaryinstitute.org

The Boundary Institute is a nonprofit scientific research organization focusing on the development of new approaches in physics and mathematics, testing new theories, and investigating phenomena related to consciousness (such as psi ability). The institute also maintains a website at www.gotpsi.org, which presents a number of informal and fun ways for you to test your own psi abilities.

Dream Gate (www.dreamgate.com)
This site has lots of information about dreams, including a dream library.

Dream Tree (www.dreamtree.com)
An interactive site about dreams, Dream Tree includes a calendar of events and workshops related to dreams.

Edgar Cayce's A.R.E.: Association for Research and Enlightenment
215 67th Street
Virginia Beach, VA 23451
1-800-333-4499 or 757-428-3588
http://edgarcayce.org/
Email: are@are-cayce.com
Facebook: www.facebook.com/edgarcayce

This membership organization promotes the study, application, and dissemination of information from the psychic readings of Edgar Cayce. Edgar Cayce's A.R.E. publishes books, downloadable audio, apps, and a blog. The organization holds workshops, conferences, and study groups and maintains a Facebook page.

Esalen Institute
55000 Highway 1
Big Sur, CA 93920
1-888-837-2536 or 831-667-3005
www.Esalen.org

An alternative education center founded in 1962, the Esalen Institute is devoted to the exploration of human potential. The institute offers five-day and weekend classes in a number of disciplines and traditions.

Rhine Research Center
2741 Campus Walk Avenue, Bldg. 500
Durham, NC 27705
919-309-4600
www.rhine.org
Blog: http://rhineonline.blogspot.com/

This is the organization founded by J. B. and Louisa Rhine. It conducts laboratory and field research as well as hosts programs and publishes the *Journal of Parapsychology*. It has a blog, too.

Institute of Noetic Sciences
101 San Antonio Road, Suite 200
Petaluma, CA 94952
707-775-3500
www.noetic.org
Email: membership@noetic.org

This membership organization sponsors research, conferences, retreats, and publications on psychic phenomenon and the potential of consciousness.

Institute of Transpersonal Psychology
1069 East Meadow Circle
Palo Alto, CA 94303
650-493-4430
www.itp.edu

A graduate school devoted to psychological research and education that probes the mind, body, spirit connection, the Institute attracts students from all over the world for both the PhD and Master's degree programs. They offer programs to students in residence and the option, through their Global Division, of studying online from home.

Interlude Retreat (www.Interluderetreat.com)
This is a cyberspace retreat! Discover the meditation of the week, a thought of the day, a great bookstore, and more.

International Association for the Study of Dreams
1672 University Avenue
Berkeley, CA 94703
209-724-0889
www.ASDreams.org
Email: office@asdreams.org

This membership organization publishes the journal *Dreaming*, the magazine *Dream Time*, and the monthly e-newsletter *IASD E-News*. It also holds conferences.

The International Society for the Study of Subtle Energies and Energy Medicine
(ISSSEEM)
11005 Ralston Road
Arvada, CO 80004
303-425-4625
www.issseem.org
Blog: www.issseemblog.org/

ISSSEEM explores the application of subtle energies to the experience of consciousness, healing, and human potential. A bridging organization for scientists, clinicians,
therapists, healers, and laypeople, ISSSEEM encourages the exploration of the practices of energy healing.

Intuition Network (www.intuition.org)
The purpose of the Intuition Network is to help create a world in which people feel
encouraged to cultivate and use their inner intuitive resources. The site contains
transcripts of the *Thinking Allowed* television series. It also provides lists of intuition-
related publications, study groups, and email newsgroups.

Intuition Newsletter (www.LynnRobinson.com)
Sign up for Lynn Robinson's monthly email *Intuition Newsletter*. It's filled with book
reviews, intuition and spirituality resources on the internet, and inspiring quotes as
well as articles about developing your own intuition.

Kripalu Center for Yoga and Health
P.O. Box 309
Stockbridge, MA 01262
1-866-200-5203 or 413-448-3152
www.kripalu.org

Kripalu offers a large number of experiential yoga, self-discovery, holistic health and
spiritual programs, and workshops designed to provide participants with tools to aid
them in their growth.

The Lucidity Institute
2155 Spencer Street
Napa, CA 94559
www.lucidity.com
Email: contact@lucidity.com

Founded in 1987 by lucid dreaming researcher Dr. Stephen LaBerge, this institute holds workshops on lucid dreaming, supports research, and provides information on how to use lucid dreams to enhance your life.

The National Guild of Hypnotists, Inc.
P.O. Box 308
Merrimack, NH 03054-0308
603-429-9438
www.ngh.net

This organization provides seminars, workshops, referrals, and an annual convention in addition to training for members and other professionals.

Omega Institute for Holistic Studies
150 Lake Drive
Rhinebeck, NY 12572-3212
1-877-944-2002 or 845-266-4444
www.eomega.org

Omega is the largest holistic education provider in the United States. Highly regarded for its pioneering work in holistic health, meditation, yoga, transformational psychology, spirituality, world music, and art, Omega offers workshops, conferences, and retreats at its Rhinebeck campus, in Texas, the Caribbean, Florida, New York City, and other locations.

Parapsychology Foundation
P.O. Box 1562
New York, NY 10021
212-628-1550
www.parapsychology.org

This organization, founded by Eileen Garret, maintains a speaker's bureau and offers grants for research and study in parapsychology. It has an excellent library.

Soulful Living (www.SoulfulLiving.com)
Each month, Soulful Living explores a unique theme of spiritual interest by presenting the thoughts and ideas of best-selling authors and highly regarded experts from diverse fields of soul study. Transformative tips and techniques are shared to help enhance the quality of life. The site has easy-to-use links to many spiritual resources.

Spirituality and Health (www.spiritualityhealth.com)
You may have seen *Spirituality and Health* magazine on your newsstands. They also have a terrific website that offers self-tests, guidance on spiritual practices, original writing from leading authors in the field, and reviews of the latest resources for people on spiritual journeys.

Touching Spirit Center
P.O. Box 1133
Woodstock, NY 12498
845-684-5052
www.touchingspirit.org

This center offers training in intuitive development and healing.

Well-Known Psychics on the Internet

You can learn a lot by reading what psychics themselves have to say. Many of them teach, publish newsletters, or offer downloadable podcasts or audio files.

Sylvia Browne
Facebook: www.facebook.com/pages/Sylvia-Browne/196312131222
Twitter: twitter.com/#!/Sylvia_Browne
www.sylviabrowne.com

Sonia Choquette
Facebook: www.facebook.com/TrustYourVibes
Twitter: twitter.com/#!/soniachoquette
www.trustyourvibes.com

Chip Coffey
Facebook: www.facebook.com/pages/Chip-Coffey-Psychic-and-Medium/90338070683
Twitter: twitter.com/#!/chipcoffey
www.ChipCoffey.com

John Edward
Facebook: www.facebook.com/pages/John-Edward/116996081651003
Twitter: twitter.com/#!/psychicmediumje
www.johnedward.net/

John Holland
Facebook: www.facebook.com/pages/Psychic-Medium-John-Holland/62144330803
Twitter: twitter.com/#!/jhollandmedium
www.JohnHolland.com

Terri and Linda Jamison—The Psychic Twins
Facebook: www.facebook.com/thepsychictwins
Twitter: twitter.com/#!/PSYCHICTWINS
www.psychictwins.com

James van Praagh
Facebook: www.facebook.com/JamesVanPraaghOfficial
Twitter: twitter.com/#!/JamesVanPraagh
www.vanpraagh.com

Lynn A. Robinson
Facebook: www.facebook.com/lynnarobinson
Twitter: twitter.com/#!/LynnIntuition
www.LynnRobinson.com

Doreen Virtue
Facebook: www.facebook.com/DoreenVirtue444
Twitter: twitter.com/#!/DoreenVirtue444
www.angeltherapy.com

Lisa Williams
Facebook: www.facebook.com/lisawilliamsmedium
Twitter: twitter.com/#!/lwmedium
www.lisawilliams.com

Suggested Reading

There's a world of wisdom right at your fingertips. All you have to do is check it out—at the library or from your nearest neighborhood or online bookseller. Here is just a small sampling of the tremendous resources that are available to you.

Adamson, Eve and Dream Genie. *The Complete Idiot's Guide Dream Dictionary*. Indianapolis: Alpha Books, 2007.

Andrews, Synthia and Colin Andrews. *The Complete Idiot's Guide to the Akashic Record*. Indianapolis: Alpha Books, 2010.

Ban Breathnach, Sarah. *Simple Abundance: A Daybook of Comfort and Joy*. New York: Grand Central Publishing, 2009.

Berkowitz, Rita, and Deborah S. Romaine. *The Complete Idiot's Guide to Communicating with Spirits*. Indianapolis: Alpha Books, 2003.

———. *Empowering Your Life with Angels*. Indianapolis: Alpha Books, 2004.

Brennan, Barbara. *Hands of Light: A Guide to Healing Through the Human Energy Field*. New York: Bantam, 1988.

Budilovsky, Joan. *The Complete Idiot's Guide to Meditation, Second Edition*. Indianapolis: Alpha Books, 2002.

Chopra, Deepak. *The Way of the Wizard: Twenty Spiritual Lessons for Creating the Life You Want*. New York: Harmony Books, 1995.

———. *Ageless Body, Timeless Mind*. New York: Three Rivers Press, 1994.

Choquette, Sonia. *Diary of a Psychic: Shattering the Myths*. Carlsbad, California: Hay House, 2003.

———. *The Psychic Pathway: A Workbook for Reawakening the Voice of Your Soul*. New York: Harmony, 1995.

Day, Laura. *Practical Intuition: How to Harness the Power of Your Instinct and Make it Work for You*. New York: Broadway Books, 1997.

de Beauport, Elaine, PhD. *The Three Faces of Mind: Think, Feel, and Act to Your Highest Potential, Second Edition*. Wheaton, Illinois: Quest Books, 2002.

Eden, Donna and David Feinstein. *Energy Medicine: Balancing Your Body's Energies for Optimal Health, Joy, and Vitality*. New York: Tarcher, 2008

Gerwick-Brodeur, Madeline and Lisa Lenard. *The Complete Idiot's Guide to Astrology, Third Edition*. Indianapolis: Alpha Books, 2003.

Delaney, Gayle, PhD. *Living Your Dreams: The Classic Bestseller on Becoming Your Own Dream Expert*. San Francisco: HarperSanFrancisco, 1996.

Dossey, Larry, MD. *Healing Words: The Power of Prayer and the Practice of Medicine*. San Francisco: HarperOne, 1997.

Edward, John. *After Life: Answers from the Other Side*. New York: Sterling Ethos, 2010.

Gawain, Shakti. *Creative Visualization: Use the Power of Your Imagination to Create What You Want in Your Life, 25th Anniversary Edition*. Novato, California: New World Library, Nataraj, 2002.

Hamilton-Parker, Craig. *The Psychic Handbook: Discover and Enhance Your Hidden Psychic Powers*. London: Random House U.K. Ltd., 1995.

Hanh, Thich Nhat. *The Miracle of Mindfulness: A Manual on Meditation*. Boston: Beacon Press, 1996.

Holland, John. *Born Knowing: A Medium's Journey—Accepting and Embracing My Spiritual Gifts*. Carlsbad, California: Hay House, 2003.

Ihnen, Anne and Carolyn Flynn. *The Complete Idiot's Guide to Mindfulness*. Indianapolis: Alpha Books, 2008.

Jeffers, Susan. *Feel the Fear ... and Do It Anyway, 20th Anniversary Edition.* New York: Ballantine Books, 2006.

————. *Feel the Fear ... And Beyond: Mastering the Techniques for Doing it Anyway.* New York: Random House, 1998.

Judith, Anodea. *Chakra Balancing.* Louisville, Colorado: Sounds True, Incorporated, 2006.

Kabat-Zinn, Jon. *Wherever You Go, There You Are: Mindfulness Meditation in Everyday Life.* New York: Hyperion, 1995.

Kasl, Charlotte Sophia. *If the Buddha Got Stuck: A Handbook for Change on a Spiritual Path.* New York: Penguin, 2005.

Klimo, Jon and Pamela Heath. *Handbook to the Afterlife.* Berkeley, California: North Atlantic Books, 2010.

LaBerge, Stephen, PhD. *Exploring the World of Lucid Dreaming.* New York: Ballantine, 1991.

Lerma, John. *Into the Light: Real-Life Stories about Angelic Visits, Visions of the Afterlife, and Other Pre-Death Experiences.* Pompton Plains, New Jersey: New Page Books, 2007.

Long, Jeffrey and Paul Perry. *Evidence of the Afterlife: The Science of Near-Death Experiences.* San Francisco: HarperOne, 2011.

Louden, Jennifer. *Comfort Secrets for Busy Women.* Naperville, Illinois: Sourcebooks Trade, 2003.

Lynne, Carole. *How to Get a Good Reading from a Psychic Medium.* Newburyport, Massachusetts: Weiser Books, 2003.

Maisel, Eric. *Fearless Creating: A Step-by-Step Guide to Starting and Completing Your Work of Art.* New York: Tarcher, 1995.

McMoneagle, Joseph. *Memoirs of a Psychic Spy: The Remarkable Life of U.S. Government Remote Viewer 001.* San Francisco: Hampton Roads Publishing, 2006.

McTaggart, Lynne. *The Field: The Quest for the Secret Force of the Universe.* New York: Harper Perennial; Updated edition, 2008.

Monroe, Robert. *Far Journeys.* New York: Broadway Books, 1992.

———. *Journeys Out of the Body.* New York: Broadway Books, 1992.

———. *Ultimate Journey.* New York: Main Street Books, 1996.

Moody, Raymond Jr., MD. *Life After Life.* San Francisco: HarperOne, 2001.

Morehouse, David A. *Remote Viewing: The Complete User's Manual for Coordinate Remote Viewing.* Louisville, Colorado: Sounds True, Incorporated, 2011.

Moss, Robert. *Dreamgates: An Explorer's Guide to the World of Soul, Imagination, and Life Beyond Death.* New York: New World Library; 2010.

Naparstek, Belleruth. *Staying Well with Guided Imagery.* New York: Warner, 1995.

———. *Your Sixth Sense: Unlocking the Power of Your Intuition.* San Francisco: HarperOne, 2009.

Pliskin, Marci, CSW, ACSW, and Shari L. Just, PhD. *The Complete Idiot's Guide to Interpreting Your Dreams, Second Edition.* Indianapolis: Alpha Books, 2004.

Radin, Dean, PhD. *The Conscious Universe: The Scientific Truth of Psychic Phenomena.* San Francisco: HarperOne, Reprint edition, 2009.

Rand, William. *Reiki, The Healing Touch.* Southfield, Michigan: Vision Publications, reissue 2000.

Rippentrop, Betsy and Eve Adamson. *The Complete Idiot's Guide to Chakras.* Indianapolis: Alpha Books, 2009.

Robinson, Lynn A. *Listen: Trusting Your Inner Voice in Times of Crisis.* Connecticut: Globe Pequot Press, 2010.

———. *Divine Intuition.* New York: DK Publishing, 2001.

———. *Trust Your Gut: How the Power of Intuition Can Grow Your Business.* Chicago: Kaplan Publishing, 2006.

Roman, Sanaya, and Duane Packer. *Opening to Channel: How to Connect With Your Guide.* Tiburon, California: H. J. Kramer, 1993.

Ronson, Jon. *The Men Who Stare at Goats.* New York: Simon & Schuster, 2009.

Rosanoff, Nancy. *Intuition Workout: A Practical Guide to Discovering and Developing Your Inner Knowing.* Boulder Creek, California: Aslan Publishing, 1991.

Schulz, Mona Lisa, MD, PhD. *Awakening Intuition: Using Your Mind-Body Network for Insight and Healing.* New York: Three Rivers Press, 1999.

Scott, Laura, and Mary Kay Linge. *The Complete Idiot's Guide to Divining the Future.* Indianapolis: Alpha Books, 2003.

Sheldrake, Rupert. *Morphic Resonance: The Nature of Formative Causation.* Rochester, Vermont: Park Street Press, 2009.

———. *Seven Experiments That Could Change the World: A Do-It-Yourself Guide to Revolutionary Science.* Rochester, Vermont: Park Street Press, 2002.

Siegel, Bernie. *Faith, Hope and Healing: Inspiring Lessons Learned from People Living with Cancer.* New York: Wiley, 2009.

———. *Love, Medicine and Miracles: Lessons Learned about Self-Healing from a Surgeon's Experience with Exceptional Patients.* New York: William Morrow, 1990.

Sinetar, Marsha. *Do What You Love, the Money Will Follow: Discovering Your Right Livelihood.* New York: Dell, 1989.

Stein, Diane. *Essential Reiki: A Complete Guide to an Ancient Healing Art.* Berkeley, California: Crossing Press, 1995.

Targ, Russell, and Jane Katra, PhD. *Miracles of Mind: Exploring Nonlocal Consciousness and Spiritual Healing.* Novato, California: New World Library, second edition 1999.

Targ, Russell. *Do You See What I See?: Lasers and Love, ESP and the CIA, and the Meaning of Life.* San Francisco: Hampton Roads Publishing, 2010.

Temes, Roberta. *The Complete Idiot's Guide to Hypnosis, Second Edition.* Indianapolis: Alpha Books, 2004.

Tognetti, Arlene and Carolyn Flynn. *The Complete Idiot's Guide to Tarot Spreads Illustrated*. Indianapolis: Alpha Books, 2006.

Tognetti, Arlene and Cathy Jewell. *The Complete Idiot's Guide Astrology Dictionary*. Indianapolis: Alpha Books, 2010.

Van Praagh, James. *Talking to Heaven: A Medium's Message of Life After Death*. New York: Signet, 1999.

Waggoner, Robert. *Lucid Dreaming: Gateway to the Inner Self*. Newburyport, Massachusetts: Moment Point Press, 2008.

Walsch, Neale Donald. *Conversations with God: An Uncommon Dialogue, Book 1*. New York: Putnam, 1995.

Wise, Anna. *The High-Performance Mind: Mastering Brainwaves for Insight, Healing, and Creativity*. New York: Tarcher, 1997.

Your Astrological Birth Chart

You can use your astrological birth chart to illuminate your life's path. Because an astrological birth chart really is a map of the heavens at the exact time and place of your birth, it is a wonderful intuitive tool for self-knowing. Exploring your chart can help you tune into your true nature, explore your own potential, and make a deeper connection to your psychic intuition.

Take a Look

To see what an astrological birth chart looks like, we've included one here for someone we feel is very connected to Universal energy—humanitarian and peace advocate Mahatma Gandhi. Looking at Gandhi's birth date, October 2, we see he is a Libra, the zodiac sign of balance. In interpreting a birth chart, astrologers look at where the planets appear in the astrological signs and houses.

What Do You See?

For now, we want you simply to look at this astrological map of Gandhi's personal moment and place of manifestation on the earth plane. Before doing any research to identify what each symbol and its placement means, meditate on what this map of Gandhi says to you, and record your impressions in your journal.

The birth chart of humanitarian and peace advocate Mahatma Gandhi.

Mohandas Gandhi
Natal Chart
Oct 2 1869 NS
7:11 am LMT -4:38:24
Porbandar INDIA
21°N38' 069°E36'

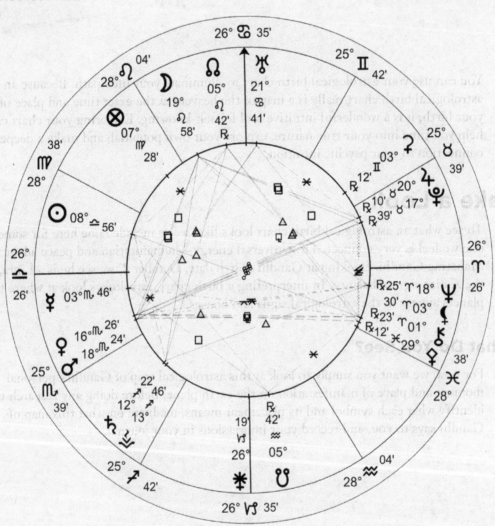

The birth chart of humanitarian and peace advocate Mahatma Gandhi.

Intuitive Birth Chart Insights

Now, let's look again to examine closely the birth chart meanings for one of human-kind's greatest humanitarians and explorers of essential human nature, Mahatma Gandhi.

Gandhi's Sun, the planet of personal identity, resides in the mystical twelfth house of the spiritual self. His Sun is in harmonious Libra, shaping a life path of spiritual growth through justice and equality. His Moon, the planet of inner self, resides in courageous and determined Leo in the tenth house of service and career, supporting Gandhi's drive to pursue his life's mission through service to others. And Uranus, the planet of innovation and change for the masses, resides in sensitive, nurturing Cancer in the ninth house of beliefs and truth to foster this spiritual leader's ability to encourage others to follow the course of liberation from oppression and prejudice.

You can see how an astrological birth chart may provide valuable clues and insights into your unique life path. What you may already sense about yourself intuitively will be enhanced by looking at the meaning of your birth chart.

Looking at Your Birth Chart

When you are ready to create your own birth chart, be sure to have the following information:

- Your date of birth, including the year
- Your place of birth, both city and state or country
- Your time of birth, as exactly as possible

You can have your birth chart done for a nominal fee at a metaphysical bookstore, look online for a website that generates free charts, or make an appointment with a professional astrologer who can assist you in making birth chart interpretations.

Once you have your own birth chart in hand, begin your exploration of it by using your psychic intuition. Meditate on your chart, as you did with Gandhi's chart. How does your birth chart look to you? Are symbols clustered together or spread out? Are some houses full or empty? How much activity do you see in the center of the chart?

Before you continue on by doing research to unlock the meanings of the symbols in your birth chart, record these early intuitive responses you have to the image of your astrological birth chart in your journal. Later, after you have decoded your chart (perhaps with the aid of an astrologer), return to these early journal comments and see how revealing they are on an intuitive level.

Remember, your astrological birth chart can reveal much about your past lives, present life, and even your future potential, but it does not tell you how you must act or who you will be. How you manifest the potential you see intuitively in your birth chart is the essence of your free-will journey through life. You, not the stars, create your life path!

Index

Intuitive Awareness Bonus Offers
from author Lynn A. Robinson

Special Offer for Readers of
The Complete Idiot's Guide to Psychic Intuition, Third Edition

Free Booklet

"7 Intuitive Tips That Can Change Your Life Right Now!"

http://lynnrobinson.com/consultations/bonus

Enter the password: *LynnBonusOffer*

Free Monthly Intuition Newsletter

- Access to NEW "Ask Lynn" column
- Advance previews of upcoming events
- Special offers just for subscribers
- How to develop your intuition articles, resources, and inspirational quotes.

  Sign up at http://LynnRobinson.com

15% Discount on Psychic Readings—Mention this book.

Lynn's unique insight can help you …

- Make better decisions.
- Clarify your next steps.
- Move ahead with confidence.
- Understand the mindset of others.
- Align your life and work with your values.

Connect with Lynn!

Twitter:	http://twitter.com/LynnIntuition
Facebook:	http://facebook.com/LynnARobinson
Email:	Lynn@LynnRobinson.com
Phone:	1-800-925-4002